The Hope of the Stone Man

A Novel by

Edward Mooney, Jr.

Stone Man Press
California USA

This is the Third Book of the "Stone Man Trilogy"

Book 1 - **The Pearls of the Stone Man**

Book 2 – **The Journey of the Stone Man**

Book 3 – **The Hope of the Stone Man**

This book is

© **2002-2016 Edward Mooney, Jr.**

Stone Man Press

is the imprint of the author,

Edward Mooney, Jr.

Prologue

The streaming lights of sunset bring richer colors - and cast deeper shadows. In some places the colors create brilliant clarity; the contrast and thicker shadows hide other areas. As the rays illuminate the deeper places the dust particles, remnants of the day's activities, float by, effortlessly shifting, almost in unison, on every gentle movement of the breeze.

Joining the visual symphony of gentle lights and wafting dust particles are hints and clips of sounds from far away. The melody brightens and fades as clouds drift by, and as the instruments producing tunes move closer or further. A singer, a soprano from far away, adds lyrics. The gentle rhythm of human breathing provides harmony. A sharp noise, followed by a delightful aroma of food cooking, punctuate the closing bars of the symphony.

"Tim! What are you doing? Are you sleeping in the garage?" A woman's voice echoed. There were tones of frustration in her words. A door slammed.

"Huh? What? Sleeping? No, just, uh, taking a break." The befuddled man shifted in his lawn chair. He pushed the brim of his baseball cap up on his head, then squinted as he noticed how low the sun was on the horizon. He followed the paths of a dusty ray into the garage – it was illuminating the often ignored corner of his garage. A bright green car rolled by; music streamed from its open window.

"Taking a break? Tim, dinner is almost ready. You've been out here for hours." The woman turned slowly as she scanned the room around her.

"Hours? Well, there's a lot to do, Shannon." The man began to rise from his chair, then slowed. He stared into that forgotten corner of the garage, as if in a trance. He rubbed his eyes and tried to focus. His confusion evaporated.

"Yeah, I can see that - and not much has been done." Shannon said with a note of frustration tagged on to the end of her words.

"I actually got a lot accomplished…" Tim's voice trailed off as he took a step toward a glowing object in the deepest recess of the garage. Shannon began pointing at objects here and there.

"Well, the pile of newspapers is exactly where it was this morning. Your tools are still all over the workbench…" Shannon turned to point across the room, but didn't finish her thought. She stared at her husband, then lowered her arm.

"I know…" Tim took one more step forward as he rubbed the stubble on his chin. His gaze remained on something.

"Are you okay?" Shannon's tone changed, almost to a whisper.

"Look at the light…" Tim stepped over to the ray nearest him, then took a breath. He turned back and looked out toward the horizon. He followed one particular ray into the back corner. He pointed at a non-descript cardboard box that seemed to be glowing with an eerie orange hue.

"I see it, and the dust blowing across it. I always wanted to get some kind of light fixture in that corner." Shannon shook her head.

"No, no. Not the light. That box – it's like it's glowing or something." Tim waved his hand in front of the particular ray of light. The glowing box appeared to turn off and then on again.

"Do that again…" Shannon stepped over next to her husband. Tim waved his arm in the same way, and the box appeared to turn off and then on - for a second time.

The couple stood, staring, in silence for a moment. Both of them drew a deep breath at the same time. Just then a car passed their driveway and interrupted the light beam, making the box appear to flicker. Tim and Shannon jumped a bit in surprise.

"Whoa…we need to slow down. It's just a beam of light hitting an old fruit box. Maybe I'm not all the way awake yet." Tim chuckled a bit. He rubbed his chin.

"Yeah, I know you're not awake, but that box really does look like it glows, like from the inside." Shannon's voice was barely above a whisper. Her gaze was locked on the orange box. She smoothed her hair, as if she were about to meet someone important for the first time in many years. Together they walked slowly over to the shelves in the far corner.

"Do you remember…uh…what's in it?" Tim asked with a pause in the middle of his sentence, as if he were afraid to ask the question.

"No, I don't. I thought it was your box. I know how you hate it when I go through your stuff. Isn't it your box?" Shannon asked nervously.

"I don't remember it. I thought it was your box, and believe me, I've been told in no uncertain terms to not go through your stuff – and I don't." Tim chuckled. He reached up to grab the box. His hand was a few inches from it when he felt a tug.

"Tim, stop. Wait." Shannon sounded frightened. She had grabbed his arm. Tim retracted his hand back to his side.

"Shan, relax. It's not like a magic box or something. There's no genie in it. We just shoved it up here when we moved in years ago and forgot about it. How many times have we done that?" Tim asked, confident of the answer.

"But this one is different. There's something about it, I don't know. Why would it glow?"

"Maybe because there's paint on the box that reflects the sunlight at a certain angle? Maybe there's a simple, scientific explanation?" Tim smiled and reached for the box again.

"Wait." Shannon grabbed his arm. Tim shook his head then lowered his arm for a second time. He turned toward his wife.

"Honey, I mean it. The science is probably pretty simple..." Tim sighed.

"You're lecturing me about science? You? The guy who barely passed any science classes in high school? The guy who had to copy my chemistry papers?" Shannon shook her head.

"Hey, we agreed you wouldn't tell anybody about that..." Tim frowned.

"Like who else can hear?" Shannon continued to stare at the fruit box. Just then the door to the house opened. A teenage boy stuck his head out. Tim and Shannon were both mildly startled.

"What are you guys doing?" The boy asked. Tim and Shannon both shrugged.

"Just talking. Not much." Tim replied as he took a deep breath.

"Oh. Well, um, we're in here waiting. So, Mom, are we going to eat sometime soon? Is the dinner, like, going to burn or something?" The boy asked. Shannon sniffed, looked surprised, then turned and walked quickly toward the door.

"Tim, just wait. Let me check on dinner. I'll be right back." As the door closed behind Shannon, Tim extended his arm toward the box, paused, and then pulled it down. He rubbed his chin again.

"I guess one can't really be too careful..." He raised his eyebrows and shook his head - he knew that Shannon's fear had gotten to him. The sun disappeared behind the house across the street and darkness filled the half-cleaned garage.

The door to the house opened, and Shannon poked her head out. Shannon squinted into the darkening room, then flipped the light switch on. The fluorescent fixture flickered and glowed.

"Tim, dinner's on. That box has sat there for years, and opening it can wait until after we eat. I don't want to waste this – I made lasagna, and you know how much work that is." Shannon said as Tim turned and smiled.

"Oh, not much comes between me and a pan of lasagna, so you won't get an argument!" The door shut as Shannon's head disappeared into the house. Tim walked to the same door, then paused. He looked back and noticed that the glow from the box seemed to remain, even with the fluorescent lights on.

"Don't go anywhere, Mister Orange. You have the next appointment, right after my seven o'clock date with Miss Pasta..."

- - -

"So, what were you guys doing in the garage?" The teen boy at the table asked as he took a bite from a plate full of lasagna. His portion was much taller than anyone else's serving at the table. Shannon sat down, holding her own plate. She shook her head as she looked at the boy's plate.

"I know you're hungry, son, but you can always go back for seconds. You always seem to forget that." Shannon shook her head.

"Oh, don't worry, I will. This is 'firsts'." The teen almost dropped a glob of tomato sauce from his lower lip. He leaned forward and caught it, making a slurping sound.

"Gross! Mom, how can anyone eat with this food machine sucking at the table? Can't he eat like in the garage or something?" A younger teen, a girl, sounded exasperated. Her brother smiled broadly at her, showing a huge portion of noodles and sauce in his mouth.

"Joey! Give it a rest. Show some manners at the dinner table." Tim said gruffly as he raised his fork. A large portion of noodles slid off his fork and hit his plate. Red sauce flicked all over Tim's cream-colored shirt. Shannon sighed.

"I don't know why I even bother making lasagna anymore. I don't know where I went wrong. I tried to teach everyone how to behave at a table..." Shannon stared at her husband. Tim, wiping his mouth, cringed and shrugged.

"Sorry – it was an accident…" The growing red on his face was almost as deep a shade as the tomato sauce.

"Seriously, both of you. There is nothing wrong with taking a normal portion, or fork full, and going back for more." Shannon shook her head as she placed a small bite of food into her mouth.

"A growing boy's got to eat, Shannon. I remember eating like that. He'll get over it." Tim shook his head, looked down at his paunch and sighed.

"Yeah, sure, right. You still pile it on. Look where it got you." Shannon said with an icy voice as she pointed at Tim's stomach with her fork.

"Hey, careful. Watch where you're pointing that thing!" Tim smirked.

"But Joey eats it all – no one else gets seconds. You know, like the last time! There are never leftovers."

"Hey, I told you. I'm 'J.J.' now, not 'Joey'. Get it right, 'Anna'." The teen boy shot back after he swallowed. Annie huffed.

"My name is 'Annie,' and I don't know why you need to change to that stupid name – like a cartoon character or something." Annie shook her head and took another bite.

"'Joey's' a kids name, and I'm almost out of high school now. I don't think you're grown up enough to understand." Joey responded.

"Yeah, I understand. You're mister 'I-am-too-important-for-my-name-now'."

"You don't understand anything. I don't know why I talk to you." Joey shook his head as he plowed another huge portion of food into his mouth.

Tim stopped from taking a bite; his fork was motionless between the plate and his mouth. His daughter's teasing about mister 'I-am-too-important-for-my-name-now' reminded him of the old box in the garage now named "Mister Orange". He turned toward the door.

"Come on, you two. That's enough. If 'J.J.' doesn't catch on, he can go back to 'Joey'. Right, Shan?" Tim turned and stared at his wife, expecting support.

"There is absolutely nothing wrong with the name 'Joseph'. And 'Joey' is just a short form." Shannon did not look at her husband. Tim frowned.

"I'm just trying to find some peace here at the dinner table, that's all." Tim said.

"Good luck with that." Shannon shook her head. Tim turned towards his eldest child.

"What's wrong with being called 'Joe', son?"

"Dad, every guy named 'Joseph' is called 'Joe'. I want something unique."

"We knew a man named Joseph. His friends called him 'Joseph'. He was who you were named after. There is nothing wrong with just 'Joseph'. Besides, his wife called him 'Joey' sometimes." Shannon contributed.

"We know, mom. You've told us before." Joey rolled his eyes and looked at his sister. Annie smiled impishly.

"And I was named after his wife, Anne. We got that, Mom." His sister added, hardly missing a breath after her brother's pronouncement.

"An old man called 'Joey'. That would be really lame." Joey remarked. Shannon glared at her son.

"That is enough! Do not disrespect that man. You have no idea who he was."

"We do, Mom. You tell us about that story in Pine Mountain like every year." Joey said with a "tone" clipped on to the words. Tim stopped chewing and turned toward the garage. A flickering thought crossed his mind.

"Do not give me that 'tone', young man." Shannon glared. Tim turned back to the table and cleared his throat.

"Come on, guys. Let's leave it alone. If he wants to try 'J.J.', let him do it. Son, please try to extend your patience with us for another year or so, until you're eighteen and able to run your own life." Tim shook his head. Joey stopped chewing and stared at his father.

"What do you mean by that?" The younger male asked. Annie stood up and walked toward the stove.

"Nothing. Absolutely nothing. Just trying to enjoy this lasagna. Let's just ratchet the tension down a few notches..."

"And I got the last of it this time! For once!" Annie smiled as she returned to the table. Joey turned his glare toward his sister. Tim put his fork down.

"I'm going to call it a meal. Got a paunch to work on..." Tim said as Shannon turned toward her husband.

"What?" Shannon looked at Tim with a confused expression.

"You're right, honey. I need to eat less. Starting now."

"We'll see how long that lasts!" Shannon shot back.

"Anyway, Shannon, let's clean up and check that orange box in the garage." Tim returned his attention to the object in the corner of the garage.

"What orange box?" Annie asked.

"It's in the back corner, up high, to the left of the water heater." Tim rose and picked up his plate.

"Probably just old junk. That's all that is back in there – stuff we never use." Joey added as he wiped his face. He was staring at his sister's plate.

"What are you looking at?" Annie asked.

"You going to finish that meatball?" Joey asked with a lilt in his voice. Annie leaned over and licked the meatball in question.

"No. It's all yours!" She smiled. Joey turned and scowled.

- - -

Tim carefully shut the door between the house and the garage. Again, the box seemed to glow from the fluorescent lights hanging from the ceiling.

"I think I know you, my friend. It hit me during dinner. You're like a time capsule, left untouched for years. Now, if I could only remember what you hold inside..." Tim whispered just as the door opened behind him.

"What was that?" Shannon asked. She let the door close on its own. Tim was startled.

"I think I remember this box, Shan. It was how the kids were talking at dinner; you know, about their names."

"It's their box?"

"No, no, no. Think Joseph - and Anne. For reasons unknown a memory in the back of my mind triggered while they were talking about how Joey wants to be called 'J.J.' I feel like this box is connected to that house, and the stone wall, on Pine Mountain."

"Tim, we went through the boxes that Paul let us have like about four years ago, remember?" Shannon replied.

"Not quite. If you recall, something happened that weekend that interrupted the process." Tim pointed toward the kitchen.

"Oh, yeah!" Shannon's eyebrows went up. Just then Annie appeared in the doorway. She was pouting.

"Mom! Joey..." She was interrupted from inside of the house.

"It's 'J.J.'" A male muffled voice from inside interjected.

"…yeah, whatever his stupid name is - he ate my piece of pie!"

"Joey! Don't touch any more food!" Shannon shouted as she rolled her eyes. There was a grumble from inside as the door shut.

"Yep. We were interrupted, just like that, only worse." Tim nodded.

"Oh, my. That was the weekend that Joey broke his leg!" Shannon exclaimed.

"Correct. So…" Tim trailed off, expecting Shannon to complete the thought.

"You just threw the last few boxes back on the shelves!"

"Exactly. We got home from the emergency room and I had to throw the garage back together really fast, just to get the car inside. So we just put off the sorting."

"That's the story of raising kids, isn't it? Everything's interrupted by broken bones, being late to band practice, licked meatballs and pieces of pie." Shannon sighed deeply as she shook her head.

"Late to band practice?" Tim turned and looked at his wife.

"Yeah. Thursday. I was ready to go, and I kept calling her name. When I went into her room, there she was, still on the floor, talking on the phone. Know why she didn't hear me?"

"I can't imagine. Why?" Tim sounded resigned.

"She had her head under the bed, with a towel around it – from her shower."

"Her head was under her bed?" Tim asked as he reached for the orange fruit box. He gently pulled it from the shelf; a spray of dust evaporated into the air around them.

"Uh…" Tim coughed.

"Yep. And she had her earphones in – listening to her music – while talking to Jenny. All while the upper half of her body was under the bed." Tim smiled at the image as he shook his head.

"How do we humans ever make it to adulthood?" He asked as he struggled to remove the top of the old box.

"I think it's only because we wear our parents out. The grown-ups have to be the ones who remember things like band practice."

"Then how did we make it? Our parents weren't around much." Tim's voice trailed off. He looked into the semi-opened box.

"I don't know, Tim, I really don't. I guess you and I had to grow up too fast. By the grace of God, maybe."

"And with the help of Grandpa and Grandma Marino." Tim's voice was almost a whisper. He removed the top of the box completely, and stared inside.

"What?"

"Maybe I'm glad we didn't finish sorting those boxes, Shan. There's something about this box..."

"I guess we have to just live with the idea that a lot of things are just not finished until after the last kid moves out." Shannon said.

"Well, we'll see if we're able to finish things after something like twenty five years of living like this. I'm not optimistic, to be honest." Tim shook his head. He pulled an old cloth object from the orange box. Shannon's eyebrows went up.

"Oh, my, Tim. Is that what I think it is?"

"It is if you think it was Grandpa's old plaid jacket. I can't believe we still have it. It's been like, what, fifteen years?" Tim asked.

"Um, Joey's going to be seventeen. Remember my condition back when you worked on that wall?" Shannon looked into the box.

"How can I forget? That's all I worried about back then. Now I worry about that 'condition' eating his sister's piece of pie!"

"Tim, there's more in here. Look. The papers..." Shannon pulled out a sheet of notebook paper.

"Now I remember. I asked Paul if I could keep his dad's old jacket, that time we visited him on Pine Mountain when he cleaned out the old place. I don't know why I wanted it, but I did. Paul threw me an old box and said I could fill it with whatever I wanted. The box had some papers in it, but I didn't pay much attention."

"There's a pocket knife, and a small hammer…" Shannon started.

"A hammer? Let me see it!" Tim leaned in and pulled the old tool out.

"Tim…" Shannon had to step back. The tool missed her head.

"Oh, wow. The old hammer we used to use to whack stones! Man, does this bring back some memories! If a stone had a chunk on it that meant it couldn't fit into the wall, I knocked off that chunk! Grandpa showed me how…" Tim made a swinging motion with his hand as his voice trailed off. The couple looked at each other.

"Brings back a lot of old feelings…" Shannon's voice was barely audible. Tim stared at the hammer as Shannon leaned into the box and pulled out a sheet of paper.

"Sure does. I wish he could have seen our house, and the kids…" Tim mumbled as Shannon stared at a yellowed piece of paper.

"Tim…these aren't just papers. Look. Read this!" Shannon's voice went up dramatically. She pushed a paper into Tim's face.

"Shannon, wait! Too close." Tim pushed her arm back. He began to read out loud.

"That hidden stone was my father. You probably saw him as he was older, and not so angry. Son, when I was a teen he was horribly abusive. He was an alcoholic. The things he said to me, the things he did to me, are too difficult for me to write or say. Needless to say, when you are told that you are a failure, at age 10, or beaten because you tried to take his bottle of vodka when you are 14, it does something to a boy…and the man years later. I'm sorry, but I just can't write much more on that. I hope there's enough there for you to understand what I went through. There is the 'Devil Stone' beneath the 'Big Demon Stone,' I suppose.

For years I used to think the problem was like something chemical – like it's just something about the mix of nitro and glycerin, if you will. I now see that as pretty superficial. There were times when I think we bonded. We had a few laughs on that drive across America, and there were moments when I was happy to be with you.

Paul, please, don't think I forgot about how we laughed that one time at the camp fire on Catalina. We sang some great camp songs. And I remember how embarrassed you were as we walked back to our tent. I never did tell you what I did with that box. I buried it by that big rock near the beach camp – the one you climbed on so much. I didn't actually intend on leaving it there – but we got so busy trying to get back home in that rainstorm two days later that I forgot to dig it up.

I thought I was helping you, but I remember how angry you were for years after that. Please know I didn't mean anything – I just got so busy that I forgot to go back after our first attempt. Someday, let's go back. If it is still there, it'll be under a weathered-looking reddish stone. Hah – another stone connection!

So, I'm off to climb Pine Mountain with Tim and Shannon tomorrow. Yes, I know you're worried, but I now know that there are times in a man's life when he has to confront his fears and find the courage to climb anyway. I'm not sure if you remember how afraid of heights I am. Well, that's why I have to go up that mountain. My fears have run things"

"Where's the rest? Is this all?" Tim almost shouted as he reached into the box. A piece of paper tore.

"Whoa, Tim, hold on! Let's not just tear things apart. These papers are old and they were important to Grandpa. He really spilled his feelings. I think we need to call Paul

Marino - he'll want to see this." Shannon struggled to take the box from her husband and put it on the nearby workbench.

"Do you still have his phone number? Doesn't he live in San Diego? He and Meredith?" Tim asked.

"Yes, Meredith is still his wife. And, yes, I'll find his number. I know he'll want to read this. I wonder if he has ever read these."

"It's worth a try. Besides, we haven't talked to him in a long time…"

"I'm going to sort through these. They're just thrown in here. Can you get me a couple of notebook binders from my sewing room? They're in the cupboard in the back." Shannon asked. Tim nodded and walked quickly toward the door. As he opened it, teen voices could be heard.

"I don't want to watch stupid reruns of 'Gilligan's Island', Annie!"

Tim turned and looked at Shannon, who smiled.

"Someday. It'll get better someday…" Shannon said quietly.

PART ONE

Echoes from Long Ago

Chapter 1

"Paul? Are you there? Should I keep reading?" Tim asked as he pulled the cell phone closer to his ear. He shrugged as he looked over at Shannon, who was sipping a cup of coffee.

"Uh, yeah…" The voice from the phone was very quiet. Tim cleared his throat.

"'So, I'm off to climb Pine Mountain with Tim and Shannon tomorrow. Yes, I know you're worried…'"

"Wait. Back up. What was that part about the box?" Can you read that again?" Paul asked hesitantly.

"Uh, yeah. Let me find it…" Tim scanned the old piece of paper on the table in front of him.

"Oh, don't bother if it's hard to find…" Paul said.

"No, it's okay. I found it. It's only one page; I just had to find the sentence."

"And I remember how embarrassed you were as we walked back to our tent. I never did tell you what I did with that box. I buried it by that big rock near the beach camp – the one you climbed on so much. I didn't actually intend on leaving it there…"

"Wow. That came out of left field..." Tim could barely hear Paul's voice.

"Left field? I don't understand." Tim frowned. Shannon put her cup down and waved her hand at her husband. Tim looked across the table, still holding the phone to his ear.

"What – is – going – on?" Shannon mouthed, not saying the words. Tim shrugged. He grabbed a nearby envelope, from an already-opened letter, and scribbled the words "HE SOUNDS CONFUSED" on it. Shannon frowned and shook her head. She grabbed the paper and pen, then wrote, "ABOUT WHAT?"

Tim shushed his wife with a finger to his lip. He mouthed the word "LATER". Shannon huffed and picked up her cup again.

"Sorry, Tim. See this from my point of view – you and I haven't talked in years and getting a phone call out of the blue is a real surprise. But the call being laced with the words of my father kind of hits me, well, a bit in the emotional department, if you know what I mean."

"I can imagine, Paul." Tim waved at his wife as he continued, pointing at the phone. As he spoke he looked at Shannon. "Hearing from us is one thing, then hearing your father's words is like an emotional double whammy." Shannon's eyebrows went up and she nodded in understanding.

"Yeah, that's what it feels like. Especially after like, I don't know, maybe ten years since we last talked."

"I'm sorry we lost touch. Life has been one thing after another. The kids…" Tim started.

"Yes! Your kids! I'm sorry, I forgot their names. What are they?" Paul was much clearer.

"Hah! You should know the names - Joseph and Anne. Well, Joey wants to be known as 'J.J.' now. He's seventeen, so you know how that goes." Tim smiled at the same moment his son entered the kitchen.

"What? Who's he talking to, Mom? What did he mean by that?" Joey, with a pout splashed across his face, stood next to the kitchen sink with an empty dirty plate in his hand. Shannon put her index finger up to her mouth.

"I'll tell you later. Nothing to worry about…" Shannon said in her most soothing voice.

"Yeah, but he's talking to someone I don't know - about me." Joey continued.

"Son, it is someone you kind of know, but he's not really talking about you. He's telling our old friend Paul about our family. That's all." Shannon strained to keep her whispering voice.

Tim frowned at his son, who was still standing at the sink. He put his finger up to his lip, as his wife had done. He turned his attention back to his phone conversation as Paul started speaking again.

"I'll bet they've grown up a lot since we last saw you. Was that when we were cleaning out my parents' place?" Paul's tone lightened a bit.

"That was it, and that is, in a weird way, how we came across these papers. There was a box in our garage. I thought it was Shannon's. She thought it was mine. We wondered if it belonged to one of our kids..." Tim was cut off by an insistent voice.

"Wait, did you guys go through one of my boxes in the garage?" Joey turned from the sink.

"...can you hold on a minute, Paul? I have to, uh, check something." Tim glared at his son.

"Sure..." Paul replied. Tim put his left hand over the phone's mouthpiece.

"Joey, what's the problem? I'm on the phone here. It has nothing at all to do with you, and I mean that. It was not your box." Tim tried to whisper, but did not do well.

"How do I know that? No one asked me about the box. You guys looked into it without even asking me. Hey, it could have been Annie's box. It's not just about me." Joey was not backing down. Tim did not notice that his hand was no longer over the mouthpiece.

"Yes, I know. Joey, we can talk about how we need to respect your stuff more after I finish this phone call. Get it?" Tim gave his son a stare as he lifted up the phone. He immediately realized that Paul had heard much of the conversation. Joey shook his head and walked out.

"It's just wrong. No respect." Joey grumbled as he went around the corner. Tim returned his attention to the phone. Shannon put her hands over her face and shook her head.

"Paul, I'm sorry. Joey's going through a 'phase'…he thinks he can run things now that he is seventeen. I guess we all did that." Tim drew a long sigh.

"Believe me, I completely understand. I went through the same thing with my son." There was a pause in the conversation. Tim heard a sigh come across the phone.

"Sorry, Paul. I didn't mean to dump this old emotional baggage on you."

"No, no, it's okay. It's just odd, hearing my father's words again, and then hearing Joey's, um, I don't know…uh…"

"Tantrum? Hissy fit?" Tim found himself smiling. Paul chuckled.

"Hah! Yeah, I guess that would cover it. I hate to say it, but that sent a chill up my backside. It seems like yesterday I was talking to my father like that. Remember my story about our cross-country road trip in a 1948 Woody? What a journey that was…" Paul asked.

"Oh, yes, yes, I do remember. You guys had some tense moments across a bunch of states!" Tim smiled.

"Leading to one huge tense moment in Wyoming. Believe me, those conflicts were a lot worse than what I just heard." Paul had a tired sound in his voice.

"Well, thanks for saying that. Sometimes we wonder if we're making a mess of this, or if we're actually helping him. I'm sorry you had to hear that." Tim turned and looked at Shannon. She was slowly shaking her head as she stared out the kitchen window.

"Not to worry, Tim. I felt for you; I knew your hand had slipped off of the phone. Someday, just to make you feel better, I'll have to give you the details about a certain run-in I had with gang of motorcycle thugs at a motel in the Midwest – if you've forgotten. I am positive my father was mortified that day." Paul laughed gently.

"Whoa. Weird. I know exactly how he felt. Yes, he was definitely mortified." Tim said; his voice was shaking. Shannon looked over at her husband.

"What?" Paul replied. There was a pause in the conversation.

"Paul, can I read another couple of sentences from your dad's letter? This is just too unreal." Tim asked.

"Uh, I guess we've gone too far into this for me to say no.... Hold on..." Tim heard a rustling on the other end of the phone.

"Are you okay?" Tim asked.

"Yeah, sorry. I decided to pour myself the occasional glass of wine I reserve for tough days. I might need this. Can I put you on speaker phone? I want Meredith to hear this."

"Sure, no problem. Let me know when you're ready." Tim signaled to Shannon and pointed at the refrigerator. He mouthed the word "soda" then smiled. Shannon nodded, walked over to the refrigerator and pulled out a cold drink. She opened it and handed it to her husband.

"Is he okay?" She whispered as she pointed at the phone.

"Oh, yeah. He just wants Meredith to hear this part." Tim took a sip of his drink.

"Put it on speaker phone. I want to hear."

"I don't know how to do that – and you know that." Tim whispered.

"Here, give it to me." Shannon extended her arm.

"Wait. He's back…" Tim answered.

"Well, let me hear it." Paul said in a monotone.

"Well, it's not too far after what I read to you earlier. Your dad wrote, '*Do you remember dealing with the motorcycle gang in the Midwest that one day?*'"

"No way! You have to be making this up. Is this in his handwriting?" Paul interrupted.

"Hey, Paul, I'm not a writer. I couldn't make this stuff up. And why would we? Yeah, it looks like his handwriting to me.

He kind of wrote like he was printing, right? Not really a script?"

"That was him. Wow. I have to see this. Is there more?"

"Oh, definitely - a lot more. But I'll just finish the part about the motorcycle gang. And after we're done I can scan a couple of pages and send that in an email message, if you want."

"Please do that, yes." Paul said quickly.

Tim picked the page of writing up. Shannon reached across and moved the soda can, away from the papers piled around Tim.

"Go ahead...read on." Paul took a breath.

"So, Joseph Marino continues..."

"You got them mad. You were scared and I could tell you were looking to me for strength. Son, I was just as frightened as you were, and yet I had nowhere to hide. I had to be the rock you could hide behind, and I knew it. Sadly, my anger toward you for that moment added yet another stone to our wall. I felt like you forced me to go into my dark, ugly place of fear."

Tim placed the paper back on the table. Shannon turned it toward her and stared at it.

"Oh, my..." Paul whispered.

"You okay?" Tim asked.

"Uh, yeah, but I'm not sure I can, um, talk, uh, any more tonight." Tim heard Paul take a gulp, as if from a glass of liquid.

"Shannon and I debated if we should call you. If this brings you pain, I am really sorry..." Tim was unable to finish his thought. Shannon reached across and grabbed the phone. She quickly pushed two buttons on it.

"Hi, Paul – it's Shannon. I really didn't want to hurt you. That's not why we called."

"Oh, hi, Shannon!" Paul said over the speakerphone.

"Hi, Shannon!" A woman's voice chimed in.

"Meredith! It is good to hear your voice again!" Shannon said with a smile. Tim recognized that smile – it was one she used to put on a happy face when she was worried that she was hurting someone, or about to hurt someone.

"As it is for us." Paul responded. An awkward silence filled the room.

"I really didn't want to do this, Paul. Shannon thought you'd want to read this stuff, but I thought you'd want to just let all of this stay buried in the past..." Tim started. Shannon glared at her husband.

"Wait, Tim - just wait. I can imagine how this put the two of you in a tough spot, but there's no guilt here. You haven't done anything wrong. I know I sound like it brings up old hurts, but the better part of me realizes I need to read this. Am I making sense?" Paul asked.

"Yes..." Both Tim and Shannon said, almost at the same time.

"So, turning to the technical side, since I'm a computer guy, how many pages of my dad's writings did you find?" Paul asked.

"Which notebook?" Shannon asked.

"What? It's more than a few pages? He wasn't much of a writer..." Paul chuckled.

"Well, Shannon went through the orange box and found a couple of those spiral-type notebooks, mostly full, and a sealed letter, which is probably a bunch of pages long." Tim reached over and opened a notebook.

"Shannon, what is this stuff? Is it like a story, or a letter?" Paul asked.

"I would say that the notebooks are like a journal. Yeah, in fact he starts out by talking about how he wasn't sure if it was a real journal, but he was going to write it anyway. I have to say I smiled when I read it – it was his quirky way, the way he talked. It was like he was here in our kitchen. I got kind of emotional." Shannon sat back and looked away.

"Wow..." Paul sighed.

"Oh, I feel bad that I read some of it. It belongs to you. After a bit I decided I shouldn't really be reading it..." Shannon leaned back into the speaker as she sounded anxious. Tim glanced at his wife. She was biting her thumbnail. Tim gently pulled her hand away from her mouth.

"No, no, Shannon. Don't worry. I meant it – there is no guilt here. Of course you'd want to read it. You knew my parents pretty well that last year...you know..." Paul replied.

"I do know. That was the year we built the stone wall – we call it the 'Year of the Stone Man'..." Shannon said, very quietly.

"I think we should get together." Paul suggested. Tim opened his mouth to answer but was cut off.

"I think we should. We live in Saugus now, near Santa Clarita. Where are you?" Shannon asked.

"We're in Huntington Beach. We moved from San Diego a few years ago. I'm not sure we want to meet in between – I don't know about places in Los Angeles." Paul said.

"Huntington Beach, huh? I once knew a guy who had a boat there. Do you live near a harbor?" Tim asked.

"Oh, right on it. I just got a boat and I'm trying to get it seaworthy. Wait, hey, Tim, didn't you work on engines or something?"

"Well, or something. I was trained on jet engines. Now I run an automotive engine machine shop." Tim wanted Paul to be impressed, for some reason.

"So, if I waved some dollars in front of you, could you look at an old marine engine?" Paul hesitated.

"Well, you don't have to wave too many greenbacks, but, sure. I imagine that they're really just the same engines mounted in a ship's hull. I guess we'll meet in Huntington Beach, then. I don't mind looking it over." Tim smiled.

"Just don't forget the scribblings of the Stone Man!" Paul said. The smile on his face shined through his words across the telephone line.

"Here, let me give you our address..." Meredith interrupted.

Chapter 2

"So, have you been around boats much, Tim?" Paul asked as he pointed down toward the dock. Bobbing gently in the water was an older looking watercraft.

"Well, a friend of mine and I built a raft when we lived in Pine Mountain Club. We found old boards, nails and some rubber inner tubes. We'd drag it down to the golf course lake and try it out. That was fun until security rousted us. I don't suppose that really counts, does it?" Tim smiled quickly as he studied the planks on the dock, watching his step.

"Hah! Not even close, my friend. We lived in San Diego for years and I learned a lot from business partners who owned some larger ships. I crewed for about a decade before I got my own. This is my second boat....just got it." Paul reached over for a line and pulled the boat a bit closer to the dock.

"Not bad." Tim rubbed his chin. For the first time in his life he realized he was a bit fearful of being on the water. He stared at the water lapping up on the hull.

"Tim? You okay? Climb aboard!" Tim turned and noticed Paul was already on the deck of the craft.

"Well, uh, okay..." Tim hesitated and put his foot forward.

"You'll be fine. Just grab on to that railing there. Watch your foot on the gunwale." Paul pointed.

"A gun? What?" Tim was surprised.

"Hah – no, no guns here. We're not the U.S. Navy! Just make sure your foot is solid on the top of the deck, there..." Tim did just as Paul suggested. He was "on deck"!

"Hey, that wasn't as hard as I thought!" Tim felt proud of himself. At that moment the boat surged a bit in the water and he had to grab for the railing. Paul reached out and steadied the novice sailor.

"Once you get your 'sea legs' you'll be just fine, Tim. We're all a bit 'green' when we first find ourselves on a ship. Not to worry." Paul said in a quiet, reassuring tone. Tim felt grateful for the assurance.

"I suppose, but forgive me if I'm a bit, well, skeptical?" Tim smiled.

"Hah! I really do understand. It was about 12 years ago that I had a similar experience. Trust me on this." Paul moved toward the center of the back of the deck.

"I guess I'll have to! So, where the heck is the engine on one of these things?" Tim asked as he looked up and down the top side of the boat.

"You're standing on it! It's under the deck. Here...let me...step back a minute, Tim..." Paul leaned over. Tim looked down and saw the outlines of horizontal doors on the deck. He stepped aside.

"Oh, sorry..."

"That's okay. We all have to learn the first time. Boats aren't quite like cars, which we all seem to be familiar with...." Paul opened the large doors, exposing an engine.

"Now this is something that looks familiar. It looks like a V8 engine!" Tim exclaimed.

"Yep – it's a Mercury!" Paul sounded proud.

"Whatever it is, it looks a lot like a V8 my shop just installed in an older car. Is this the original engine?" Tim asked as he squatted to get a closer look.

"I think so. I know the boat's older, but it's what was available." Paul sounded apologetic.

"Oh, hey, it's more than I could afford. I'd be excited to have a boat of my own, so don't feel bad, Paul. It would be kind of fun to tinker with, and tootle around the bay in."

"Oh, I have ambitions bigger than 'tootling around the bay', Tim! This is an ocean-going vessel!" Paul leaned over and tapped on the edge of the cabin. A piece of wood fell off. Tim leaned over, picked it up and handed it back to Paul.

"Maybe after a little work, huh?" Tim smiled.

"Well, that's why I wanted you to come over. I had a guy over to look at the engine and he said I should just pull it and install a new one. Do you have any idea how much that would cost?" Paul took a deep breath.

"Well, in a car that would run deep into the thousands, for sure. But in a boat? I can guess it would be a lot more. Not sure pulling this engine out of the hull would be cheap or easy." Tim squinted as he looked at some rubber hoses. He ran his finger along one and followed its path.

"It's a lot more. I thought I'd get your opinion before I moved forward." Paul looked toward his house and shielded his eyes with his right hand.

"Well, hand me the tool box, over on the dock. Let's take a quick look." Tim pointed. Paul walked over and picked up the red steel object. As he placed it beside Tim he knelt down on the other side of the engine compartment door.

"Tim, now that the ladies are back in the house, can I be honest about this?" Paul's tone of voice changed. He sounded far more serious. Tim looked across the engine at the man.

"Well, as I tell my customers, honesty from both directions always makes a job go smoother. What do you mean?" Tim opened the red box.

"As I said, this is my second boat..." Paul paused and looked back at the house.

"Yeah. Second boat." Tim repeated. He grabbed a rag and started wiping the joint between the engine block and the head. He looked carefully at the rag. Paul noticed what Tim was doing.

"Find something?" Paul asked.

"Oh, no, just checking for gasket leakage. Doesn't look too bad. So, it's your second boat..." Tim reached under the forward end of the engine.

"Oh, yeah, right. Well, we had to get rid of our first boat. It came between us. Cost a lot of money. You know how it is – a lot of married couples fight over dollars." Paul picked up a wrench and started spinning it in his hand.

"Believe me, no one knows about that idea better than me. Shannon and I have never had more than a few dollars a month extra at any given time in the eighteen years or so that we've been together. Every extra buck we could scrounge went into a down payment on our house in Saugus. It was the smallest amount we could use to get into the deal. Now? Hah! Let's not go there." Tim examined a few wires leading to the engine block.

"Well, I sold the old boat when we moved here. I told Meredith that I'd get another boat only if it didn't screw up our budget, like the old one did. Tim, that old bucket had us at each other's throats."

"So, you found some money and bought this?" Tim pointed at a small flashlight in the tool box. Paul handed it to

39

him. Tim clicked the device on and pointed it into the deeper areas of the engine compartment.

"Not exactly." Paul said softly. Tim looked up. The light was still shining inside the compartment.

"Not exactly?" Tim asked.

"Well, it's like this. On the weekends I often get side jobs with small companies – I work on their computer networks."

"Yeah. I've fixed a motor or two on the side for some extra cash." Tim pulled on a metal bracket, then nodded.

"Well, I worked for like ten months on a network, and the guy's business went south. He owed me a bundle."

"I've seen a few clients 'disappear,' as I call it. We do the job and we never hear from them. Yep, I get it." Tim answered as he signaled for a screwdriver. Paul picked one up.

"Here…" Paul handed it to Tim.

"No, a Philip's screwdriver. The other one." Tim pointed.

"Oh, sorry." Paul handed over the other tool.

"Hey, it's okay. I probably wouldn't know a router from a keyboard if I had to fix a computer." Tim smiled. He placed the screwdriver into the end of a screw and turned slowly, then returned to the starting point.

"Well, the guy needed more work, and I told him that I had to have some kind of payment first..." Paul started. Tim put his hand up.

"Let me guess. I'm looking deep into his payment." Tim pointed into the engine compartment. Paul nodded.

"Yep. Now here's the thing. The guy told me that this boat is in tip-top shape. We started it, and got it over here just fine. The next weekend, when I went out to start it, nothing." Paul sighed.

"Let me guess again. Meredith was standing on the dock as you tried cranking it." Tim started to return the tools to his red box.

"Um, no. You're wrong on both counts. Merrie was standing next to me on the deck as absolutely nothing happened. Nothing at all. No cranking, no clicking."

"Don't you love it when that happens? Ever notice it always happens when you want to impress someone?" Tim smiled. Paul smiled half-heartedly.

"Well, we didn't have a good night that Saturday, Tim." Paul looked away.

"Well, since this is Saturday, I can say you'll have a better night tonight." Tim smiled.

"What do you mean?"

"What you described fits my suspicion. Bad battery cable. Fried. We can get a new one and this baby should fire right up. I can't find much else wrong from my once-over.

41

Sure, maybe it could use some spark plugs, but who knows? Can't guarantee anything, but a few bucks worth of cable should get it started."

"Great! Let's do that! There's a marine shop down the street..."

"Paul, I have to warn you. I've seen small problems like this hide big problems, so don't get your hopes up too much. I need to hear this beast running. Been a while since I've worked on a carburetor engine..." Tim wiped his hands on an old rag hanging out of his tool box.

"She'll fire up! I believe it!" Paul said as he stepped off of the boat. Tim followed.

Chapter 3

"Ready? I'm at the helm - just give the signal." Paul announced from behind the boat's wheel. Tim finished installing the new cable.

"Helm? I have to learn some of this boat lingo. Looks like a steering wheel to me." Tim replied. He stood up and wiped his hands.

"Hang around long enough and you start using the right words, Tim. I'm ready for..." Paul grinned, but it faded as he saw two women walking toward the boat. Tim noticed the change and looked over toward the house.

"Looks like a possible storm off of the port bow, Captain..." Tim whispered out of the side of his mouth, just loud enough for Paul to hear.

"You've picked up the lingo mighty well, First Mate..."

"Turn on the ignition, Paul." Tim said.

"Right. All set."

"Crank her over, Captain!" Tim announced in a loud voice. Paul turned the key. Nothing happened. Tim looked quickly at the helm.

"Tim, it's not happening..." Tim jumped up and walked to the control center. He went back to the engine compartment, then stood up, slowly.

"Sorry, Paul. I messed up. Hold on. I disconnected the ignition, just to be sure. Wait for my signal..." Tim reached in and fumbled with wires.

"Roger..."

"Turn it over, Paul!" Tim said anxiously, in a not-so-loud voice. Paul turned the key. A loud roar came from the open compartment. The engine was alive! Both Tim and Paul looked toward Shannon and Meredith. The women had stopped walking toward the boat. Both had big grins on their faces; Meredith sent a "thumbs up" sign to her husband. Paul responded in kind.

"Tim! What should I do?" Paul said in a loud voice.

"Let her run for a bit. I'm listening!" Tim shouted back. The engine sounded smooth, Tim thought, but there were a few irregularities.

"He said he wants to listen to it for a bit!" Paul shouted to his wife on the shore. He pointed down at Tim.

"We can hear it here, too!" Meredith responded.

"Shut it down, Paul!" Tim said, loudly. Paul turned the key and the engine settled down and stopped. Tim closed the doors to the engine compartment.

"Let's start her one more time, just to be sure." Tim pointed at Paul. Paul nodded. He turned the key and the engine started. It was much quieter on deck with the compartment closed.

"Sounds good, Tim!" Paul smiled.

"It does. Not perfect, but not too bad. Go ahead and shut it down." Tim picked up a few tools and started to put them into his tool box. Paul shut down the engine. Silence engulfed the boat once again, save for the creaking of wood against water. The two women on the shore started applauding. Paul smiled gently.

"Well, it looks like the audience appreciated the concert!" Tim said as he gently rubbed a scratch on his left hand. At that moment Meredith cupped her hands around her mouth and started to speak.

"Dinner's ready! Come and get it!" Meredith's announcement caused Tim to pause the inspection of his hand. Meredith and Shannon turned and walked toward the house.

"It's that late? Whoa – I lost track of time…" Tim said as he looked toward the western horizon; sure enough, the sun was getting low in the autumn sky. Tim noticed clouds building on the horizon.

"Isn't that the way it is when you're consumed by a project? But it was worth it, Tim. The hum of that engine was like music to my ears, my friend." Paul said as he walked toward the dock. Tim followed, still concerned about the scratches on his hand.

"My hands remind me why I got out of working directly on engines. They sure can get scratched up easily. I hate wearing gloves while working, but maybe…" Tim felt a hand against his chest as he was nearing the edge of the boat. Paul was standing between him and the dock.

"Tim, thanks. I mean that. You may have saved my marriage." Paul said quietly as he looked toward the house.

"It's probably not that bad. I can't believe that Meredith would allow an old boat to come between you and…" Tim was interrupted.

"My friend, it IS really that serious. I promised her that we would not spend over a certain amount per month on this tub. That marine mechanic I told you about gave me an estimate of about eight thousand. Let's just say that was not even close to being 'in the ballpark'."

"Eight thousand? For what? The engine seems solid enough to me – yeah, I know I don't know anything about boats, but I can talk about engines." Tim was surprised.

"Well, there are a few other things, but the engine was the big issue." Paul replied.

"That's how it usually is with cars, too." Tim noticed that Paul was not turning to step on to the dock.

"Listen, Tim. Can you talk it up in there at dinner? Just say some positives about the boat? Talk about how great the engine sounds, stuff like that?" Paul's eyes were pleading with Tim, even more than his words.

"I feel a little weird about that, Paul. Sure, I'll say what I know, but…" Tim started.

"That's all I ask. You don't have to lie. I don't want it to sound fake, either. Not too much, just be upbeat." Paul interrupted. He turned and stepped on to the dock. Tim took a deep breath and followed. Much to his surprise, moving off of the boat was not as tough as he had feared.

Chapter 4

"Hey, that smells familiar!" Tim exclaimed as he stepped through the back door of the house. As he slid the door shut behind him he noticed the boat bobbing gently in the dock outside. A crisp red, white and blue flag gently fluttered on its small mast on the rear of the ship.

"Meredith showed me how Grandma Marino used to make tomato sauce, Tim!" Shannon smiled.

"Whoa, so that really is an old familiar smell!" Tim smiled as he turned toward the kitchen table. The table was set with a nautical theme. Each plate had signal flags and anchors on it. The colors of the flowers in the center matched the plates.

"Nice table, huh, Tim?" Paul asked with a smile. Tim nodded.

"All these years I've tried to remember what she taught me. Grilling the onions was the step I left out. Do you remember how I made Grandpa Marino a meatball sandwich after Grandma..." Shannon stopped herself in mid-sentence. She glanced at Paul. An uncomfortable silence filled the room. Paul pulled a chair from the table and spoke up.

"...after my mother passed away. It's really not a problem, Shannon, but thanks for being worried about my feelings. Yeah, I miss them, but after seventeen years it's not as raw as it used to be." Paul sat down next to Tim at the table.

"I wasn't sure." Shannon said in a quiet voice.

"Well, it is why we're here together, isn't it? Actually, thanks for breaking the ice. Isn't it strange how uncomfortable we are talking about those we loved who've passed away."

Paul waxed philosophical. He looked at Tim who was still looking at the boat outside.

"I know it's true in our family. To be honest, I still have problems talking about my father. He died from lung cancer – on my birthday." Shannon's volume decreased as she finished her sentence.

"I never really knew if your dad accepted me or not." Tim responded. He was still watching the small American-style flag on the rear of the boat. There was another uncomfortable silence in the room.

"You seem fascinated with something on the boat, Tim." Paul asked.

"Uh, oh, yeah. The flag. It's an American flag, but the stars are not there. An anchor and a few stars?"

"A yacht flag…used at sea. It's called an ensign. Very common on boats."

"The flag reminded me of your father. You know that he used to have a flagpole near the stone wall we built. I remember him putting up a few different flags. A connection you have with your dad…the yacht flag." Tim said.

"Well, you should fly a flag on your ship when out and about. It's an old custom to identify your country of origin, that sort of thing, on the high seas. As to my father, I have a lot of his flags, but I don't really collect them."

"High seas? Like to make sure you're not a pirate or something?" Tim turned to look at Paul.

"Believe it or not, that's still kind of valid, Tim. Out on the ocean laws are a bit different. Once you get away from land the rules change. The captain of a ship becomes like the president and courts and judges and juries. Well, not on small boats like ours – but on the big boys, yes."

"Weird. I had no idea." Tim looked across the room and noticed something familiar.

"One learns a lot, and has to, when one brings a boat into the family." Paul leaned over and reached for an empty glass. He reached for a pitcher in the center of the table and poured some lemonade.

Meredith cleared her throat. Paul stopped pouring and looked over at his wife. Tim noticed that she was shaking her head. He turned away, uncomfortable with the not-so-hidden message. Tim's gaze returned to the familiar object on the wall.

"Uh, so, what are those things in the picture frame next to the photo of your parents, Paul?" Tim pointed.

"What? Oh, that. Meredith framed a few of my mother's notes. Do you remember my father finding them after she passed away?" Paul answered. Tim nodded.

"Tim, you remember. I think Grandpa handed one of them to you, absent-mindedly. Remember that day when you were working on the stone wall?" Shannon said to her husband. Tim stood up and walked to the display on the far wall.

"Hey, Shan...I remember this one! We were in their kitchen when Grandpa read it! It was their anniversary!" Tim exclaimed as he pointed at the pink note.

"You are kidding me! I remember that! The one about the ducks, right?" Shannon asked, moving toward her husband.

"Yeah, that's the one." Tim answered.

"Oh, my! Tim, look above your head." Shannon pointed. Tim looked up and noticed two small ceramic mallard ducks, facing each other, on a small display shelf. The male duck had a thick, faded lipstick mark on its beak.

"Wow. It's like seventeen years just disappeared..." Tim mumbled.

"Come and get it!" Meredith called out as she placed a bowl of pasta on the table. Tim backed slowly away from the wall display, then turned toward the table. Shannon stayed, carefully reading the anniversary note. He tripped over a purse next to a chair in the center of the room but was able to catch himself before falling.

"Hey, careful, Tim!" Paul blurted. Tim felt the red flush rising in his face as he made his way to the chair at the table.

"Wait..." Shannon said quietly. It was obvious that she was crying. She had her hand over her mouth.

"What's wrong?" Tim stopped short of the table and turned toward his wife.

"I have a missing piece! You have to hear something! Now; please, bear with me. Maybe you'll understand in a minute." Shannon said with urgency. She stepped over to the chair Tim had just tripped over then reached past her purse to a large cloth bag behind it.

"That's not a problem, Shannon. Dinner has to cool down a bit anyway." Meredith said in a consoling voice. Still in her apron, she walked to the edge of the dining room area. Paul turned toward the living room as well. Shannon pulled a very old looking notebook out of the bag, then sat on the chair close by.

"Meredith, can you read that pink note, out loud? We need a woman's voice. Wait until I give you the signal..." She asked. Shannon quickly scanned through numerous pages of the old notebook, as if she were looking for something in particular. Meredith looked at Paul, shrugged and started walking.

"Sure, I guess..." She said as she walked past Shannon on her way toward the framed papers on the wall.

"I know it's here - somewhere..." Shannon whispered.

"It's okay – take your time. We're baffled here, Shannon. What is...?" Paul started as he stepped into the living room. Shannon interrupted him.

"Found it! Tim, come here and read this – after Meredith reads. We need a male voice." Tim walked over and took the notebook from his wife. Shannon pointed to a passage. Tim nodded.

"Yeah, I see…" Tim acknowledged.

"Tim, wait until she finishes her part. Meredith, read the note - out loud!" Shannon said excitedly.

"Okay…uh…" She started.

Happy anniversary, Joey!

I knew you'd still have our ducks on the table in the morning. I'm sad that I can't be there this time. If you look at the male duck, he's sporting a lipstick kiss. It's for you. I'll be watching you and loving you – today and always.

Love, Annie

"Tim…" Shannon whispered as she pointed.

"Yeah…" Tim cleared his throat and started reading.

OCTOBER 11

Yes, there's a date, right there, which totally messes up my impeccable journaling system. I'll bet that Mary from the Post Office would cringe if she could read this lousy excuse of a journal. I'm, sure she'd never make it past the first page.

Oh, well, none of it really matters. What does matter is that it's our anniversary, and the first one since you left. Yes, I got your pink note about this day, and I saw the lipstick on the male duck. I almost went in and got your lipstick, put it on and kissed the female duck. Oh, what the heck, maybe I will.

You know what? I'm not going to tell you if I did it! Just take a peek down from heaven and see for yourself. I love you still…

All eyes in the room immediately turned toward the two ducks on the shelf. All four people walked over and looked at the shelf. Paul reached up and gently took down one of the ducks.

"That's the male, Paul…he's more colorful. We've seen the lipstick on him." Meredith corrected her husband.

"Oh, yeah. Here…" Paul replaced the male duck and gingerly picked up the other.

As Paul brought down the female duck everyone leaned in to look at the front of the beak.

"My Lord. Look, there it is. It's faint, but it's there." Paul said in a hushed tone.

"It looks like it was just dabbed on. The male's kiss mark looked like your mother actually kissed the duck. This was drawn on..." Meredith added.

"I can't see my father putting on lipstick to do that! I'll bet he used one of my mother's lipsticks like a crayon." Paul smiled.

"Yeah, that was not him...not on his mouth, I mean..." Tim added with a nervous chuckle.

"Well, now that the show is over, should we have dinner?" Meredith asked as she pointed to the kitchen with both hands. Paul gently replaced the female duck and nodded. Each person quietly made his or her way back to the dinner table.

Chapter 5

"So, shall we 'retire' to the living room? What do you think, Tim? Shannon, I hate to say it, but I really want to look at what you have in that cloth-lined magic bag of yours." Paul gestured to his right.

"I guess the living room would work for me. That was great penne, Meredith!" Tim said with a smile. He pushed his chair back.

"Thanks. Let's just stack our plates in the sink here as we move to the living room. They can start soaking while we investigate this relic from Pine Mountain." Meredith walked over and deposited her plate, then filled the sink with water. The others followed her example.

"After we read that passage it dawned on me that maybe I shouldn't have read his journal – I do feel like it belongs to you." Shannon was very sheepish. All four picked out places to sit, on the couch or on chairs.

"No, no, no, Shannon. What I said earlier still stands. You cared about my parents, and you were there with them at the end, so I know you understand the emotions in these writings. I've never forgotten that someone was there for them in their last days, and you two were those people. Please, all is well." Paul waved his hand as he sat down at the end of the couch.

"Thanks; I did need to hear that. When we found the papers, in that orange box, they were all just thrown in there, like packaging materials. I went through them, sorted the loose ones and straightened out the bent notebooks. Well, I did the best I could." Shannon pulled the cloth bag from beside the chair as she sat down.

"I believe you. When you texted that cell phone photo of the box as you found it, I was a bit embarrassed, to be honest." Paul admitted.

"Why?" Shannon asked.

"It looked like how I packed boxes that month we had to get all of my parents' stuff out of the house. I just threw stuff into whatever box was lying nearby at the end. I'm pretty sure I created the mess you ended up sorting out. I guess I should be the one saying 'sorry'." Paul said apologetically.

"I understand. We had to clean up my father's place in Pine Mountain a few years ago and we did a bit of that, too. I wonder what our kids will find after we're gone." Shannon sighed.

"Oh, I'm sorry about your father…" Meredith extended her hand. She sat in the chair next to Shannon.

"Thanks. That was a rough time…" Shannon shook her head. Silence filled the room. Tim drew a breath and opened his mouth. He paused.

"Well, uh, it might have been a bit of my fault, too, Paul. I do remember what happened. I asked you if I could keep your dad's old plaid coat, the one he wore while working on the wall. You nodded and told me to just throw whatever I wanted into a box. I saw the orange one, and dumped it in there. I also took the little hammer we used to break some of the stones, and one of his Boston Red Sox hats. He wore those a lot." Tim sat in the middle of the couch.

"Oh, don't I know that! Whenever we went to New England to visit family he had a couple of those in the car or in his suitcase. I still have one or two around here somewhere." Paul smiled and nodded.

"I'm glad you have a couple. I want to keep the one I have, but I was willing to give it back…"

"Oh, no, no. Keep it." Paul shook his head.

"Will do..."

"Now, Shannon, tell us about what you found." Paul leaned back.

"I think you pretty much have a grasp on it. A few old spiral notebooks. Altogether I call these 'Joseph's Journal,' mainly because, well, that's what he called it that at the beginning. Or what I guess was the beginning. Then there were the loose..."

"You guess?" Paul interrupted.

"Not really. Your dad kind of answers your question at the beginning, but he didn't really date things the way journals usually are, so that's what I mean." Shannon chuckled. Paul nodded.

"I interrupted you – what did you mean by 'loose'...?"

"The rest of the papers made up what looks like a letter – a letter to you. We scanned that one page and sent it in an email, but there were more pages. We have it all here." Shannon gestured at the bag.

"I'm sorry, I'm jumping all over the place. Let's start with his journal. Tell me about it." Paul said, taking a deep breath.

"Well, instead of me telling you, let me read his words, from the beginning, to you. Let your dad tell you about it." Shannon opened to the first page of a notebook and cleared her throat.

Chapter 6

The Journal Of Joseph Marino, A Retired, Bald, Overweight Old Guy Who Is Supposed To Be Building A Stone Wall But Can't Find The Energy.

TUESDAY

There, this thing has a starting point. I guess I am supposed to call it a journal, but I'm not really sure what to write here.

For about two weeks now I've been staring at this sheet of paper, not exactly sure how to start writing. I can't believe that today I wrote something. Mostly I've just scratched the stubble of my beard and watched the mockingbird in the tree next door. But today we have a title! Yeah, I know the title probably sucks, but there it is.

You know what? Note to future editor, if anyone does that to these scribblings: I decided I want that title to stay just like it is. All I give permission to do is edit it in case I capitalized a word I wasn't supposed to capitalize. I decided I'm not going to spend any time trying to look those kinds of things up.

WEDNESDAY

Okay, so I didn't write a whole lot on my first day. To be honest, watching a mockingbird sends me into the emotional dump. Mockingbirds were Annie's favorite. I can remember her telling me about how those little things can imitate all kinds of things, like a lawn mower or a dog. Well, I'm not sure about the dog part, but yesterday Mocker (as I call him) imitated my neighbor's lawn mower really well!

I turned to call Annie, to have her come over to hear Mocker, and that ended my writing efforts for the day. And guess what? There's that bird again, trying to distract me from writing this thing. Hold on a minute while I close the window.

Yes, I know I'm wandering. Why in the heck would I write asking you, the reader, to "hold on" while I closed the window? Heck, will there ever be a "reader"? Like you were in this room with me? Shoot, if you were here I'd be kind of embarrassed. I'm not half the housekeeper Annie was. Heck, I'm not a housekeeper at all. I'm now an official "house messer."

Well, when I sat down today the choices presented to me boiled down to either writing about the mockingbird or describe in intimate detail how I suck down soda, or chips (or both), wondering why I would want to write anything. Who would want to read anything I would have to say?

I think I'm just going to quit for today. I caught myself just staring at on old family picture. At least I wrote a little more than I did yesterday.

THURSDAY

Okay, it's not much but at least now this journal idea is moving. Yeah, I've decided to call it a journal. I'll try to write every day, and I suppose that's how a journal works. I looked the word up in the dictionary. Comes from French – for "day". If nothing else, I'm learning something.

So, now we have a title, a bit about mockingbirds, and some sordid details about my inability to clean up my own messes, for what all of that is worth. I can now tell people that this thing isn't blank anymore. Just getting the title down seems to have started the engine. I have to thank Mary down at the post office. She was asking about what I was doing with my time, besides building the stone wall, and I, well, decided to kind of lie. I told her I was writing a book.

Isn't that what all old guys do? Don't we all write down our important thoughts and the wisdom gathered from having lived on this Earth for almost 80 years?

I've never written a journal before, and I'm really not sure where this is going, to tell you the truth. How are you supposed to do a journal? Who do you go to ask? Yeah, sure, I could call a retired English teacher friend of mine, but that's uncomfortable.

I can imagine THAT conversation. "Hey, Heather! How are you doing? Yeah, it's been years! Oh, Annie passed away. Yes, she was a nice lady. Thanks for saying that. By the way, can you give me some advice on how to write a journal?" Sure, I'd sound sane. Or not.

Okay, I'm done for today. That was not productive.

SATURDAY

I know I skipped Friday, but I really had nothing to write, to be honest. I sat for a while looking at the paper and nothing happened. I got angry – felt it's a waste of time to just sit and stare at paper when there are no words coming. I still don't know why I'm doing this. I mean, do I have some deep thoughts that will bring peace to the world, or change the course of human history? I don't think so. This old high school teacher knows that greater minds than his have busted many pencils and pens and crumpled millions of pieces of paper for a long time in those fields and come up empty-handed. So I went outside and stacked a few stones on the wall.

I guess I need to change the title of this journal now that I've started back on the wall. Nah, let's leave it like that. Did you read that, future editor? Don't change the title! It's how I want. I also decided that even if a word should or should not be capitalized, leave it just the way I wrote it. It's my writing. Leave it alone.

I figure I'll try to work on the wall for a while, then try to find some meaningful words to scribble here. Maybe if I write long enough something worthwhile might come out of it.

This is looking more and more like that old story about having a thousand monkeys working on typewriters for a thousand years – eventually they'll produce something like "The Grapes of Wrath" or another piece of real literature. But there's only one monkey and I'm not using a typewriter.

My apologies to John Steinbeck – he has always been one of my favorites. John, I'm sure a million monkeys in a million years could not create anything close to what you wrote. I think that was the iced bourbon and lemonade in me talking. I had three of them and I really need to stop for today.

- - -

Shannon stopped reading and looked at Paul; Tim and Meredith looked over as well. His sighs were audible. Paul reached across and gestured to see the notebook. He look up and down the pages she had just read.

"Wow. Those are his words – it's his 'voice'. That's his handwriting. This is amazing. I had no idea he wrote any of this. Heck, I had no idea he wrote much of anything except for a short note or a shopping list. I can really see that he was lost after my mother...uh...passed away." Paul's voice faded.

"Paul, he mentioned the old family picture..." Meredith gestured toward a dark corner of the room. Behind a darkened lamp sat a black and white photo in a wooden frame. Paul, Tim and Shannon looked over as Meredith reached up and turned the lamp on. The warm glow illuminated the portrait of a happy family.

"I know that is the one he referred to. It was on his desk. It was the only one he kept out - for years." Paul whispered. He seemed entranced by the photograph. Shannon opened her mouth, then paused.

"Did you notice that he wondered why he was doing this, writing this journal? I think, in his own, flawed way, he was trying to tell you something with all of this, Paul. It's a guess, but after reading through a lot of this that idea came up. I believe he didn't understand why he kept writing, but I think he just pressed on, hoping somehow some meaning would appear." Shannon offered. The room grew quiet.

"Paul?" Meredith asked in a soft voice. Her husband was staring out of the window. Shannon looked at Meredith and shrugged.

"Uh-huh…yeah…" Paul whispered as he looked at the old photograph.

"All's well, honey?" Meredith whispered.

"Yeah. Just hard hearing my father's voice again, my father's words echoing in our house."

"It was a bit higher pitched this time…" Meredith smiled as she looked at Shannon.

"A bit…" Shannon contributed.

"John Steinbeck. Huh!" Paul mumbled. After a pause Meredith looked over at Tim.

"So, it seems like you had some luck with the boat's engine today, Tim? I don't know much about those things but it sounded good to me." Meredith glanced again at her husband.

Chapter 7

"Well, uh, yeah, we did fix a few minor problems." Tim shifted in his seat and glanced over at Paul. Uncomfortable silence remained.

"What was the biggest problem?" Meredith asked.

"Uh, there was a fried cable." Tim noticed that Meredith looked confused.

"Fried?"

"Sorry, I mean there was an electrical cable that was corroded. It was the one was that went to the positive terminal of the main battery. It was a simple fix, and the battery seemed fine, so it started." Tim elaborated. He noticed that Paul was now looking at him.

"We had a bit of an embarrassment as we turned the switch a bit too early – we forgot to re-connect the control panel wires. Tim thought it was prudent to do that before he worked on things." Paul added.

"Yeah. I don't want engines starting when my hands are down inside of them, so I always try to make sure the circuit is broken somewhere, besides where I'm working." Tim felt a bit more comfortable talking, now that Paul had joined in.

Tim noticed that Shannon was returning the notebooks and papers to the cloth bag.

"I'm glad to hear it. I've had some, um, how shall I say it? Anxiety? Boats can consume a lot of money and time, and that worries me." Meredith said as she watched Shannon tidying and sorting the notebooks and papers. Paul glared at Tim.

"I've heard that, but other than building a scrap wood raft as a kid, I don't know much about boats…" Tim felt a bit "on the spot" and uncomfortable.

"Oh? Don't you work with engines and mechanical things?"

"Oh, yeah, sure. A boat's motor is not very different from a car's, but, well, I mean…"

"Honey, I think he means he's never owned a boat and doesn't know about what costs are like. Is that it, Tim?" Paul threw out a lifesaver.

"Yeah, that's it. But I can say that the engine is solid. Perfect? No, but she definitely has some years left in her. No head gasket leaks, stuff like that." Tim shifted in his seat again, then looked at Paul. The older man nodded gently.

"That sounds good. I can imagine that 'head gasket leaks' are not good at all…" Meredith said.

"Oh, no, not something you want in any engine…on a road or on the water. It's not…" Tim started.

"Tim used to work on jet engines, too, so if he says an engine is solid, it probably is..." Shannon interjected. Tim pointed at his wife and nodded.

"I like to think I know the internal combustion engine. Jet engines? Well, you're not considering mounting one of those in your boat, are you, Paul?" Tim offered a smile.

"Jet engine? Whoa, no...no...no." Paul smiled, half-heartedly. He shook his head.

"So, is the boat ready for her maiden voyage? Paul said the two of you would be taking her out soon!" Meredith smiled. Tim turned and stared at Paul. There was another uncomfortable silence.

"Uh, I don't, um...know..." Tim was at a loss for words. Paul had not mentioned actually going out on the boat for a test run, or any other voyage.

"Well, uh, Tim and I didn't have much of a chance to discuss that, Merrie. We kind of got consumed with fixing the wiring..." Paul shifted in his chair.

"A boat trip?" Shannon said as she finished straightening the papers in her lap. Paul noticed the notebook still lying beside her, on the arm of the chair.

"Sure. Just a day trip. Maybe we could all go?" Paul asked. Tim looked at Shannon.

"Tim and I will have to talk about it, Paul." Shannon said as she looked at Tim with an intense stare. Tim understood – Shannon wasn't about to say anything, but he wondered if her fear of the ocean was boiling up.

"Oh, definitely. I understand." Paul replied as he looked over at Meredith.

"I'd be up for it..." Meredith offered. She fidgeted with her bracelet.

"Wait. There's tension here, and it's not about my father's journal. It's not fair to Tim and Shannon..." Paul started.

"What's not fair?" Shannon shot back.

"There's a back story to this boat that you're not aware of. I told Tim a bit about it. We've not had a lot of good luck owning boats in the past, Shannon."

"That's an understatement." Meredith said, softly.

"So you're trying again?" Shannon asked.

"As I told Tim, someone gave me the boat as payment for a computer network project. Merrie wants to sell it and just get a small skiff that we can use to motor around the harbor. I want to see if we could keep this boat." Paul explained.

"My idea is to put the money from selling this boat in the bank and use that to maintain a smaller boat. It was the money and the time that came between us the last time, years ago, in San Diego." Meredith looked out the window.

"I get it – so Tim's looking at the boat is your way of checking out the idea of keeping it." Shannon said.

"Both, actually, Shannon. We agreed on a plan. We would have an expert give us an opinion. We got one. That marine services guy said the engine needed thousands of dollars' worth of work. When you guys called, and I knew Tim worked with engines, I thought it would be helpful to get a second look." Paul continued.

"I get it, Paul, but what confuses me is why the other guy would say that about that engine. It's an older engine, sure, but it's in good shape. It needs only minor work. Maybe marine engines are different. Maybe I could do some compression tests, and there could be a cylinder that is a bit off, but not by far..." Tim straightened up in his chair.

"Oh, no, Tim..." Paul interrupted. Tim continued.

"Look, you two have a lot riding on this. It's no big deal to do a compression test. You invited us for the weekend, and I do have a compression test kit in my truck. I'm sure I can rig it to work. A compression test tells a lot about an engine's health." Tim gestured toward the front of the house.

"Well, okay, if it's not a big deal..." Paul responded.

"Oh, no, it doesn't take long at all." Tim sat back.

"Then we can discuss a boat trip..." Shannon offered. She was staring right at her husband. Tim nodded with understanding.

"Of course. We wouldn't do it this weekend, no. It wouldn't be an overnight thing, either. Just a few hours out and a few hours back." Paul explained.

"We'll see…" Shannon whispered.

"But we forgot another reason you're here. How about hearing more wisdom from the Bard of Pine Mountain?" Paul pointed at the journal in Shannon's lap.

"Well, I am excited about sharing his scribblings. That was my reason for wanting to visit. Your dad really opened his heart in these pages. He was an amazing man!" Shannon opened the journal again.

"It's the most anticipated book in this household, Shannon! I'm sorry about checking out emotionally earlier – I just didn't expect that he ever did anything like this. Sort of hit me broadsides…" Paul said.

"Here. I'll read from where we stopped, after the anniversary ducks. A week at a time, is that okay?"

"Sounds good to me. Sitting around the living room, listening to a story. Sort of like my childhood…" Paul sighed.

"Childhood?" Shannon asked.

"When I was a kid my mother used to sit in front of the kids, gathered on the floor, and read. Even kids from down the street would come visit for that. She'd make some popcorn and set a whole bowl down in the middle of the room. Hah! I remember how she laid out a sheet first. We kids were so messy!"

"Maybe I'll pop some corn for desert?" Meredith asked as she rose. Paul nodded and continued.

"She'd pull out a book. When I was little it was one of those 'Little Golden Books.' I can still remember 'Scuffy the Tugboat'!" Paul smiled.

"Well, that's an appropriate book to remember!" Tim gestured with his hand toward the dock behind him. The sound of corn popping filled the room, followed by the aroma of butter.

"Hah! I guess so! As we got older, she read us chapter books that she bought for us or brought home from the library. I still have one of them somewhere – 'Paddy the Beaver.' Who would have known that we'd be sitting here, decades later, listening to a story book written by that woman's husband...?"

"You only have a few?" Shannon asked.

"Yeah. We used to have boxes and boxes, but as we got older my dad gave some of them away. I vividly remember him handing over one or two of those boxes." Paul said.

"What made those boxes memorable?" Shannon leaned forward.

"Well, one box in particular stands out. After my first-ever Boy Scout camping trip to Catalina Island with my dad, he decided that he wanted to take my mom, my sister and I back for a weekend trip. He felt pretty guilty, so..." Paul stopped suddenly; he turned away.

"Guilty? About what?" Tim wondered. Paul paused.

"Well, it's not important." Paul took a deep breath. Tim looked at Shannon who raised her eyebrows. Meredith cleared her throat; it could be heard from the other room. There was an uncomfortable silence in the room.

"So, what about the box, dear?" Meredith called out from the kitchen. Paul turned back toward Tim and Shannon.

"Uh, yeah - *that* box. My mom thought it was odd, but he wanted to take a box of books on our trip. He got a cardboard box, which was labeled with our last name, filled it with all kinds of novels, and he carried it out there – along with our typical luggage."

"Why in the world did he do that?"

"I knew, but my mom didn't quite understand. A bit earlier, on our first trip to the island, we met this unusual kid on Catalina. He was really shy or something - kind of strange, actually. He was a little older than I was, maybe a late teen or something. He hung around the dock, like a shadow. Just stood there, looking at everything." Paul ran his hand through his hair; he appeared to be uncomfortable.

Meredith returned to the living room bearing popcorn. She handed a small bowl to each person.

"I think your father did something really outstanding. You really need to tell them about what happened." Meredith said.

Chapter 8

"You have to remember that on our way back from camp, well, my dad and I were pretty angry with each other." Paul sighed and paused. Meredith looked at her husband.

"You don't have to go there, Paul. It's okay to just tell them about the books..." Meredith said as she scooped some popcorn for herself. Paul nodded.

"To make a long story short, as the saying goes, my dad left a paperback novel sitting on the dock as we were getting ready to make the return trip. He put it down to help me get into the boat, but forgot to pick it up again. This kid saw the book, picked it up, turned away and started reading it. Right there on the dock. My dad didn't know what to do."

"He wanted the book back, but he didn't want to take it from the kid?" Tim asked.

"Exactly. I could tell – I saw my dad stare at the kid. I remember Dad pointing, then raising his arms, but not saying anything."

"What happened?" Shannon asked.

"Well, it was almost instantly, some really old guy, I think he ran the gas station on the dock, was watching and yelled at the kid to give the book back. I remember the old guy calling out, 'Hey, Peg Leg! The man wants his book back!'"

"'Peg Leg'?" Tim asked.

"Yeah. That's what he called the kid. As soon as the old man said that both my father and I looked down at the kid's legs. They looked normal, but he did have only two toes on one foot, sticking out through the sandals. I can still remember the look on my father's face. He looked really sad." Paul shook his head; he seemed uncomfortable.

"So, your dad got the book back, I presume." Tim said.

"Oh, yeah. That kid handed it to him, really quickly, and ran off. He ran funny, I remember. My dad called out to him, said he could have the book, but that kid was gone - fast." Paul paused again.

"Then you went back to Catalina a while later..." Meredith said.

"Right. I think my dad felt bad about the kid. So he loaded up a box of our old books. I remember him telling me that he had a hunch the kid couldn't read well, so younger books would be okay. My mom helped, of course, but my dad really didn't want to talk about it much. She came and asked me what I thought was going on, so I told her about 'Peg Leg'."

"Was the kid there on the second trip?" Tim asked.

"Not when we arrived. We had to take the box to our hotel. My dad wasn't sure what to do if he didn't see the kid."

"Maybe just leave it at the dock?" Shannon offered.

"Yeah, but I think my dad wanted to see the kid again. Then he went off for the day to get the other box..." Paul trailed off.

"Two boxes of books? I'm confused." Shannon asked.

"No, something else, Shannon. Not sure Paul wants to go there." Meredith answered.

"No, I don't. I'm sorry; it's a personal thing." Paul looked down. Tim looked at Shannon and shook his head. Meredith intervened.

"Moving ahead, his dad came back that night, not happy at all. It was not a good way to end what was supposed to be a fun overnight outing."

"No, it wasn't good at all." Paul whispered while shaking his head.

"The next morning they went back to the boat dock. Do you want to take it from there, honey?" Meredith asked.

"Yeah, I suppose. Thanks. We were walking down the dock and my dad spotted 'Peg Leg'. Dad pulled a book out of the box and walked up to the kid. When the kid saw my father he froze. My dad had to pull the kid's hand up and put the book into it. We watched from a few feet away. The kid nodded, and dad handed the box to the kid. 'Peg Leg' grinned from ear to ear. Can you guess what happened next?" Paul smiled gently.

"I'm going to guess he ran off again?" Tim offered.

"Yep, hugging his new box of books." Paul nodded.

"I wonder whatever became of that kid." Shannon asked.

"I have no idea. Any time that kid came up in conversation, I always noticed a change in my father's voice." Paul replied.

"I think I can understand why." Tim responded.

Chapter 9

"Well, where did I leave off in 'Joseph's Great Journal'? I believe it was on a Sunday, right after the wedding anniversary..." Shannon began.

SUNDAY

I did something really strange today, Anne. I walked over to that church behind the post office and went to a service. I don't exactly know why, but I had never done that before, so I figured, why not?

Even though it's not Catholic, the pastor or minister, or whatever he's called, was really good. He talked about being lonely, and he said something that I couldn't stop thinking about - he said everyone has to deal with that at some time in their lives. On the way out he hugged me. A lady I didn't know hugged me. She said she knew you from the crafts store, and knew that you were still with me, in my heart, Annie.

The hugs were nice, but I couldn't stop thinking about what that lady said. Those words and hugs sounded like something you wrote to me in that letter you gave to Shannon. I ran (or what passes for running for someone of my age) home and dug out your note. Yes, I kept it. I put it in that old wooden box on my desk, the one right next to me that I got on a trip to Solvang. I remember how good the fudge was that used to sit in the box!

There it was – your letter. You wrote, "I have wondered what it would be like to be alone after more than a half of a century. Perhaps, this is a way I can stay with you."

As soon as I saw your note, I knew you were still here with me. And then I found a reason to keep writing in this journal, or diary, or whatever it's called. I never answered your letter! Tomorrow I'm going to change that! I'll work on the wall and then write to you!

"Oh, my. We have that wooden box upstairs in the extra bedroom!" Meredith interrupted.

"It must have been a lonely time for him…he was so connected to my mother." Paul looked over at his wife.

"The next entry, done on a Monday, mentions me. I remember handing him the note he refers to here. I didn't know what was in it, but now I have an idea. It was the first meatball sandwich I ever made!" Shannon picked up the page and continued her reading.

MONDAY

Dear Anne,

Yes, I got your note from Shannon. And yes, I remember getting up early and getting to work on the wall. I didn't know you were awake. Sorry if I woke you up. Strange, but I think a big part of what I'm struggling with over the time since you "went home to heaven," as you called it, is worrying about all the times I never apologized for stupid little things I did to hurt you – like that, waking you up. Guilt – my boogeyman.

The meatball sandwich was great, as it always was when you made them. Shannon did a pretty decent job putting it together. I can tell that you taught her!

I do remember seeing you sitting on the porch while I worked on the fence. I thought you were writing a diary, but, boy was I surprised when Shannon delivered the letter. But I still don't know what you mean by leaving letters around the house. I decided I didn't have the stomach to turn this place upside down looking for more. To be honest, I'm a little nervous about finding more. What in the world could you find to write about?

Well, now for the hard part. Yeah, it's been hard since you, well, passed. I have never found it easy to write or talk about well, that night – when you passed. I've tried the other ways of describing what happened that horrible night when I, uh, found you, but I am struggling to get myself to write those things down. I'm going to stop for right now. I think I need a stiff drink before I write any more about my feelings.

"He always had a tough time apologizing. Whenever he knew he was wrong, he'd try to explain around whatever had just happened. I remember one time, when he was wrong about me losing my bike, I noticed a tear in his eye. A dad down the street came down with my bike and apologized for his son taking it. At that moment I realized I hardly ever saw my dad apologize. Well, I learned that he apologized by trying to change the words he just spoke." Paul said, then took a slow breath.

"I get that. Apologies aren't easy for me, Paul." Tim looked down at the floor.

"For some of us they get harder as we get older. I think we hate the idea that we're not going to be perfect - ever." Paul added. He looked over at Meredith. They shared a long gaze. Tim sensed something was being said without words.

"I think I know what you meant about your dad. I had a sense, back when we were building the wall that something inside of him wanted to apologize, but it was like there was not an electronic circuit there, if that makes any sense. I dropped a load of stones once. The wheelbarrow tipped over." Tim sighed as he spoke. Paul looked over at the younger man.

"Too much sense." He said.

"One thing, and please forgive me for asking, but I never noticed him drinking back then, in his last year...um..." Tim asked.

"No offense, Tim. He didn't drink much, but started to more and more after my mom died. I noticed. It was hard. My grandfather..." Paul stopped suddenly.

"Grandfather?" Shannon asked. Paul looked away.

"Read the next day's entry...not ready to go there." Paul said.

Shannon looked over the next day's entry.

"This next one might be rough, Paul. Are you sure?"

"Let's give it a try. Yes. I'm probably doing better than you think." Paul nodded.

TUESDAY

No, it's not really a day later, Annie. It's just after midnight and yes, I'm sorry to say, I had two bourbon and lemonades, on ice. I've never been much of a drinker, but what I need to write now is a bit past my line of courage. I'm sorry, but somehow I know you'd understand.

The night you died – there, I wrote it just like it was – was one of the worst nights of my life. To feel the cold skin of someone you've lived with for a half a century is not something you'd wish for anyone. To be honest, what happened after that is a blur. I'm not sure why I can't remember much until I got home after your funeral. Everything from that night you left until I was home with our kids here is patchy. I guess it's what's called shock or trauma or something. I know it was bad because I needed two bourbons to be able to write this, and I can't remember much of it. I think I've written all I can about that night.

"You weren't kidding, Shannon. That is rough. I always wondered what he must have felt like that morning, when he, uh, found her. He never talked about it." Paul's voice was almost a whisper. A tear was sliding down his cheek.

"I wondered the same thing." Shannon responded.

"I remember that he walked around in a daze then. I wanted to find a way to snap him out of it..."

"Well, check this out. It seems he found a way!" Shannon smiled.

WEDNESDAY

Sorry, Annie. I decided I can't write much today. I'm going out to pile some stones. I think I need a distraction. I'll try again tomorrow.

"I always thought that my mother cooked up the stone wall project just to get my father to do something. She knew he didn't do well unless he had something to work on. I think she knew it had to be attached to her somehow." Paul speculated.

"I think she told me she had one in front of her house when she was a girl, Paul." Shannon offered.

"Oh, there was a small one in front of her old house, sure. But she didn't start talking about it much until her last year or two. Yeah, she mentioned it, in passing, but that was all she talked about at the end." Paul explained.

"I've discovered that Marino men look for a physical task whenever they're feeling overwhelmed..." Meredith commented. Paul leaned over and frowned at his wife. She smiled gently.

"We're not from the Marino family, Meredith, but that rule fits males in our family, too…" Shannon stared at Tim. Tim stopped chewing popcorn and smiled.

"Hey…" Tim responded.

"Close your mouth…" She whispered. Tim complied.

"What's next, Shannon?" Meredith asked.

"It seems we have more clues here. Paul may be on to something. And look at this." Shannon picked up the notebook and pointed out two dark reddish-brown smudges on the page. She kept reading.

THURSDAY

Well, I'm back, Annie. I jammed my thumb (and got a nasty gash to boot) trying to position a rock on the wall yesterday, so forgive my crappy handwriting today. Yes, I put some ice on it. Yes, I took two aspirin. Yes, I cleaned it with soap and water before putting a Band-Aid over the wound.

I'll make this short tonight – my hand does ache. In your letter you asked if I would finish the stone wall. The two drops of blood to the right of this paragraph are my answer. As I was putting the bandage on the cut two drops fell.

I've been staring at those two drops. Maybe I read too much into things, but they kind of remind me of us. They're connected by little strands, but they are definitely two distinct drops. Maybe it's a fitting answer to your question. As long as my heart pumps, I'll keep trying on that wall.

But you do know me. If there are times when I'm not up to it, I hope you'll forgive me. I am seeing that I have up and down days. I guess this isn't going to be a short one – the blood drops just, well, affected me.

I've not been too excited about that question you asked about loneliness, but yes, it has been hard since you left. Sorry, that is how I look at it. I can't get myself to "call it like it is" – maybe someday. When I stop and think of how the days stretch out ahead, without you, well, I, well…

I think I'll go take a shower and get some sleep now.

"It seems like yesterday that my mother would ask me about washing cuts on my finger. That is exactly how she used to do it. Strange that my father and I can connect on this issue…" Paul sighed.

"It seems to me that we're all like those blood drops. We're separate, but connected. Distinct, but all made of the same thing, when it comes down to it." Meredith commented. Paul nodded.

"Well, we're up to the Friday of that particular week." Shannon drew a breath and read on.

FRIDAY

Annie, I went into the post office again today and Mary asked, once again, how my writing was going. I was really excited to tell her all about my "book" – and I called it a journal. She smiled and asked me what format I was using. I stood there with my mouth open and shook my head. I said, "Um, I just write down whatever I want to."

Mary laughed and asked if I use daily headings and titles. She told me she has been keeping a journal since she was a teenager (and that was a while ago, but don't worry, I didn't say that to her). She then went on to tell me about how these things should be designed. Designed! Hah! Here I was, all proud of having written like 8 pages and now I have to go back and re-do everything. No, ma'am. Sorry, Annie. I'll just keep writing like this. I figure some high-powered editor can "format" all of this.

"So, what do his entries look like?" Paul interrupted.

"Pretty messy. Mostly he just titles the day of the week. There's no way to know what date he actually wrote this stuff, unless he mentioned it, like for their anniversary." Shannon explained as she raised a page so Paul could see it. She lowered it and continued her reading.

I did feel bad that I haven't been putting the actual dates on each entry, just the day, like today is "Friday", but then I thought, what does it matter? I don't think any of this will be used in any kind of legal document (note to any future lawyer: none of this is true, unless it would make me a lot of money, then every word is true).

"Hahaha! There's a laugh! A lawyer! You know, he did have a sense of humor. Sometimes I forgot, but he did." Paul blurted out, then motioned to Shannon to continue.

Anyway, you went on to ask me about Tim and Shannon, about being "their parent". I'm not sure how to answer that one, Annie. I am trying to listen, as I know you've told me to do for decades, and to offer whatever advice I can, but I'm not sure how much else I can do.

"I wish I could have told him how much he did for me. My father, well, he was out of the picture early in my life." Tim interrupted in a quiet voice.

Shannon looked at her husband, nodded slowly, and then continued.

You said I'm a warm and caring man, and you made me cry when I read that. No, it's not a bad thing. This is one of the reasons you mean so much to me, Annie. As you know, more than anyone else, when I was a kid I was always made fun of for being "too emotional."

When I think back to when we were first married, I can see how much the trials, pains, stresses and problems of life, and living as an imperfect man in an imperfect world that seems to want us to be perfect, changed me. I am not proud of how I became hardened, and you saw it more than anyone else. I sometimes wonder if every human being has like some sort of "pain storage system" and my "container" is smaller than what other people have. I don't know.

"Um, wait." Paul had his hand up. A tear appeared on his cheek.

"Paul?" Meredith asked in a kind voice.

"Just feeling something here..." Paul whispered as he shook his head.

"We'll wait..." Shannon said quietly.

"It's hard. The older I get the more I understand my old man, and the more I feel terrible about how we used to fight. I could never see things from his point of view. What you just read, right there, makes my point. I feel, more and more, like that in the last decade or so. We've had a lot to cope with; my container is pretty full." Paul grew quiet.

Shannon looked at Meredith, who signaled for her to continue.

I remember how you told me that I learned how to not "feel" things sometimes because I could only take so much, like whenever Paul had a "boo-boo." I'm not proud of that, Annie.

I'm trying with Sarah and Paul. Tim and Shannon, too. That's all I can say, but right now I'm kind of raw about, well, you know. You aren't here now. I'll do what I can.

Sorry, but I have to get to bed. I always start writing these things with a lot of energy, but it runs out quickly. Of course, I'm not writing about baseball or world history – this stuff kind of hits too close to home. Or way too close. When I read your mention of Chocolate Chip Creek it pushed me over the edge. So, is there one over there, in heaven?

"Oh, gee. I remember going to the place that they called 'Chocolate Chip Creek'!" Paul exclaimed. "It's back in Maine, where they grew up. My mother used to make a batch of Toll House cookies and then give one to my dad, saying 'that's for Chocolate Chip Creek!'"

"Seems like they tried to stay in touch with how they saw each other as kids." Meredith added.

"Here's the entry for that week; your dad mentions something I never really understood. What was up with the flags?" Shannon asked before reading on.

Oh, and I flew a Swedish flag on my flagpole today, just for you. No, I didn't leave it up after dark. I wouldn't want to start an international incident!

Thanks for that note, Annie. It meant a lot to me and I just wish I could tell you.

"That's an easy answer, Shannon. When I was a teen he put up a flag pole behind our house, not the place on Pine Mountain. I was there when he put it in the ground – I helped him pour the bag of cement."

"Really! He took that pole to Pine Mountain?"

"Well, it was a different one - the old one was pretty worn out. The new pole was one of the first things he did after they moved there. But that first one was one of the few projects we worked together on.

"It was his tradition!" Shannon added. Paul nodded.

"He told me that when he was in middle school he built a crude flagpole, or what passed as one, and nailed it up on the fence behind his parents' place. He found some old rope and a couple of hooks. He found scraps from my grandmother's sewing and made flags of different countries. He'd fly them every now and then." Paul paused.

"Sounds nice..." Shannon interjected with a smile. Paul sighed, started to speak and then stopped. He tried again.

"One day, as he walked home from school, he watched as his father broke the pole in half and used it to stoke a fire, to burn weeds. There, in the fire, was the flag he had made. It was Sweden - one of his favorites. My dad liked blue and yellow together; it really wasn't for the country, he just liked seeing a pretty flag fluttering." Paul grew silent.

"Oh, my. Horrible." Shannon whispered.

"Yeah. I guess my grandfather tore into my dad – called him all kinds of names, wondered what was wrong with him for not flying only the American flag. My mother told me that my father was in deep shock that day." Paul sighed.

"Ouch..." Tim said, quietly. Paul leaned forward and looked at the family photo in the corner.

"She was waiting in the woods nearby. They were going to meet and look for rocks at the creek together. That's what she told me. She used to collect rocks."

"That must have hurt your mother, too." Shannon said. Paul nodded.

"That's why my mother always urged him to hoist the Swedish flag. It was her way of, well, I guess...you know." Paul trailed off.

"I understand; she wanted to heal an old wound of his." Shannon offered. Paul nodded, then rose from his chair. He walked to the garage door, opened it and went through. The door closed behind him.

"Is he okay, Meredith?" Shannon asked. Meredith nodded, stood up and headed for the garage. Before she could reach it the door opened quickly. Paul walked back in carrying an envelope. He opened it and pulled out an old blue and yellow flag. After unfolding it, he held it up high.

"Here it is. My father's flag. Sweden." Paul announced.

"Maybe it's time we brought down the flag for this particular evening..." Meredith said as she rose from her chair.

Chapter 10

Tim rose early that Sunday morning; he rarely slept well when he was not in his own bed. He gently pushed himself out of bed as he looked over at Shannon, who appeared to be sound asleep. He looked across the room for his pants, then decided he was definitely awake for the day. Gazing at the clock he noticed it was a few minutes before six.

He walked to the window and scanned the harbor. He noticed that the sun was just barely making its appearance on the eastern horizon. The dark water was gently lapping along the dock, and few birds had stirred. The quiet amazed him.

Tim reached for his pants, hanging over a nearby chair, but something outside caught his attention. There was a light and movement in the boat next to the house – Paul's boat.

"Shann..." Tim whispered. He quickly closed his mouth, remembering his wife was asleep. He turned toward her; though he was unaware of it, she had turned to face him.

"It's Paul. He slept on the boat last night." Shannon yawned.

"What? I thought everyone just went to bed."

"Well, I know why you didn't hear it. As soon as your head hits the pillow you're out. I'm not so lucky. I heard the fighting."

"Meredith and Paul? Huh." Tim shook his head as he finished pulling his pants on.

"Oh, yeah, no mistake about it." Shannon placed her head back on the pillow.

"About the boat?"

"That was the center of the drama, yes." Shannon rolled over; she was now facing the back wall.

"The last I remember, Paul showed us his dad's flag, and we went to bed."

"Oh, that was the spark…" Shannon mumbled then paused. Tim realized he was not going to get more out of her. He pulled on his polo shirt and slipped into his flip-flops. He closed the door quietly behind him and walked toward the back door.

As he strode toward the boat, a flutter above the cabin caught his attention. A blue and yellow flag hung limply from the small mast near the control center. It hadn't been there the night before. It appeared that someone had haphazardly used twist-ties to secure it. Looking past the cabin, Tim noticed that the red, white and blue American flag with the anchor on it was still at the back of the boat.

He took a deep breath as he stepped on to the boat. He stopped for a moment and congratulated himself, silently, that he hadn't slipped or jammed his thumb or something worse. Just then the boat rose a bit and Tim grabbed a nearby railing.

"So, how long does it take to get those sea legs everyone talks about?" Tim whispered, almost inaudibly. A voice from his right answered his question.

"Give it about three years, maybe. If you're lucky." Paul said in a monotone. He was slouching behind the ship's wheel. It looked as if he'd been sleeping there.

"Oh, hey, I didn't see you there." Tim wasn't sure what to say.

"Well, I saw you." Paul had a navy blue and white San Diego Padres baseball cap pulled down over his face. His voice sounded worn, and much older than what Tim remembered from the previous night's talk.

"Are you okay?" The Swedish flag caught Tim's eye. A slight breeze wafted by and billowed out the cloth a bit.

"I suppose. Welcome aboard the 'Dog House' – my new working name for this old tub." Paul shifted slightly.

"Dog house?" Tim asked.

"Come on, Tim. You heard the fireworks last night."

"Well, uh, a bit..." Tim lied. Sometimes he hated how hard he slept. He missed so many dramas because of that. At least that's what Shannon told him back when they lived in a crowded apartment building.

"That's my 'flag of independence' now." Paul pointed up to the blue and yellow cloth. His hat was still pulled down over his face.

"Independence?"

"Yep. Welcome to the 'Republic of Marinoland.' I was thinking of calling it the 'Principality of Paul' but, hey, I was raised to believe in democracy. So, 'Marinoland' it is."

"But it's on the water..." Tim was sorry he let that slip, even as the words were coming out of his mouth. Paul pushed his hat back, shook his head, sighed and stared at Tim.

"A mere technicality, my friend. I live here now." Paul pulled his hat back down.

"What about your house..." Tim started.

"I now call that castle the 'Dictatorship of Meredithia.' That's how she wants it, so that's how she gets it. It's my way of flipping her off. If she wants war, I can dish it out as much as she can. She'll have to get her own flag. Probably all red with a pitchfork on it."

"Do you think your dad would want you to use his flag this way?"

"What?" Paul pushed the hat back up on his head again.

"I remember what he wrote, what Shannon read last night. He said, 'I flew a Swedish flag, just for you. No, I didn't leave it up after dark. I wouldn't want to start an international incident!' It was something like that. I figure this would be, uh, like an international incident?" Tim looked at the house. Paul stared at Tim.

"What in the world are you talking about?"

"You just described two countries at war with each other, and it seems to me that this flag started it. It just feels wrong. I don't know. I'm guessing here – your dad wouldn't like this. I'm no diplomat, just a mechanic." Tim offered, hesitantly.

"My father? One lousy old flag and you bring him into this?"

"Well, we were talking about him last night. I noticed how his words hit you pretty hard, Paul..." Tim used a softer, more consoling tone.

"Yeah, well, it seems no one else noticed how hard it was..." Paul sat up and stared out into the harbor.

"I think we all did. I know some of it hit me hard, and you had a much longer history with Joseph Marino than I did."

"Yeah, let's just call him 'Joseph' from now on. He left me with a pile of emotional crap to deal with when he died, and then he comes back to haunt me with his stupid diary..."

"He called it a journal..." Tim interrupted.

"Yeah, whatever. In fact, I don't want anything around that reminds me of him right now. Here..." Paul stood up on the seat and reached toward the Swedish flag. He tugged at it.

"Careful, Paul...that's the radio antenna mast..."

"Who the hell cares? It won't be my boat any more after next month, so screw it." Paul tugged harder – the flag gave way. There was a muffled 'crack' heard.

"Uh-oh..." That was not good, Tim thought.

"Here, you want it? You want this old rag of a flag?" Paul pulled on Tim's arm and thrusted the object into Tim's hand.

"Paul, please...don't..." Tim gently smoothed the flag out.

"Don't? I should have done this years ago. Anything that reminds me of my father has to go. Once and for all. I've had it." Paul looked around and found an old, sweat-covered Boston Red Sox hat next to some towels, toward the rear of the boat.

"I understand why you're upset..."

"Upset? You want to see upset? Here – this filthy, stinking Boston hat! It just screams 'Joseph Marino.' Over it goes!" Paul threw the blue, white and red hat as far as he could. It spun gently and landed without much fanfare in the water about fifteen feet from the boat.

"Paul, no. I thought..."

"Thought? Me and the Red Sox? Hell, no. This is my team, and he hated that. I'd wear a San Diego hat to his place just to irritate him." Tim looked up at the hat.

"I had no idea, Paul. He never mentioned that. I'm sorry. I wonder if his journal is hitting you pretty low." Tim said. He noticed that Paul was glaring at him.

"You think? Yeah...a lot lower..."

"Paul, maybe I don't know what I'm talking about – I'm just saying what I think Shannon would say." Tim mumbled as he looked down. He heard Paul sigh.

Paul walked over to the rear of the boat – what he once told Tim was called the "stern" – and splayed out on a bench covered with a foam pad.

"My friend, how can I describe what it was like to grow up with that man as a father?"

"Was it really that bad? I'm not arguing with you - just asking."

"Bad enough that anything that says "dad" on it, well, I want it nowhere near me." Paul said just as the sun shimmered on the two men. The intertwined letters, "S" and "D" on Paul's hat seemed to shine. Tim tried to hold back a smile.

"What are you smirking at?" Paul was a bit more agitated.

"Your hat."

"What about it? That's my team." Paul shot back.

"What's the name of the team?"

"What?"

"The name. San Diego…" Tim started then pointed at Paul.

"Padres. So what?"

"Hey, I only took one year of Spanish, but I get it. What does the Spanish word 'Padre' mean in English?"

"Father…so what…" Paul paused as the message sunk in. He sat up, removed his hat and stared at it. He gently dropped it over the edge of the boat. The hat made a mild splash as it hit. Tim leaned over – the hat was floating next to the hull.

"Could your father have been worse than mine?" Tim asked as he sat directly across from Paul.

"Yours? I'd be willing to bet my dad was the worst of the two."

"I'll tell you what. Let's make this interesting. I'll bet you one baseball hat that mine sucked worse than yours." Tim pointed into the water.

"That's too easy! Hey, you can just have the hat. Here…" Paul leaned over and pulled it from the water. It was dripping wet. He sat it on the floor between the two men.

"No, I mean the loser gets the hat. The loser is the guy whose father was the better dad of the two. I'm a Dodgers fan, so I wouldn't want a Padres hat." Tim shook his head as he pointed at the wet cap.

"Deal. You know what? Give me the worst story about your dad. I mean it. I'm the home team here, so you get the first 'at-bat'." Paul pointed at Tim.

"Okay, yeah. Um, I don't know. I don't have many stories - just one, really." Tim took a deep breath and looked at the flag in his hands. He re-folded it, and smoothed it gently.

"Maybe one is all it takes?" Paul asked.

"Yeah, well, the worst thing, I guess, was that he almost killed me, like maybe three times. Beat me up. Pretty bloody. I woke up in the hospital. My dad drank, every day. I had to watch as he beat my mother up, like all the time." Tim noticed his own hand was shaking.

"What?" Paul whispered. There was a new softness to his voice.

"Yeah, beatings. One day, when I was like a freshman in high school, I came home to find my mother crying on the couch. She had a black eye."

"He hit her?" Paul was almost whispering.

"Yeah. That day, well, I looked around and most of our furniture was gone." Tim paused, unable to say much more. Paul leaned forward. His mouth was open.

"Gone?"

"Uh-huh. He took all of our money and just walked out. I haven't seen him since. I think it's been way over 20 years now. I don't even know if he's alive anymore." Tim's voice became very quiet. He stared at the deck.

A strange silence engulfed the boat. The lapping of water and the sound of a distant seagull were the loudest sounds. Tim noticed Paul's hand reaching out; he squeezed Tim's arm, then pulled back. Tim looked up in time to notice Paul picking up the soaked San Diego Padres hat.

With one motion Paul swung the hat around and on to his own head. The splat of water was noticeable, and small streams rolled down Paul's head.

"Paul...you didn't get your 'at-bat'!" Tim said.

"No need to. You hit a grand slam, and the best I've got is a bunt. My father missed all of my concerts when I was in middle school." Paul whispered, then looked out into the harbor. He was searching for something.

"I'm sure that was hard, too..." Tim offered.

"It depends on how you define 'hard', Tim." Paul looked back at the deck.

"I suppose if you remember it, and can't get it out of your mind, that would be hard..."

"What you just described isn't a memory. I'll bet you lost sleep over it." Paul said in a kind tone.

"Yeah. I went to counseling for a while. I had nightmares..." Tim answered as Paul looked out across the harbor again.

"I was angry at him, but I never had nightmares about my father missing my concerts." Paul whispered.

"That could be hard, I suppose..."

"No, it wasn't." Paul pointed as he found what he was looking for. He stood up, took off his hat and shoes, and then jumped into the water.

"Paul! What...?" Tim shouted.

With only a few strokes Paul reached the object. He retrieved it, turned and came back to the boat. He held the soaked cloth up high. The red and white "B" glistened in the morning sun.

"I'll even wear a Red Sox hat now. That's how much you beat me." He said, almost out of breath.

As Paul climbed on to the deck he donned the old, soaked Boston hat. A piece of seaweed slid down the side of his face. Tim thought he noticed that tears were mingling freely with the harbor water.

"Well, I guess I can wear a Padres hat, then." Tim said as he picked up the other hat and threw it on to the top of his head. It landed at a goofy angle.

"Tim, I needed you here this weekend, and I now see it had only a little to do with the engine. I'm really sorry about what happened with your father." Paul grabbed Tim's arm.

"Thanks. I had a crappy dad, but for a short time I had a really good grandfather who taught me how to build a stone wall."

Chapter 11

"Paul, I really think you should keep this flag. It meant a lot to your dad. He'd want you to take care of it. You were important to him." Tim hesitated and then extended the flag toward Paul.

Paul stared at the cloth for what seemed like a long time to Tim, then gently took the flag. Almost ceremoniously, Paul walked over to the seat next to the ship's wheel and placed the neatly folded cloth on a side board. He ran his hand over the blue and yellow cloth, then stared out toward the harbor. Tim wasn't sure what to say, or if he should say anything.

"I was important to him? I'm not so sure about that, my friend. How would you know?" Paul asked, gruffly, while shaking his head. Tim paused.

"Because I heard him say it..." Tim said, almost whispering.

"What?" Paul turned toward Tim.

"Yes, he said it. I remember the first time..."

"The first time?" Paul interrupted.

"Yes. We were working on the wall. You had just gotten into your car - I remember you driving off. He stopped and watched you as you drove down the driveway."

"I remember. Yes, I remember that day. I saw him in the rear view mirror. I wondered what he was looking at. I felt like he was staring at me. I wondered if I had left something on my rear bumper. I got out and looked. Nothing was wrong."

"You waved and he waved back. That was the day." Tim responded. Paul's eyes widened.

"What did he say?" Paul whispered.

"Well, he wasn't talking to me. It was like I wasn't there. I'll never forget, it was like he was calling out to you."

"Calling out?

"He said, 'Paul, come back. I don't know how to fix this, but I have to, somehow.'"

"Oh…" Paul whispered. He appeared to try to speak, but the rest of the words were garbled.

"Your dad was crying, and the only reason I heard him is that I was holding one handle of the wheelbarrow – he had the other one. I remember feeling like this must be tearing him up, because he didn't care if I heard what he said. It was like I wasn't there." Tim took a deep breath.

"…wasn't there…" Paul repeated Tim's words as he ran his hand through his wet hair.

"He seemed to only see you. I said something to him, but…he didn't hear me."

"So why the hell didn't he call out to me?" Paul clenched his fist. Tim noticed a tear steaming from the older man's right eye.

"Paul, take a breath. Hold on a minute." Tim put his hand up.

"So, why didn't he?" Paul continued.

"Let me ask you a question. I think you'll understand from your answer…" Tim started.

"What?"

"Play along with me for a minute."

"Okay, if you're going somewhere with this…" Paul seemed to calm down a bit.

"I think this'll make my point."

"Then ask away."

"So, how did you feel at that very moment, standing by your car? Did you really worry about something being on the bumper? Honestly?" Tim asked.

Silence filled the boat, except for the gentle sounds of the water around them. Paul opened his mouth to respond, but could not.

"What?" Paul asked. He looked as if he did not understand the question.

"I saw your face. You waited there. You wanted him to call out to you."

"Damn right I did. Yes. I wanted him to say something, anything…but he said nothing. Not a damned word. He was the usual distant man I saw every day of my life." Paul grumbled.

"Paul, wait…" Tim took a breath, then sat down.

"Wait for what? What are you getting at, damn it?"

"I'm going to ask you one more question, and it's kind of brutal. Take a minute to think about your answer. Don't say whatever hits your mind first. Okay?" Tim put his hand up, as if he were signaling a stop, then took a deep breath.

"Okay. Whatever." Paul nodded.

"So, why didn't YOU call out to HIM?" Tim asked in a calm voice. Paul opened his mouth, then stalled. He turned away.

"Tim, he was the father. It was his job to do it, not mine."

"There you have it. Two men, both with the same problem on the same day. He later told me that he thought it was your job, as the son, to reach out."

"Damn it. I hate this." Paul said under his breath.

"I understand." Tim tried to console his friend.

"No you don't. You couldn't." Paul shot back.

"What?"

"What you just asked me. Why I didn't call out to him…"

"Yeah…" Tim nodded.

"Meredith asked me that same question less than a mile after we drove off that day."

"So you knew where I was going with this, Paul."

"Yeah. I was afraid you were going there."

"There must be something behind this, if two people notice it like seventeen years apart." Tim said.

"Now, let me ask you a question. What did he seem like to you?" Paul turned toward Tim and spoke with a very quiet tone.

"What do you mean?" Tim asked.

"You said he was like a 'really good grandfather.' I saw someone different. He wasn't a man that allowed his son to get very close. That's my perspective."

"I've always been confused by how you've talked about him over the years. Like how the two of you butted heads all across the country when you drove that old car west."

"Yeah, that was the tipping point, I think. That was the point that drove us apart." Paul said with a resigned tone.

"I'm no psychologist, but I think the problem was there long before you took that drive." Tim said as Paul nodded.

"Probably true."

"Can I say something that might upset you, Paul?" Tim was hesitant. Paul turned and looked at the younger man.

"Hell, isn't that what we've been doing since the sun rose?" Paul looked across the harbor and noticed how the day had brightened.

"Okay, then. What if I told you that you remind me a lot of your father?" Tim bit his lip and stepped back. Paul smiled, slightly.

"Huh. A decade ago I would have wanted to punch you out. And maybe even more recently."

"But not now, right?" Tim feigned a smile.

"No. It's not you, Tim. There's a woman standing in the window over there who told me the very same thing last night. And a number of other times over the last twenty five years." Paul sighed and sat down hard on a padded bench.

Tim turned to look toward the house. Standing in the window were two women. Tim could tell that one was Shannon, and guessed the other was Meredith. Tim waved. Shannon opened the sliding glass door and called out.

"Breakfast is ready, guys!"

"I know what my father would do."

"Go get breakfast?" Tim guessed.

"Yep. And in this way he and I are exactly alike." Paul said.

"Can I ask you one more question, Paul?"

"Hey, why not? What hasn't already been covered?" The older man shrugged.

"Well, how would your father deal with your mother after an argument like you had with Meredith last night?"

Paul looked into Tim's eyes, started to speak, and then stopped. He nodded and looked down.

"I guess I bought this problem. My dad would probably pout for three days before trying to make some half-hearted attempt to patch it up. It was always my mother who had to extend the olive branch."

"Well, here's your big opportunity to walk a different path." Tim said, quietly.

Paul smiled as he rose and walked toward the port side of the boat. He stopped just short of the edge and turned toward Tim.

"Thanks for the talk, Tim. Turning the tables, can I ask you a tough question?"

"Hey, I guess I owe you…"

"It dawned on me as you described my father on that day back then - how you've been able to deal with your situation, I mean, with your father? If this has been hard for me, your issues must have been brutal on you." Paul's voice was kind.

"Someone told me something really wise a long time ago and it helps me every day.' Tim took a breath. Paul leaned in.

"What was that?"

"Never forget that the person you were when you were a child, many years ago, is not the person you are now." Tim said in a very quiet voice.

"Sounds right. We grow, we learn, we adapt."

"Well, your father changed, too. But it's not just about them - sometimes we don't allow our parents to change. We only know how to deal with them as we did when we were little. That's how it breaks down. Maybe they can't deal with us as we grow up, either. I don't really understand it much, but that's what I'm going with."

"I think that makes sense…he was still overwhelming to me when he was old." Paul whispered.

"As for me, I think that my dad had a nasty childhood. Well, I know he did. He couldn't deal with seeing me as a kid

– it probably brought back painful memories. He didn't know how to cope. I don't either, sometimes. I'm lost when I'm dealing with Joey sometimes. Oops…I mean 'J.J.'" Tim smiled and shook his head. Paul smiled.

"Ah, the 'I want a new name' problem…" Paul responded. Tim nodded.

"Yep."

"Let's go get some pancakes, 'Zach'!"

"Right behind you, 'Zeke'!" Tim responded as they stepped off of the boat.

Chapter 12

"Official announcement here! Listen up! From this point forward, I am to be called 'Zeke'." Paul made the pronouncement as he slid open the door to the dining room. Shannon and Meredith, busily setting the breakfast table, looked at each other. Tim, following close behind, responded.

"And I am to be called Zach."

"Okay, I can tell that great things were accomplished on the boat this morning…" Shannon said with a twinge of sarcasm in her voice.

"You are just jealous that you didn't get a new name!" Tim smiled at his wife.

"Well, then, I'll be 'Marilyn Monroe'!" Shannon moved a plate across the table.

"Actually, Shannon, or Marilyn, we did accomplish some important things. Tim and I had a good talk."

"About names?" Shannon asked. Tim looked at Meredith. She had her back turned to the others, and appeared to be working with food on the stove. Tim touched Paul's arm.

"Paul..." Tim whispered and signaled toward the older woman.

"Yeah...sorry. Not easy for me. Not sure..."

"Just walk over and say you're sorry. Nothing fancy. Just try it. But watch out – she may not understand what you're doing..." Tim whispered. Shannon stopped adjusting plates and looked at the two men. She walked over to Tim as Paul walked slowly toward Meredith.

"Tim, what are you doing?" Shannon leaned over and whispered.

"We talked about grudges and taking first steps. Let's see how this goes..." Tim whispered as he shrugged.

"Merrie..." Paul started, tentatively.

"What? Just sit down. Breakfast will be ready soon." She replied in a distant, icy tone of voice; she did not turn around.

"Listen, Mer..." Paul started, in a quiet voice. Meredith interrupted him.

"I said the food will be ready soon. Just sit down."

111

Paul looked over at Tim. Tim nodded and gestured to keep trying.

"Mer, Please. We don't have to do it this way..."

"I fix the breakfast. You eat it. Yes, we have to do it this way. You don't like it when things change." Meredith turned and picked up a plate. Tim noticed a tear streaming down her face. It was obvious that Paul noticed, too.

"Well, maybe it's time some things change. I know this isn't really about the bacon and eggs." Paul sounded very kind.

"What are you talking about?" Meredith turned and faced her husband. A greasy spatula was between them, in Meredith's right hand.

"It's about last night. I know this'll be a shock, but I want to apologize, I want to be the first to say I screwed up last night." Paul offered.

"Is this a new way of coming out on top? You look good for apologizing, so you win?" Meredith's voice grew colder. Tim and Shannon turned toward the back sliding glass door, away from the older couple. Shannon shrugged. Tim nodded and touched his wife on the upper arm.

"No. Please listen. I'm trying to do this a different way – not the way my father did things."

"What the hell are you talking about?" Meredith shot back. A red streak appeared on Paul's neck. Shannon pointed at Paul as she nudged Tim.

"Tim..." She whispered.

"Shh. He can do this, Shan. Hold on..." Tim said as Paul continued.

"Let me put this plain – I can be a stubborn ass sometimes. I will dig in my heels and wait for everyone else to apologize first. I cannot see that I cause my own problems. I did all of that last night!" Paul's voice was rising but it was evident that he was trying to control it.

"What?" Meredith shook her head in confusion.

"Meredith, out on the boat - Tim and I talked about my dad. His journal hit me hard last night. Unfortunately, I'm too much like my dad. He was stubborn. I am stubborn. Because of that we stayed apart for the rest of his life. I saw that this morning. We don't have to go that way."

"No...we don't." Meredith whispered as she shook her head.

"Do you remember that day we drove away from the old house on Pine Mountain when my dad was building the wall? Remember that I stopped because I saw him staring at me?"

"Yes..."

"I stood there, waiting for him to call out, to apologize, to say, I don't know, 'I love you', or just about anything. We stared at each other." Paul appeared to be fighting tears.

"I remember..." Meredith's voice was calmer. Shannon turned and looked at Tim, tilting her head with a confused look. Tim nodded and put his finger to his lips.

"Neither one of us was willing to make the first move. Because of that we drifted further and further apart. Then he was..." Paul stopped and cleared his throat.

"Are you okay?" Meredith put the spatula down and touched her husband's arm.

"Yeah." Paul nodded and took a deep breath.

"Take your time..." Meredith said softly.

"...then he was, he was...gone..." Paul drifted off. He turned and looked out the window. Shannon looked at Tim. In unison they gently touched each other's arms.

"So much unfinished..." Meredith said softly.

"That's my point. I'm trying to do this type of thing differently, I mean, between us...now..." Paul stumbled with his words.

"I suppose I should give it a try, too..." Meredith responded.

"You're a lot better at it than I am. I'll have to learn how to do this as we stumble and fall. We've never had any good examples around." Paul shook his head.

"But maybe if we just keep trying it will feel more and more natural." Meredith added.

"I hope so. It's not feeling very natural right now." Paul half-smiled.

"Is the bacon burning?" Shannon asked, tentatively.

"Oh, no..." Meredith returned her attention to the stove.

"Well, we all like 'crispy' bacon, right?" Meredith turned with a pan of well-done bacon strips in her hand.

Chapter 13

"Where did you learn how to do that, Meredith? Quickly throwing together omelets using crumbled crispy bacon, cheese and onions was brilliant! I would have just seen a failed meal – but you pulled it together!" Shannon smiled as she scooped up the last of her portion.

"Yeah...good stuff!" Tim added while chewing.

"Tim, not with your mouth full!" Shannon whispered.

"Oh...yeah..." Tim nodded.

"My mother left me a cook book, but it was an unusual one, Shannon. She called it the M.U.M. – the 'Messed Up Meals Cookbook'." Meredith pointed to a large binder on the counter.

"What?"

"My mother was probably the most klutzy person ever to inhabit a kitchen. No matter what she cooked, something went wrong..."

"I can attest to that..." Paul interjected. Meredith nodded and did not argue with her husband.

"Here…I'll show you what I mean…" Meredith reached over.

"Was this meal in there?" Shannon asked? Meredith nodded.

"Yep. Right there on page seventy eight. 'Burnt Bacon Surprise.'"

"No way!" Shannon leaned over to look.

"You have to know, my mother was a social butterfly. She would spend hours on the phone and not notice how a roast or a soup was burning. She realized she was doing it and came up with quick solutions."

"Amazing…" Shannon added.

"The neat thing is, over time, my dad would purposely ask for dishes like this "Burnt Bacon Surprise'…" Meredith's voice trailed off as she looked closely at the end of the recipe. She put on a pair of glasses.

"What's that?" Shannon asked.

"I've read these recipes dozens of times but I never noticed that every one of them ends with a personal note."

"Like what?" Paul asked.

"Like this one here, in the 'Burnt Bacon Surprise': 'Last ingredient – sprinkle liberal doses of apologies…and learn how to hang up the phone when Mildred calls.'" Meredith looked at Paul and touched his arm.

"Interesting. Paul's dad has those kinds of things written in his journal, too." Shannon added.

"That's right – you've read all of his entries." Paul said as he took a bite of toast.

"It seems that their generation was willing to write down what they had a hard time saying out loud." Meredith said.

"Do you feel up to hearing more from your dad, Paul?" Shannon asked as she opened the notebook in the chair by her side. Tim leaned over and shut it.

"Not sure if we need any more fights, Shannon..." Tim whispered.

"Tim, no. Let her read. I think you had some good advice out there on the boat. I'll try to see my father as a different person now. Maybe I can figure out how to move forward. Maybe he found a way and never told me. Now maybe he can let me in on his secret..."

"If you think so..." Tim sat back.

"Maybe, just maybe, I can find a way to work with the relationships I have left in my life. Maybe I can find a 'Burnt Bacon Surprise' in my dad's writings..." Paul looked at his wife as he signaled to Shannon.

Shannon cleared her throat and began to read.

SATURDAY

Not much to report today, Annie. I got the flu, or at least I think it was the flu. Pretty weak tonight. Yes, I drank lots of fluids and got lots of rest. All I could really keep down were some saltine crackers, but I'm feeling a little hungry now. Maybe I'll warm up a bit of soup to go along with the crackers. You know how much I like cheddar cheese on crackers, well, that's not real appetizing right now. THAT is how sick I am!

"Well, that's not the best way to finish a breakfast, Shannon!" Paul laughed. Meredith chuckled. Shannon continued.

I'm feeling strong enough to get over to the desk and write this, so you can see that your "prescriptions" still work. I'll try to write more tomorrow.

SUNDAY

I'm sorry, Annie, but I'm still feeling a bit under the weather. I mostly slept through the day – that helped a lot. I have to make the drive to Bakersfield tomorrow. I didn't want to tell you this, but the teens got into a bit of trouble and I have to go to court. No, not Shannon. Tim and that jerk that hangs out with him, Isaiah. I swear, sometimes I wonder about Tim. Why would he hang out with Isaiah I will never understand – he is a real troublemaker. I hope that someday Tim will really step back and ask himself why he makes the decisions he

does. Remember when we had a talk about why I made
some bad choices? Yep. He needs that.

"I don't know why I hung out with Isaiah; it still makes me
sick to think about him. What was wrong with me? All these
years and I still can't figure it out." Tim said with a frustrated
tone. Paul looked over at him.

"Was he older, Tim?" Paul asked.

"Yeah, a little, but he always acted like he was like thirty
or something. Why?"

"You told me that you had no father around. Maybe you
needed an older brother and he was available...?" Paul
asked. Tim sat back and nodded.

"It's possible. Yes..." Tim whispered while nodding.

"Tim, sometimes we get desperate for companionship,
then we latch on to anyone who pays attention to us, even if
it's negative attention. I've learned that the hard way myself."
Paul looked down at his plate.

"Oh, really?" Meredith asked with a lilt in her voice.

"Present company excluded, dear!" Paul, still looking
down, smiled gently.

Shannon continued reading Joseph's words.

Strangely, I know what you'd want me to do in that
courtroom. I'm just going to shut my mouth and let you do
this your way. You know how hard THAT will be for me.

I'll let you know what happens tomorrow, after court. I'm
going to try to not bite my tongue too much.

Meredith cleared her throat and smiled.

"Whoa. Hold on," Paul put his hand up. "Here, I'll say it
before you do, Mer. That sounds like us, right?" Paul looked
at his wife.

"I won't argue with you...but maybe your father was
further along on this lesson?" Meredith said quietly, a small
smile on her face. Paul opened his mouth to speak, but
paused.

"I know this will shock you, but I think you're right." Paul
nodded as he whispered.

"It's like Grandpa Marino is here at the table..." Shannon
added as she returned to the writing.

MONDAY

Well, you got me again, Anne. I was getting ready to go
to Bakersfield. I decided to look professional and wear a
tie. On my way out I started to slip on my favorite coat,
you know, the one with the patches on the sleeves that
you gave me? Guess what I found in the pocket? Of
course, you know. There it was – a pink envelope.

"I always wondered where my mother got the idea to put notes around the house like that..." Paul said in a quiet voice.

Before I reply to what you said, I need to tell you that you'd have been proud of me today. I asked the judge to let the boys work off their punishment by helping me build your stone wall. He should have seen his look – he must have thought I'd lost my sanity.

"Well, that explains a lot I that didn't understand. I thought my dad would ask the judge to throw the proverbial book at you guys, Tim." Paul interrupted.

"Like I said, Paul. People change. We have to accept that and let them change..." Tim smiled.

"You told him that?" Shannon asked with a surprised tone.

"Uh, yeah..." Tim sat up and looked uncomfortable.

"So, you DO hear some things I say to you?" Shannon shook her head but was smiling.

"And I now see he's not the great psychologist he makes himself out to be!" Paul said with a big smile.

"Hey, like I said, I heard someone say it..." Tim shrugged and blushed. Shannon stared at her husband while gently shaking her head.

"'Someone', huh?"

"Um, go ahead and read some more, dear…" Tim flashed a smile. Shannon looked down at the papers.

Hold on while I get the letter from my pocket. I'm back. Sorry, but I'm not sure I can reply tonight. Yeah, those nasty symptoms have reared up. No, not the flu. I'm pretty much over that. The tears are clouding my vision…so, until tomorrow, please know that I love you.

"The notes really did hit him." Paul said quietly.

"Oh, yes. The emotional roller coaster gets a bit faster and harder now. Make sure your seat belt is tight." Shannon said and then continued reading.

TUESDAY

I'm not sure how much I can write, Anne. You brought up how I found you in the garden, when you wrote that I saved your life. I, well, I haven't thought much about that day since then. To be honest, I thought you were gone. I ran to the phone and called, and in my head I was cursing the fact that we lived so far from a city, and how hard it is to get an ambulance into Pine Mountain Club. I felt like I had made a lousy decision to move there, and it would cost you your life.

"Wow. Hearing my father blame himself...amazing." Paul whispered. Shannon continued.

We were in luck that day – there was an ambulance driving out of town after dropping someone off who had come home from the hospital. Wow, I can't believe how clear my memory is of those hours. Every minute felt like an hour. I couldn't tell if you were breathing. Hold on a minute.

"What happened?" Paul sat up and urgently asked.

"Hold on..." Shannon said with a reassuring tone. She had to take a breath.

WEDNESDAY

I had to take a walk, Annie. Remembering that day in the garden was not easy. I've tried very hard to not think about those minutes that became hours that became days. Unfortunately, I walked out by the very spot where you collapsed, and a flood of memories crashed back in. It's actually the middle of the night now. I guess it is Wednesday, so I wrote WEDNESDAY at the top of this paragraph.

I have to say that my walk around the garden allowed me to see that God granted me a real gift – to be able to be with you for a few more months. You mentioned that you learned how to let go of everything that is meaningless. Strangely, that seems to be a lesson I'm learning. Sadly, one of the most important things was you, and I had to let you go.

"Tim, you called it like it is. He did change, and I couldn't see it. Letting go of everything that is meaningless. I need to find that myself." Paul looked down at his plate. He sighed as he picked up his fork and played with some crumbs.

"Well, Shannon called it..." Tim looked at his wife.

"That's okay, Tim. You gave it to Paul. I can let it go..." Shannon smiled. Paul picked up a glass of orange juice and started to drink from it.

Paul and Sarah mean a lot to me, and I am trying to reach out, but, well, you know how hard that is for me. I won't quit on that, but I'm not sure I can tell them all I want to say. Too many problems in the past – too many misunderstandings, and, well, I suppose just too much stubbornness. That seems to run deep in the family.

Paul coughed - he choked a bit on the juice. Meredith jumped out of her chair and started patting her husband on the back. Tim rose, but didn't leave his chair. He noticed that Meredith got to her husband quickly.

"Honey?"

"Hack...ugh...hold...on. I'm okay..." Paul was finally able to take a clear breath.

"What happened?" Meredith asked softly.

"I'd like to blame the juice, but that part about stubbornness, well, you know. Too close to home there." Paul wiped his mouth.

"Paul, did you hear what your dad said? He said he wouldn't quit..." Tim added. Paul nodded in reply.

"I've been thinking. What's weird is, well, he hasn't quit. He's still trying, years after his death, to get a message through. This feels like some kind of séance - like we need to ring a tambourine or a bell or something, you know, like that ride at Disneyland?"

"Or maybe we just found some old papers..." Tim answered.

"But why would he write all of this, Tim? He wanted his effort to go past the end of his life." Shannon said in a reverent tone. Tim looked down and nodded.

You mentioned scrambling after the almighty dollar. When I look back now, after all of those years, I wonder if it was all worth it. I spent long hours at school, taking on all kinds of extra duties. Yes, we needed the money, but I feel like I lost all that time when our kids were growing up.

"Oh, wow. I was never able to see that side of him, even though I've had to do the same thing – taking extra jobs. All I saw was how he wasn't there for me. I couldn't see how, well, how he wasn't there for him. He wanted to be there." Paul took a deep breath.

"Are you okay?" Shannon asked. Paul nodded.

"It's what I need to hear. Please, go on…"

I talked to Paul on the phone the other day and after I hung up I start to cry. Anne, where was I when they were growing up? What happened to all of those years? No, wait. What happened to all of those decades?

"I wonder that about our own kids." Paul said quietly as he looked at Meredith.

We were just kind of shooting the breeze. I was trying, and you know I was. I wanted to find a way to connect, even if I don't know what I'm doing. He mentioned a concert in junior high school and, for the life of me, I couldn't remember. I sat down with a pen and paper and plotted out when he had been in junior high and I realized that was when I was coaching football.

"Yeah, dad, football. And I remember that you bought me a bike that year. Now I bet you used your coaching stipend for that. All I could see was myself..." Paul looked up at the ceiling.

I remember you telling me about some events at the school for our kids – and I remember how I had no time to get to those moments. How many years was I unable to go to the open houses or back to school nights at their schools because I was too busy at my own school? I used to think that being a teacher was good for the family. I was off from school when they were off, and stuff like that, but now I see that, for most of the time, I could not be a part of their school experiences.

"I used to hate him for being a teacher. He could never get to my school. My mom always showed up. Duh, it makes sense now. Teachers are the people in society who aren't allowed to show up at their kids' schools because they have to be there for other parents. Is that irony or what?" Paul remarked.

I'm not sure if I ever thanked you for being there for them. I have to admit I feel bitter – no, not toward you, but toward, I don't know, maybe our system in general. All my life I heard, "work harder, work smarter, earn more," and every time we got a bit ahead there was always a bill due, or an unexpected expense.

I feel like someone in the financial world has rigged a system so you work harder and harder just to stay even. They don't want you to get ahead – I figure that if you get ahead they don't control you, and they want to control you. They make money off of you borrowing from them. Maybe I'm just a grouchy old man, I don't know.

"Now my father and I can really relate. Yes, dad, absolutely. If you were a grouchy old man then, I am one now. But you wrote the truth." Paul said.

Shannon cleared her throat and kept reading.

I remember one time so well; it was when I taught summer school. This one hurt a lot. I had squirreled away a little money so we could make it through the summer without me getting a second job, and they asked me (at the last minute) to take over a class. You were all excited about how we could go to Zion National Park and camp, and we had to cut that down. We could get ahead, I said. Put some money in the bank, I said.

"Your son is still trying to do the same thing..." Meredith reached over and tapped her husband on the forearm.

We camped for a week and, when we got home, we discovered something. Do you remember? There had been a water leak in the front yard and we needed a plumber to re-do a major pipe. Remember how much it cost? Yep, the same amount I had earned working in summer school. Remember how I never reconciled all of that? If we had just stayed home, would the expense have proven unnecessary? I have to find a way to let that go.

"There it is again. Find a way to let it go. Good advice, Dad. Your leak at the house is a boat in a dock to me." Paul reflected.

"One more line on these pages..." Shannon mentioned.

I really have to get to bed. Everything is getting blurry...

"Wow. Finally. My father and I are actually communicating." Paul said quietly.

"It doesn't matter if it is by voice or on paper – the message matters." Meredith added.

"I see that, but I think I need a break. Tim, shall we look at the boat a bit more? Maybe we can figure out what we need for a maiden voyage?" Tim nodded

"Sure."

"Can we hear more from my dad later, Shannon? I think bite-sized is what I need from this." Shannon nodded as Paul and Tim took one step toward the back door.

"Um, hold on, guys. How about cleaning up breakfast dishes first?" Meredith smiled. Paul paused, looked down, and then nodded. He picked up his plate and walked to the sink. Tim and Shannon followed the example.

"Thanks for breakfast, honey." Paul kissed his wife.

"Thank my mother…" She smiled in return as she turned on the water faucet.

"Strange how our parents are always there to haunt us…" Paul shook his head as he picked up a wet baseball cap.

"Would we want it any other way?" Meredith answered.

Chapter 14

"Can you think of anything we've missed?" Tim asked Paul as he scanned the clipboard in his left hand.

"Well, we ran through the engine, the controls, the electrical system, and the radio. I'm not sure how we can check the hull, but I haven't seen any leaks."

"And the roof, or whatever you call it, looks solid." Tim tapped on the flat area above the main cabin.

"We'll just call it the roof, Tim. You haven't been picking up on the marine terminology at all, my friend!" Paul smiled. Tim nodded as he handed the old wooden clipboard to Paul.

"I guess I'm a, what did you call it? A 'land lubber'..."

"I think you might be the best example of one of those that I've met in a long time." Paul smiled.

"But I know engines..." Tim added with pride.

"But you know engines." Paul nodded in agreement.

"Well, we have a pretty good list of parts here. If we can get these things installed this old tub might be ready for a maiden run. That is what you called it, wasn't it?" Tim asked.

"Maiden voyage, yes. Well, at least for us."

"How long do you think it'll take to get the parts? I can schedule another weekend down here. We should be able to get all this done in a day or two." Tim asked.

"Oh, I think my contact at the marine store can get this together in a week or two. None of these things are really unusual." Paul tapped on the list.

"He's not the guy who has been trying to talk you into a complete engine replacement, is he?"

"Actually, yes. Why?"

"I made a couple of calls about this particular engine. It's a rare beast, and it's in good shape. I think your friend may be trying to get his hands on the engine for another reason. It's a high demand power plant. I'm just worried about this guy dealing straight with you, Paul."

"Really?"

"Think about it. Boat engines, car engines. They're the same thing, really. Paul, this happens in my line of work a lot. Not with me, but I've seen it happen."

"I guess so. I've dealt with some shady characters in the computer business, too."

"I believe it – it's the human condition. People push the limit, see how far they can get with things and not get noticed. They don't think they're wrong unless they get caught." Tim said in a matter-of-fact way.

"You knew someone like that a long time ago...really well." Paul nodded.

"My dad? I really didn't know him long enough..."

"No, I was thinking of your old friend. Forgot his name – the idiot you hung out with on Pine Mountain."

"Oh, Isaiah...yeah. That was how he lived every day of his life. Take what he wanted, as long as he didn't get caught. I realized years later he learned that from his father. Man, what a piece of work he was." Tim shook his head.

"I guess we all learn from the examples of our parents." Paul looked toward the house.

"That's what I've learned by coming down here this weekend." Tim answered.

"Yup…" Paul nodded.

"Well, that brings me back to my point. Your contact may be seeing a possible gold mine here." Tim pointed at the engine compartment. "If he could get you to put in a new engine, he'd make a bundle, and then he'd make another bundle selling this one to someone else."

"Maybe I'll go over to the marine store in Newport Beach instead."

"I could be wrong, Paul, but it makes me feel uncomfortable. I've got no skin in this game, if you know what I mean. If you want to replace the engine, I won't make anything. If you want to fix it with these minor parts, I still won't make anything. Heck, it would actually be easier for me to just tell you to replace the engine. Less skin off of my knuckles." Tim flashed his left hand, which had three small bandages on it.

"No, I'll make the drive to Newport. A friend recommended a marine shop there. I'd rather not work with someone who I have to always wonder about." Paul was adding some numbers to the list on his clipboard.

"So we'll set up a weekend and get this done. Maybe in two or three weeks?" Tim took off his hat and rubbed his head.

"Sure. That would be about right. Meredith and I will bring along a cooler for the first trip – some sandwiches, chips, apples, drinks, stuff like that. What do you and Shannon like for a picnic style meal? It's on us."

"Well, we're pretty easy about that, but, to be honest…" Tim stopped in mid-sentence. He was not sure how much to say, or how to say it. He looked toward the house.

"Honest about what?" Paul was writing on the clipboard.

"I'm not sure I can get Shannon to ride along. Um, well, she…" Tim paused. Paul looked up from his writing.

"A problem?"

"I guess so. Can we keep something between us?"

"Sure. What's up?"

"Shannon's terrified of the ocean. She wouldn't have a problem just cruising in the harbor, but out on to the Pacific? No way, no how. She'd probably jump overboard as we left the harbor entrance." Tim said quietly.

"Yeah, that would be a problem."

"Yep. I'm not sure how to do this, I mean, she'd want to come down here again, and she'd be happy to ride in the harbor, but, well, you get my drift…"

"I do. Let me talk to Meredith. Is that okay? We can figure something out."

"I guess. Maybe they could do something while we take it out on to the open water and come back in." Tim responded.

"Tim, I don't want to do it that way. I have a destination in mind."

"There's someplace you want to go on the first trip? I though maiden voyages were just out and back?" Tim asked.

"Well, yes and no. Yes, I have a very specific place in mind. No, they don't have to be out and back trips." Paul reached into a map case next to the ship's wheel and pulled out a nautical chart. He spread it out on the flat surface on top of the cabin.

"This is it?" Tim asked.

"Hold on...yes..." Paul found a few objects to hold down the rolled-up map.

"Hey, cool. A neat map! I've always liked maps!" Tim exclaimed.

"On a ship they're called charts, but, yeah, it's a nice map. There. That is Catalina Island, about 26 miles off the coast." Paul pointed with his pen.

"So, you want to go there? To Avalon?" Tim pointed at the major city on the southern end of the island.

"No, no. Here..." Paul pointed at the other end of the chart.

"Parson's Landing?" Tim asked.

"Exactly." Paul stepped back.

"What's there?"

"You don't remember, do you?"

"Remember? I've never been to Catalina." Tim shrugged.

"Do you remember our phone call a few weeks ago? When you found the orange box?" Paul asked.

"Yeah, sure. Oh, wait...something your dad wrote..." Tim's energy level went up.

"You've got it. What he wrote, what you read to me over the phone - I've burned into my memory." Paul sounded very intense.

I never did tell you what I did with that box. I buried it by that big rock near the beach camp – the one you climbed on so much.

"So you want to go back and find that box?"

"Yes." Paul clicked his pen and made an ornate "X" mark on the chart.

"'X' marks the spot! So, we're going after pirate gold, huh?" Tim chuckled.

"Not really gold, but maybe it is for me. Well, maybe blue."

"Blue? What? So, what's in this treasure chest?"

"It was painted blue. Can I get back to you on your question? I'm still struggling with the idea that I might be able to get it back. It's kind of personal. I hope you can, you know, cut me some slack."

"Hey, sure, I understand. Old, hard stuff here…"

"By the way, I decided something about an hour ago. It was tough." Paul grew quiet and looked around.

"About the boat?" Tim said, quietly. Paul looked over quickly.

"How did you know?"

"Well, it has been a major topic of the weekend…"

"After our talk today I decided this boat will stand between Meredith and me forever, and there's no reason for that. We have to be together on this, or we can't have it in our lives. She's not interested in boating."

"That is tough. It's your dream…"

"She was once, too, and she has seniority." Paul said. Tim nodded, in a knowing way.

"Like how I gave up my old Monte Carlo for Shannon. She needed a minivan."

"Sounds about right…" Paul started rolling up the chart.

"So, we go to Catalina to pick up a blue box – if it is still there…"

"If it is still there…" Paul repeated in a whisper.

"And…?" Tim asked.

"When we return I'll put the boat up for sale."

"But you live on a harbor, you have a dock…or a jetty or a pier of whatever this is…" Tim stumbled with his terms as he pointed. Paul smiled.

"Hah! It's just a dock, Tim. And we can buy a small boat just to get around the harbor. She wouldn't mind that."

"But, first..." Tim started, then looked at the older man next to him.

"But first I want to try to find this thing, this blue box. I hope you can trust me on this – it's worth a lot to me. More than I can say."

"I guess I'll have to. It's nothing illegal is it? Not like Coast Guard ships will be tailing us or anything?" Tim smiled.

"Oh, no. I'd be too embarrassed if that happened. What's in that old box is probably only valuable to me. But to me, it's really valuable..." Paul returned the smile.

"Okay, then. We'll be off to 'Parson's Landing' to find some buried treasure, then back here to sell a boat! Sounds like a plan. Wait. How long will that trip take?"

"We'll be there and back in the same day. Don't worry. No side trips." Paul sounded confident.

"That should work. It'll be just you and me, and this old tub, the...uh, um, what's the boat's name? Don't boats have names?" Tim asked.

"They most certainly do! Right now it's called the H-N-L-J-U." Paul slid the paper chart into its case.

"The what?"

"Like I spelled it. The H-N-L-J-U. Look at the stern of the boat. Stern is 'back' in land lubber language."

"Hey, I've learned that much. But what does the name mean?"

"I don't have a clue. I was going to rename her, but decided not to - now that I'll be selling it. I'll leave that honor for the next owner. For now, I just call it the 'Hunniljoo'." Paul walked over and stepped off of the boat. He was carrying the clipboard. Tim followed.

The two men moved to the rear of the ship. There, across the back, in red paint done in a strange font style, were five letters...H, N, L, J, U.

"I guess we can name it whatever we want, as long as it goes along with the letters." Tim suggested.

"What do you mean?"

"Well, something like, 'Her Nostrils Look Just Ugly?'" Tim proposed.

"Oh, you can do better than that."

"'He's Nothing Like...um...'" Tim struggled and quit.

"'He's Nothing Like Jerry's Uncle'?" Paul smiled.

"Who's Jerry?" Tim asked.

"Don't know. Just picked it out of thin air."

"Maybe it belongs back in thin air..." Tim smiled.

"Got it. It fits today's theme! 'He's Not Like Joseph's Understudy'!"

"What's an 'Understudy'?" Tim asked.

"That's someone who is an assistant, like to a famous actor. If the actor is out sick during a play, the understudy fills in. And you know who Joseph was."

"I get it, but, boy, that clunks. It reminds me of when we dropped an engine block on the garage concrete once. Not a pleasant sound." Tim smiled.

"Well, we've got two or three weeks to come up with something better, I guess."

"Man, I'd love to find out what the original meaning was. 'Harry Never Liked Jelly Underwater'?" Tim joked; Paul smiled.

"On that upbeat note, let's get some lunch. Maybe we can hear more from my father…" The two men walked up the dock toward the house.

Chapter 15

"Man, I'm hungry. I wonder what's for lunch. I could use a nice burger, or maybe a submarine sandwich…" Paul said as the crossed the back patio.

"I've been dreaming about a bacon cheeseburger, but I could go for some pizza." Tim added.

"I wouldn't argue with that." Paul slid open the door leading into the house and suddenly stopped. Tim almost ran into him from behind.

Shannon and Meredith were seated at the kitchen table, looking at papers – old papers. Lots of papers. The table was covered with scraps, pages and lists. It seemed as if the two ladies were re-arranging something.

"Well, hello..." Paul exclaimed. Tim stepped around his friend.

"Hmm. Hadn't counted on paper for lunch." He said very quietly.

"So, do you want it fried or with cheese and bread?" Paul turned and whispered.

"I vote for take-out...or delivery." Tim smiled.

"We hear you. Are you guys complaining or something?" Meredith did not look up from her stack of papers.

"Complaining? Oh, never!" Paul replied. Meredith removed her glasses, looked up and stared at her husband.

"Never? So you've been drinking?" She asked.

"Oh, no, no, no..." Paul smiled as he walked by the table.

"We were just concerned that we are interrupting some important literary work." Paul scanned the table as he said as he walked over to the kitchen sink. Tim followed behind. Paul turned the water on and reached for a bar of soap. Tim paused and looked at a yellowing page.

"Meredith has quite a talent as an editor – she found some problems in all of this – things I missed." Shannon said.

"She's good at that. Without her I would have never finished my Master's degree. I mean that." Paul nodded and stepped over to the refrigerator.

"She thinks some of these pages from your dad's journal are out of order and she's found forensic ways to put them back as they should be. I guess the word is 'forensic'..." Shannon pointed at the table in front of her.

"That sounds like my dad." Paul smiled as he handed a towel from the refrigerator to Tim, then stepped aside.

"We also found a lot of odd papers in here, too. Like a shopping list." Shannon pointed to an old scrap in the corner. Paul picked it up and started to read.

Gloves – size large
Hammer - heavy
Band aids - assorted
Toilet paper – the usual
Bread - white
Mike and Ike – 10 boxes

"What the heck? Mike and Ike? I get the other things but, whoa, I really didn't know my dad! My father liked candy? TEN boxes? And why does it look like someone else's handwriting?" Paul looked at Shannon, who covered a smile on her face.

"I think there is someone in this room who can explain that item, dear." Meredith turned toward the sink. Tim had stopped washing and was looking down. The back of his neck was getting redder by the minute.

"He kept that? Crap. Remember, I was a lot younger back then..." Tim started as he dried his hands.

"Weren't we all?" Paul responded with a smile.

"I used to be addicted to those candies..." Tim started.

"Used to?" Shannon said with a lilt.

"Okay, used to be MORE addicted to those candies." Tim said, emphasizing one word while looking at Shannon.

"So, is this your handwriting...?" Paul asked, handing the paper to Tim. Tim pulled it away and looked down.

"Yeah. It was a joke. He noticed how I had a box of those candies with me whenever we worked on the wall. He once told me we'd have the wall done in a week if I stacked stones as fast as I downed those candies. So I said if you want that, get me more candy." Tim turned and watched Shannon pull something from her purse.

"Like these?" Shannon smiled and waved a brightly-colored box in the air. Tim was in full blush.

"Yeah. So, when he was getting his keys, I noticed the note lying on the table. He was going to drive over to the store in Pine Mountain, so I added that line. He picked the paper up on his way out and shoved it into his pocket."

"Well?" Meredith asked.

"Well what?" Tim answered.

"Did you get the candy?" Paul continued with his wife's train of thought.

"What if I don't want to answer that?" Tim mumbled.

"That's okay, sweetheart. Grandpa Marino can answer that for you – look at this note..." Shannon sounded a bit too sweet as she pushed a scrap of paper across the table.

Hi, Tim,

I did notice you really increased the speed with stacking rocks after I got all of those boxes of candy, but I didn't think they'd only last a week. Not sure how many more weeks I can afford to pay you like this!

Smiles,
Grandpa Marino

Everyone in the room broke into laughter, except for Tim.

"Hey, uh, I was a growing boy..."

Paul reached into the refrigerator and pulled out two cold sodas. He handed one to Tim.

"So, are you thirsty, 'growing boy'?" He smiled as he sat down. Tim opened the bottle, shook his head and took a drink.

"I'll never be able to live that down..." He mumbled.

"That's okay, honey. That's covered under Secret Number 2." Shannon said with a smile.

"Secret Number 2, huh? Is that somewhere in that pile of papers?"

"Oh, yeah. Right after Secret Number 1."

"Why am I not surprised?" Tim took a sip of his drink.

"You know what we need? Wasn't there an old shirt of my father's in that orange box you found in your garage?" Paul asked.

"Yeah. It's in the back seat of our car." Tim responded.

"Go get it. I mean it. I have something…" Paul trailed off as he rose and walked out of the room. Tim looked at Shannon and shrugged.

"I guess you should go get the shirt, Tim." Shannon shook her head. Tim hesitated. Shannon looked at her husband.

"Don't worry. I washed it…" Tim rose and went out through the garage door. In a minute he turned with a faded and worn plaid work shirt. Shortly thereafter Paul walked in with a pair of work gloves.

"Hang the short on that chair, Tim. Yeah, like that." Paul commanded. He then placed the two work gloves on the arms of the chair.

"Paul, those are dirty!" Meredith complained.

"I'll clean the chair after we're done. Now, my father has his rightful place at this table. I figured that if we're going to hear his words, we might as well look at his clothing, too!" Paul pointed at the chair. He adjusted the shirt so the sleeves touched the gloves.

"Sometimes I wonder if you've lost it..." Meredith shook her head. All four people stared at the image in front of them.

"Most of the time you wonder..." Paul smiled. He reached over and gently touched his wife's arm. She smiled.

"I worry. I know this isn't easy stuff, Paul."

"It's not, but, believe it or not, I really do wish my dad was here right now. I'm seeing him differently now. Unfortunately, it's too late..."

"But never happening would be worse." Tim said, quietly. Paul look over at his friend and nodded.

"I hope his words can help you, too, Tim."

"They do. Maybe I can understand why my father took off. Raising kids, dealing with job problems, relationship issues, and, you know, fears. Tough stuff."

"So, where is the next part, Meredith?" Shannon asked, looking across the many papers in front of her.

"I thought these were all in a couple of spiral notebooks?" Paul asked.

"Some were. Some were shoved in. Some were torn out and shoved back in." Shannon replied. She pointed at one stack in the corner near Meredith.

"Yeah. Right, uh, here...the next unread portion." Meredith handed a number of pages to Shannon.

THURSDAY – ABOUT TWO WEEKS LATER. I THINK.

You know, I should have dated these things from the beginning. I hate to admit that Mary at the Post office was right, but I wonder if all of this will seem confusing and out of place to you. I was going to date this one, but then I said, what does it matter? We have all of time now. The days, well, they don't matter much now. I'll just keep doing this just, well, because I'm used to it. Yeah, I know. Stubborn.

"He was not good about marking time, I see." Paul interrupted.

"I'm not sure he was worried about that. I think time became meaningless to him after your mother died." Shannon said, softly. Paul nodded and looked away.

"But he used that word again - stubborn. Runs deep and wide in this family." Paul interrupted, quietly.

"Paul, did you notice what he said about time? 'We have all of time now'? Think about it. Here we are, like seventeen or eighteen years later, and these words are fresh to us..." Meredith said. Paul looked at his wife and nodded slowly.

"Go ahead, Shannon..." Paul gestured.

THURSDAY – A WHILE LATER

Well, Annie, you mentioned that you hid these notes all over the place, and I realized that at this rate it WILL take me the REST of my life to respond to all you wrote! Maybe that's okay. Maybe you have found a way to help me in my time of aloneness.

Paul coughed and sighed. Shannon stopped reading and looked over at the man.

"My mother was amazing. She worried about him so much that she set things up to care for him even after she was gone. I know she did that for you, Dad…" Paul stared off. Shannon read a bit more.

You wrote that you worried about being crazy, Annie. No way, no how. If you are, then I am, too. Hah! Maybe THAT explains a lot! Don't get upset – I'm just teasing.

"Maybe your mother saw something in him that we can't see, Paul. How long did they know each other?" Shannon asked.

"He was in high school and she was, I think, like in junior high. They grew up in the same neighborhood in Maine. They saw each other every day."

"Did they know each other's families?" Tim asked. Paul looked over at his friend and nodded.

"Yes. Why?"

"Remember what you told me about his father? How hard he was? The flagpole? I wonder if your mother saw your dad before, well, before it got hard on him..." Tim's voice trailed off.

"I never thought of that..." Paul whispered.

"I knew Tim before, well, um..."

"I told him, Shannon. I told Paul about my father. You can say it." Tim looked down.

"It changed him, and I saw it happen. But it didn't change who he was deep inside. Tim's still that boy that made toys out of wood in the garage. He's still the boy who shared popsicles with me. But I watched him build a wall between him and the outside world over the years." Shannon took a deep breath.

"My mother would have seen that, that sort of thing." Paul said quietly.

"I saw the same thing, Paul..." Meredith offered, in a quiet voice. She reached over and touched her husband's left hand, on his wedding ring. He looked down at the golden object.

"From one generation to the next. How do we break the chain?" Paul said.

"We've done better than your parents did, honey. Our kids will do even better. It takes time." Meredith said.

"I just don't know how any marriage works, ever. It seems we've got two strikes against us even before we meet the right one." Paul sighed and shook his head. He played with his wedding ring.

"You won't believe the next part of the journal, Paul. He has some words about that..."

Paul looked over at Shannon.

Someone recently asked me how we were able to stay married for those 53 years. Since you've been gone I've seen that there were only a few "secrets" to our marriage. I thought I'd tell you here what I never really said, straight out, all those years.

"You are kidding me." Paul shook his head. Shannon paused, then continued.

JOEY AND ANNIE'S SECRETS

1. We truly, deep inside, cared about each other. I saw something very special in you, something that resonated inside of me. You had a sweetness that I was drawn to. You were always kind. You were patient. I believe you saw something that felt the same way for you – inside of me.

"It's what you said, Shannon, about seeing something from a long time ago..." Paul interrupted, then quieted down.

2. We saw that each of us had flaws, and we accepted that. I know we had many. I think we learned how to give up on the idea that someone is "perfect" (that princess and the prince idea) and to see who we are, just real people. I think early on you tried to change things about me, like how I always fidgeted with my second shirt button. I remember how your chewing your nails bugged me. Over time, however, these things seemed so small, so trite, so worthless…but we did have fights over them, early on. I'm sorry about those fights.

"You've been saying this sort of thing a lot recently, honey. You say a lot of our fights as worthless. And we stopped trying to change every little thing about each other. There's hope here." Meredith said as Paul looked nodded.

Shannon picked up where she had left off.

I want to say I'm sorry over that purple dress – one of your favorites. For some reason I got really upset about it, especially after we went camping and you wore it. I have no idea why I didn't like it, and now it seems so worthless. I saw a photo of you wearing it. I feel like whatever was going on inside of me had nothing to do with that dress, but I put it on the dress. And you got rid of it. I still feel bad about that.

"I know that photo. My father was very kind to write this. I had no idea this was going on inside of him." Paul said.

My best guess now is that I never really liked purple, and when you wore it that made me feel like I didn't "control" you, or something like that. That's the best I can do. But now I see we had another secret…

"Control. There's a huge problem." Tim said in a quiet voice. Shannon nodded.
"We struggle with that, too, Tim." Meredith added. Shannon cleared her throat.

3. We let the other person be who he or she really is. After a time I accepted you liked purple, and purple dresses. After a time I liked to see you in those dresses. Maybe I was learning, and I know it took too long, that you won't hurt me just because I can't control you, and when I let go of that idea, I could accept more about the "real" you. But, looking back, I see that it took a long time to get there. I'm sorry for all of the years when my fear kept us apart.

"It seems that all marriages have to go through this. We did, right, Mer?" Paul looked at his wife, who was nodding.

Gosh, I had a flashback about being bothered about how you ate pizza – from the crust end first. I see that it scared me, and there was no reason. I hope you were able to forgive me for such stupid things. Strangely, I believe you did. That's probably another secret…

"My mother ate pizza like that all of her life. My friends used to tease me about it. But it really didn't matter."

"Notice how your dad knew, deep inside, that she forgave him? They could communicate even through the conflict, Paul." Meredith added and signaled to Shannon.

4. We knew each other, and we felt genuine around each other. Harry (remember him from when I first started teaching? I can't remember his last name) once said knowing someone else really well is being able to scratch where it itches, in front of that person.

I suppose when you go through all we went through together we had few secrets…except for some pink notes you left around just recently! I sure chuckled about that! We never really kept secrets, but, boy, you hit me with a doozy!

"Genuine. There's a secret. I suppose we're afraid to be that way with others. We might get rejected. Heck, we will get rejected. That's what makes a good marriage so precious." Meredith added.

5. Then there is fighting. Whenever we did, mostly in our early years together, we always made sure we didn't not insult the other person, or put them down. We never hit "below the belt". I know we respected those weak places that we knew we had, and never, no matter how frustrated we were, ever hit each other there. I remember we did once, early on, and saw how painful that could be if we kept at it. That's when we went back to Joey and Annie's Secret Number 1...we truly cared for each other.

"I've never felt like you hit below the belt, Paul, even in our worst arguments." Meredith touched her husband's hand again.

"You've never done that either. And you've always walked softly around my weak places." Paul replied.

6. I think we always had the long term in mind, Annie. There were times when just breaking up would be the easiest thing to do, not many, mind you, but I think we realized our marriage was bigger than just that moment.

We have kids connected to us, and grandchildren. I now see that we were an example to them. We learn how a marriage works form people whose marriages work. I give you more of the credit, considering how messed up my family was.

"I don't know how our marriage works, then…" Tim said to Shannon.

"We saw people like Grandpa and Grandma Marino and how it worked for them, Tim. Neither of us knew these things when we got together – not from our families." Shannon replied. Tim nodded strongly.

I remember how I absolutely had to drive that old car back from Maine, because I didn't want you-know-who to buy it from my father's estate. You could not talk me out of it. I was stubborn, and then I drove across the United States being just as stubborn with Paul. Yeah, I know, I shouldn't use the same word twice in once sentence, but stubborn is a word that needs to be written twice in one sentence when I think about certain aspects of my life. Stubborn, stubborn, stubborn. There, three times in one sentence, if you don't look at the fact that there's no verb there.

All four people chuckled at the sound of the word "stubborn" being repeated.

"Man, what a rough trip that was, but I think he was too hard on himself. I really pulled some stupid stunts that week or so – and he seemed to just absorb all of it. I always wanted to apologize for that journey across the country. Never did."

"I think you just did, Paul…" Meredith pointed at the old shirt on the chair.

When I was in court the day the teens were sentenced, I decided, for one of the few times in my life, to let go and take someone else's advice, Annie. It was from you, and I am so sorry you weren't around to see it. Or maybe you were. I knew you'd be compassionate to those kids.

"It was weird, but I felt like she was there that day…" Tim said. "When I looked at him, in that courtroom, I felt like I knew he was doing that for her – asking the judge to go easy on us. Huh. Now I know…"

You know I wanted the judge to throw the proverbial book at them. My heart and mind were made up. When I read your letter, and you said so many kids were dumped by their parents, I saw Tim, Shannon and Isaiah. Sadly, I remember how I wasn't there for our kids much, and now I am so thankful you were there for ours.

"That's unusual. Probably because he had been a teacher he realized that kids get all the frustrations, problems and pains dumped on them by their parents. The kids are scapegoats. Or he listened to my mother's insight..." Paul offered.

"Or both?" Shannon added.

7. Well, one big "secret" we had was that neither of us was willing to give up. Quitting was just not allowed. I do see that it takes both people to feel that way, however. You remember a certain couple...darn, my memory is hazy again...when Paul was in high school. They lived next door to us. What were their names? I know if you were here you'd remember.

"Never give up. Good words. I remember the guy next door. His named was 'James'." Paul interjected.

Oh, well (I use that phrase a lot about these kinds of things nowadays). The husband wanted to stay with his wife and she just up and left him, with his three daughters. Wait, I do remember he worked in a lab. Wore a lab coat or something like that. I think he drove a white truck.

"Yep. That was him. His wife up and drove off one day. Left him with all the problems." Paul added.

I get so frustrated when something like a lab coat or a truck pops up but not a name. Sigh. Anyway, I remember how horrified we both were, and how we could not understand why she would do that. I'll never forget how three pretty little girls went from playing outside to being shut-ins who hardly every smiled – in the same week. The world became a harsh place for them on that day.

"It's strange how what haunted my dad haunts me, too. I can't forget those faces. I've wondered about those people; whatever happened to them?" Paul asked. Shannon looked at the next sentence and stopped.

"Whoa…"

"What?" Paul asked.

"The next line…" Shannon continued to read.

I wonder what became of them.

Paul leaned back and stared at the old shirt on the chair near him. He sighed.

Strangely, I still include them in prayers from time to time. I remember how pained the dad looked, and how overwhelmed he said he felt. They moved away after a while, and I saw him once after that, at the hardware store. He told me how much guilt he felt because his girls had to lose so much, in addition to their mom. I remember all I could do was just reach out and squeeze his arm. I wish I could have done more, but that has been a common theme of my life.

"Can you hold on? This is hitting a bit too close to where I live..." Tim said, clearing his throat. Meredith turned her head toward Tim. Paul looked down at the floor.

"Tim?" Shannon asked.

"It was a mom, and I was a son, but the guilt, the pain, it's the same. I was one of those kids. No one seemed to be able to...to..." Tim stood up and walked to the back door. He opened it and went outside. It was obvious that he was wiping his eyes. Shannon stood up, wanting to follow her husband. She stood by the door, the pane of glass separating them.

Meredith reached over and picked up the last piece of paper on Shannon's placemat. She continued where Shannon had left off.

Well, I just saw a natural signal to stop writing. I really mean that – very natural. You won't believe this, but the sun is coming up over Pine Mountain. The old rock is telling me it's time to "hit the hay". Yep, the mountain still talks to me.

I'm a bit dizzy and blurry-eyed, but, for some reason, I am so glad I had this time with you, Anne. I really did have something special with you. Good night.

"I'm glad I had this time with you, too, Dad." Paul whispered while looking at the old plaid coat. A tear was making its way down his cheek. Meredith slowly stood up and walked over to Paul. She rubbed his shoulder; he gently touched her hand.

"I believe you were hungry, back when you came inside. Yes, I heard. Can I make you something to eat?"

"Thanks, honey. Maybe later. I'm okay. Really..." Meredith leaned over and hugged her husband. Paul was still looking over his father's old work coat.

"Whenever you're ready." She added.

"You know, that's one heck of a fine plaid jacket..." Paul smiled.

Chapter 16

"Here, let me just stack these pages in one place. If you don't mind, I could put a little mark on the bottom corner to indicate some kind of order..." Shannon asked as she pulled papers toward her. Meredith looked over.

"That sounds really good, Shannon. Why don't you make a first pass through and I could check your work? Maybe put a Post-It on a page that you're not sure about?"

"I can do that." Shannon nodded.

"Strange, isn't it? Paul's father actually addressed us at the beginning of all of this – I guess we are his 'editors'!"

"Yes! I was just looking at that. We'd better follow his instructions!" Shannon began to read.

Note to future editor, if anyone does that to these scribblings: I decided I want that title to stay just like it is. All I give permission to do is edit it in case I capitalized a word I wasn't supposed to capitalize. I decided I'm not going to spend any time trying to look those kinds of things up.

"Well, he didn't say anything about organizing pages, so I guess we're good!" Meredith chuckled. Paul closed the back door and walked by as Meredith joked.

"Knowing my father, and having seen my mother fix up his letters to his parents, I know he'd appreciate that!" He smiled as he headed for the sink.

"We'll just keep the title as it is, and make sure everything is in proper order. Not too hard!" Shannon said.

"How much of his journal is left?" Tim, following Paul toward the sink, asked.

"Just a few pages left. I can organize it into a nice binder and maybe..." Shannon paused and looked over at Paul, "we could get a copy of it?"

"I don't see why not..." Paul started to wash his hands, then stopped. "Wait! Maybe this could prove to be a huge national bestseller. You know, like on the New York Times' list?" Everyone chuckled.

"I'll tell you what. If you can get this published, we'll pay you for a photocopy." Tim contributed.

"Don't hold your breath..." Paul smiled as he wiped his hands.

"So, what have you two been doing?" Shannon asked.

"I think we're about ready to take the 'INHLJU'..." Tim started.

"It's the 'NHLJU', Tim. Like 'in hill juice.'" Paul corrected.

"What are you talking about?" Shannon stopped shuffling papers.

"The boat. That's its name." Paul answered.

"It sounds like just a bunch of letters. Really?" Shannon asked.

"Believe it or not, yes. To answer your next question, I have no idea why it's named that."

"Huh!" Shannon shook her head.

"Anyway, we got a lot done on the 'in hill juice'. We have a list of parts we need, and Paul just finished making up a shopping list for food and supplies for the maiden voyage. Did I get that right?" Tim asked.

"We could call it a shakedown cruise…but, yeah, close enough." Paul responded.

"I'm not so up on nautical terms…" Tim shook his head.

"Wait, whoa. What the heck is 'in-hill-juice'?" Shannon looked confused.

"The boat's name again. But it's not. The letters on the back of the boat spell out 'N-H-L-J-U'. I just call it something like 'in hill juice'. That's the best I can do." Paul answered as he opened the door to the refrigerator. "Speaking of which, do you want a juice, Tim?

"Sure. What do you have?" Tim responded.

"Orange or apple."

"I'll take the orange…" Tim reached and took the bottle from Paul.

"A boat called 'N-H-L-J-U'. Just spelled like that? Does it stand for something? That has to be one of the lamest boat names I've ever heard of!" Shannon shook her head.

"We really don't know, Shannon. I mean it. The former owner never old us." Meredith added.

"Why don't we call him and ask?" Tim suggested.

"Ahh, well, there's the problem, Tim..." Paul started. He took a sip from his apple juice.

"Problem?" Tim asked. Paul took a deep sigh and looked over at Meredith.

"You know I got the boat as payment for computer services that the man couldn't pay me for, right?

"Really!" Shannon exclaimed.

"Yep. He was a good guy but business got tough. He wanted to make good on the debt. He was like that."

"Was?" Tim asked.

"Yeah, was. Right after he signed the boat over to me he had a heart attack. Died the next week." Paul's voice was very quiet. He picked his juice bottle up, started to take a drink, but stopped.

"Oh..." Shannon whispered.

"Good guy. So, that's how this nautical stress entered our family. He told me to hold the boat and when things got better he'd buy it back. He said he'd pay for maintenance. Of course, we never wrote all of that down, and his death really threw his family into a lot of troubles. His wife and kids really didn't need me to add to the issues."

"What did they do?" Shannon asked.

"It's what they are doing – they're still dealing with it. Selling the business and their house. She's hoping to get enough money to get a small house. She and her oldest son have jobs, so they should be okay." Paul took a sip.

"What about the deal with the boat? Can she buy it back?" Tim asked.

"Oh, no. They need every dollar."

"Paul did offer to give it back…" Meredith added.

"Yeah, I did. They were having a rough time, but his wife wouldn't hear of it. She audited the books on the business, so she knew I was owed more than what the boat was worth. They're proud people. Good people."

"Sounds like it." Tim said.

"I know we were doing business together, but I actually liked Larry. We could talk. He always asked about my family. Every year he had Christmas presents for us." Paul sighed as he looked out the window. Silence filled the room.

The song of a cell phone ringing echoed in the kitchen. Each person look at the other. Paul pulled his phone out.

"Not mine…that sounds like that 'all about that bass' song…"

"That's mine." Shannon said, her face turning red.

"Who is it?" Tim asked. Shannon picked up the phone.

"Joey." She said as she pushed the talk button. Shannon walked into the living room.

"Hahaha! I get it – 'bass' – deep voice!" Paul chuckled.

"Shannon does that – personalized ring tones. Me? I just use the 'Superman' movie theme for everyone." Tim shook his head.

"Here's mine…" Paul fumbled with his phone and pushed the button. It sounded just like an old fashioned desk phone ringing.

"Why do I imagine your father would be doing that if he were still with us?" Meredith smiled.

"Well, you are wrong. I know for a fact that he hated cell phones. Never saw a use for them." Paul responded.

"Yeah, that was twenty years ago when each phone weighed as much as a brick and most of our conversations were filled with, 'can you hear me know'?" Meredith said, sparking a chuckle around the room. Shannon came back into the kitchen.

"We'll have to continue this in a couple of weeks, when we come back. Tim, we have to get home."

"Something wrong?" Tim put his drink down.

"It depends on how you look at it. My mother wants Joey and Anne to make dinner."

"So?"

"Tim, stop. Think about your two kids. Make dinner? Together?" Shannon stared at her husband.

"That explains it all. I guess we have to get going…" Tim sighed.

"Whoa, wait a minute. Hold on. I'm getting a vibe from the past here." Paul put his hand up.

"What?" Shannon asked.

"Thinking about parents from way-back-when. If I recall correctly, your mother did not get along with Tim – not at all - back on Pine Mountain…"

"How do you know that?" Shannon sounded nervous.

"Um, I remember a certain phone conversation I had with my father one night. Something about her coming over to his house yelling about Tim. She wasn't too happy with my father, either." Paul bit his lower lip.

"Oh, yes. She did that. She found out I was pregnant – with Joey. I'm really sorry, Paul, about her yelling at your dad. She was hurting pretty badly back then…" Shannon looked down at the table.

"That's okay, Shannon. Remember, Tim gave me an excellent lesson on how we have to let people change over the years…" Paul pointed at Tim and smiled. Tim blushed.

"Uh, yeah. The stuff Shannon taught me. Yes." Tim said quickly.

"That's true. She and Tim get along really well now. In fact, she often takes his side in our little arguments…" Shannon glared at Tim.

"Hey, she's a sensible woman, what can I say?" Tim managed a half-smile.

"We'd better get our stuff together; it is later than I thought." Shannon looked around the living room.

"I have most of my stuff in my duffel bag, so I'm mostly ready..." Tim said. Shannon looked across the kitchen table, with the piles of papers covering it.

"Do you two mind if I take the rest of these papers home and bring them back in a couple of weeks? I'm really into my system here and I want to do this right. Of course, they belong to you, Paul."

"That's our plan, Shannon. You do the first pass and I'll check the work, so I don't have a problem with that. Paul?" Meredith said as she turned to her husband.

"I did want to read the last few pages..."

"They'll be back. It will only be a couple of weeks. Besides, you have a lot to do to get 'He's Not Leasing Just Using' ready between now and then." Meredith responded.

"'He's Not Leasing'...?" Shannon was confused.

"That's my interpretation of the boat's name – you know, "H-N-L-J-U'!" Meredith smiled.

"Mine is 'His Nautical Lingo is Just Unpossible.'" Tim offered. The room was quiet as everyone stared at him.

"'Unpossible'?" Shannon asked.

"Hey, it has to be a 'U' word...'unpossible' isn't, um, possible."

"The scary thing is, after being married to him all these years, that makes perfect sense to me..." Shannon smiled and gathered the papers.

"Paul, I can scan and send you the last few pages this week." Tim offered.

"Okay, that's workable." Paul nodded as he watched Shannon carefully place the papers back into her cloth bag.

Chapter 17

As Tim started the car in the driveway he noticed a movement to his left. It was Paul, walking toward the driver's door. Tim rolled his window down.

"I just sent you an email about the Parson's Landing trip. Just a reminder of what to bring along..." Paul said.

"Oh, yeah, I guess we should have talked about that. I'll check it and send a reply if I have any questions." Tim responded.

"Good. I think three weeks will do it – parts, repairs, stuff like that."

"We'll look at our calendars when we get home, sometime this week after we deal with teen issues..." Tim smiled as he looked over at Shannon. The smile disappeared as he saw her scowl.

"Have a safe drive home!" Paul said as he waved and turned toward the house. Tim rolled the window back up and took a deep breath. He shifted the transmission into reverse and turned to look down the driveway.

"I know that look, Shannon. What's going on?"

"What's 'Parson's Landing'?" Shannon said with an icy tone. Tim winced. He shifted the gear into drive as he centered the car in the street in front of Paul and Meredith's house.

"That's where Paul wants to take the maiden voyage for the boat." He accelerated toward the stop sign at the end of the road, then slowed to a stop. Two directional signs were pointing, left and right.

"Now, which way did we come in? Did we come in on Edinger or Warner?" Tim looked at his wife, hoping it would distract her from where he felt she was going.

"There's no place called 'Parson's Landing' in Huntington Harbor that I noticed." Shannon replied. Tim looked down and sighed.

"Should we pull over and talk about it?"

"We have to get home. It's getting late."

"But this is going to be a long drive if our standard epidemic of silence descends on the car." Tim strained, trying to be patient.

"Is he going to take the boat out on to the ocean?" Shannon came right to the point. Tim knew his wife. He knew where this was going.

"Edinger. It was Edinger that we came in on. We'll head that way." Tim turned left.

"Well?" Shannon asked.

"Yes, he wants to take it to Catalina Island." Tim answered.

"What's wrong with just driving it around the harbor?" Shannon shot back.

"Shannon, it's an ocean-going boat, and you don't test it in the harbor."

"I'll bet some people do. Drive it around the harbor."

"I'm not much into boating lingo, but I doubt they call it 'driving'. Cruising? Sailing? Something like that."

"I don't care what it's called. You know what the problem is." Shannon said.

"Yes, but what other option is there?"

"Why are you slowing down?" Shannon asked.

"Let's stop for a few minutes...and get a soda." Tim pulled the car into a fast food restaurant.

"We have to get home."

"Only for a drink and a breather. We'll just park for 5 minutes."

"Maybe some onion rings, too?" Shannon sighed.

"Definitely onion rings, with the dipping sauce you like, too." Tim pulled into the drive-through lane. He knew it would be an "onion rings with dipping sauce" sort of stressful drive home.

"Hi! Welcome to Ole's Burgers! Can I interest you in our chili-bacon-potato-chipotle-chicken double cheese burger?" A pretty female voice from a speaker asked.

"Your what…?" Tim was surprised.

"Yes, our chili-bacon-potato-chipotle-chicken double cheese burger, on a sesame bun. It has two kinds of cheese. French fries are in the burger."

"Inside the burger? People actually eat that?" Tim was incredulous.

"Oh, it's one of our most popular orders! Would you like to try one, dear?" The female voice asked with a lilt. Tim looked at Shannon and winked.

"I think she likes me, Shan!" He whispered. Shannon frowned and shook her head.

"Sir?"

"Oh, sorry. Um, I'm not sure you have enough napkins in there – my car would be a mess, it sound like!" Tim chuckled.

"Well, come on inside then, honey!" The voice continued. Tim noticed the voice was starting to sound a bit weary.

"Tim, I think she just wants to take your order." Shannon whispered.

"I'm sorry. Let's just order two medium diet sodas, and one order of onion rings, with your special sauce. Sorry, I know it's not your biggest orders of the day, I'm sure." Tim responded.

"Every order counts. Will that be all?"

"Uh, well, make it two orders of onion rings…" Tim felt compelled to add something.

"That will be seven fourteen at the second window, dear." The voice responded.

"Thanks…oh, and don't forget some of your secret sauce." Tim said as he put the car's transmission into drive.

"It just bugs me when a clerk in a drive-through fast food place calls my husband 'honey' and 'dear'…" Shannon whispered as they came close to the service window. There was one car ahead of them.

"So, you're jealous because some teen supermodel clerk at Ole's Burgers has a crush on me?" Tim forced a smile. Just then the car in front of them drove away.

"We're next…" Shannon gestured. Tim edged the car forward, up to the window. As they pulled up an older woman with long, wavy white hair appeared. She wore heavy make-up.

"Seven fourteen, sir…" She put out her hand. Shannon turned away and smiled.

"Uh, here's a ten…" Tim handed the bill to the woman, who disappeared inside.

"You're right, Tim. It does look like your supermodel has a crush on you. Sorry to interfere…" Shannon managed a half smile as she looked the other way and brushed the hair out of her face. Tim blushed as he turned to retrieve his change.

"Here are your drinks...hold on, you wanted extra napkins, right?" The clerk reached out with two cups of liquid and two straws.

"Uh, no. That was for that chipotle potato burger thing." Tim stammered. The clerk looked over the receipt she was about to hand to Tim. She looked confused.

"But I don't see that on your order. Did I mess it up, sweetheart?" The lady asked.

"No. I mean, yes. Actually, I mean no..." Tim became flustered and took a breath. Shannon leaned over.

"Ma'am, no on the burgers, but yes on the extra napkins with our onion rings. Sorry, my husband gets confused sometimes."

"Boy, do I understand that, missy. Mine gets so bad that I don't even let him drive anymore. There's a suggestion for you for the future..." The lady smiled as she turned away to retrieve a bag.

"Maybe not as far off as she thinks..." Shannon said quietly, looking at Tim.

"Come on, Shannon...it's been a long weekend." Tim rubbed his head.

"Here you go, two double orders of onion rings. And you wanted one secret onion sauce and one chipotle dipping sauce, right?" The clerk handed a large bag into the car.

"Exactly..." Tim said as he grabbed the bag and handed it to Shannon.

"Have a great evening, honey!" The lady waved. Tim smiled faintly as he put the car into gear and drove toward the parking lot.

"Tim, we didn't order double onion rings, and we didn't want chipotle sauce." Shannon said as she reached into the warm bag of food.

"Whatever is in that bag, I'll eat it." Tim said under his breath. Shannon reached into the bag and pulled out a large cardboard box. She opened it.

"How about a chili-bacon-potato-chipotle-chicken double cheese burger, on a sesame bun?" Shannon lifted a large burger box.

"What? Good thing we got extra napkins. What in the heck happened there?" Tim shook his head and looked back at the restaurant.

Chapter 18

"Hold on a minute..." Tim said while chewing. He picked up a napkin.

"Tim, not with your mouth full." Shannon scolded. Tim stopped chewing, turned and looked at his wife. He wiped his mouth and gently shook his head back and forth. He swallowed.

"Look, I know how you feel about going out on to the ocean..."

"You know how I feel, but you agreed to do it anyway, without even talking to me about it. Do you understand why I'm upset?"

"I feel kind of caught between two sides here…" Tim answered; Shannon cut him off.

"You are caught between your wife and some man with a boat who we only slightly know? So, how do you think that makes me feel?"

"Okay, okay…I can understand how you feel. Yes." Tim said as he looked at the box of onion rings lying between them on the seat. Shannon noticed.

"Those are mine. You got your mega-lots-of-junk-on-a-bun burger. Eat your food." Shannon pointed.

"I did not order this. I ordered onion rings, too."

"You got the burger. Don't complain." Shannon put an onion ring in her mouth.

"Listen, this isn't about the food. Yeah, they screwed up our order, but something else is going on here." Tim took another bite of his burger. He studied it carefully, then raised his eyebrows. He nodded in approval.

"It's not about the food. It's about how we make decisions and how we communicate." Shannon said sternly.

"Honestly, Shannon, I don't know if that's it, either. We haven't changed much in how we do those things. I don't know why I, uh…agreed…" Tim trailed off. Someone was walking in front of the car and it caught his attention. He lowered his burger as he stared out the front windshield. Shannon noticed the movement at about the same time Tim did.

Standing squarely in front of their parked vehicle was an older man, leaning on a walker. He stopped and looked closely at the front of their car. He nodded enthusiastically and then leaned over to tap on the license plate attached to the front bumper.

"What in the world is he doing?" Shannon stared at the old man.

"Tapping our license plate, what else?" Tim shrugged.

"He's saying something, Tim." Shannon rolled her window down.

"California! Yes sir, that's California." The sound of the old man's voice drifted into the car. His sounded very sure of himself.

Tim and Shannon turned and looked at each other. Neither seemed to know what to say. Shannon opened her door and stepped out.

"Hello! Can I help you, sir?" Shannon asked. Tim could tell that she was using her "very kind and polite" voice.

"Oh, missy, that is his license plate, alright. I know it anywhere. It's California!" The old man smiled at Shannon. He stood up as straight as he could and shuffled with his walker toward the passenger side of the car. He stumbled a bit on the concrete tire block.

Tim, shaking his head and feeling a bit anxious about the man, quickly put his burger back into the box on the seat and opened the driver's door. He stepped out and walked to the front of the car. A quick check of the bumper and license plate showed no damage there. Tim did, however, notice a bug splattered across the grill. He reached into his pocket and pulled out an Ole's Burgers napkin. He leaned over and wiped the remains off of the car.

"'His' license plate?" Shannon asked, quietly. She looked over at Tim.

"Yes, it is. I have my good days and my bad days, but I know my son's license plate anywhere." The older man pointed at the front of the car. Tim dropped the napkin, quickly turned from the bug splatter and looked carefully at the older man.

"Your son?" Tim asked with a surprised tone.

"Yes, sir! I came out here looking for my son and I knew I'd find him. This is his license plate. There's the word on it, right there. It is spelled C-A-L-I-F-O-R-N-I-A. We don't see too many of those around here." The old man turned and faced Tim. As he tightened and loosened his grip on the walker he squinted hard, looking right at Tim; the older man seemed to be studying his appearance.

Tim swallowed and licked his lips. He looked at Shannon, who looked confused. Tim looked back at the older man and studied him closely.

"'We don't see many of those around here?' What?"
Shannon shook her head as she spoke to Tim. She pointed
at the car parked next to their own; it sported a California plate
as well. Tim looked across the parking lot and saw nothing
but California license plates.

"Nope. It's a long drive from California to Cincinnati,
you know." The old man said to Shannon then returned to
studying Tim. He was obviously staring.

"Um, uh, sir, we're in Southern..." Shannon started.
Just then a gray-haired man walked up quickly and interrupted
her.

"Dad...there you are!" The newcomer said. Tim turned
quickly toward the new voice. He looked at the old man in the
walker and back at the other man; Tim could see the family
resemblance. The ears stuck out a bit, like the ears of the
man with the walker, and the shape of the jaw was similar.

Tim took a breath, reached up and touched his chin.
The shape of the jaw was very familiar...

"Is he alright?" Shannon asked.

"Oh, sure. He gets confused, but he's taken care of.
He's out with us for dinner tonight, next door." The man
gestured. Tim looked over and noticed a more expensive
family-style restaurant nearby.

"Oh, that explains it..." Shannon nodded.

"I hope he didn't bother you. Dad? Shall we go back
to our car now?"

"Our car? This one?" The older man asked as he pointed. His son shook his head.

"He was no bother. Glad he's okay." Shannon said. She looked over at her husband as she stepped back toward the passenger-side door. Tim was touching his ear. Shannon stopped short of the door. The two strangers walked away, slowly.

"Dad, this way..." The old man behind the walker continued to stare at Tim. Tim was unable to look away.

"Tim?" Shannon quietly called; Tim did not respond.

"But I know that's his car..." The old man continued as he moved further away. The two strangers disappeared around a holly hedge. Tim took one, then two, slow steps toward the end of the hedge. Shannon turned quickly and came around the front of the car, to the driver's side.

"Tim?" She called a second time, this time a bit louder. Tim took another step away; he continued to touch his jaw, then his ear. Shannon stepped over next to her husband.

"What's going on, Tim? Are you okay?" Shannon reached out and grabbed his upper arm. There was a light breeze in the air.

"His jaw. His chin. His ears..." Tim said quietly.

"What?" Shannon asked softly.

"He was looking for his son..." Tim replied. Shannon squeezed her husband's arm.

"He found him, Tim. His son took him back to the other restaurant."

"I don't know. His jaw line looked really familiar..." Tim said, quietly. He was coming out of his trance.

"I think I see what's going on..." Shannon said in a very kind voice. The wind began to pick up, blowing her hair back.

"Do you think...?" Tim started, then stopped. He looked at his wife; he noticed her hair billowing.

"No, I don't think so, honey. Let's walk the other way." Shannon led Tim back toward their car.

"Maybe he was looking for another son...?" Tim said as he stopped and looked back at the hedge. The strangers were no longer in sight.

"Let's take a walk to the end of the parking lot and back, just to get some air." Shannon suggested. Tim nodded and followed his wife.

Chapter 19

"Why don't I drive us home, Tim?" Shannon asked as the two approached their car.

"I guess. Why?" Tim responded. He stopped short of the passenger side door and looked at his wife.

"I think you just took an emotional whack, honey." Shannon said, kindly. She grabbed her hair. The wind was getting stiffer.

"An emotional 'whack'?" Tim decided the wind was getting to be a bit too much. He opened the passenger side door and sat down quickly. He rolled the window up as Shannon walked around to the driver's side. She opened that door and sat down.

"I think something hit you that caught you off-guard. You know, emotionally. I think this may explain some of what's been going on today." Shannon reached for a soda, then realized it belonged to Tim – they had changed sides in the car.

"That's mine..." Tim said.

"I know." She handed the cup to him, then reached for her own. She took a deep breath as she pulled out her car keys.

"Okay. You drive. But turn the heater on - it's getting cold." Tim said in a monotone.

Shannon started the engine and adjusted the heater as she noticed a gentle crunching sound coming from the other side of the car. Shannon turned and looked at her husband just as he popped the last of the onion rings into his mouth.

"Tim! Those are mine!" Shannon exclaimed. Tim slowly stopped chewing then picked up the onion ring bag. It was empty. He turned toward his wife.

"You can have the rest of my mega-all-kinds-of-stuff French fry burger…" He said sheepishly.

"I'll pass…" Shannon shook her head as she looked down at the hamburger box between them. The hum of the heater and the car's engine filled more and more of the ensuing human silence.

Tim shifted in his seat as he looked out the window. He sighed. Shannon looked over at him.

"Hey, forget about the onion rings. I'm sorry." She offered.

"If you want, we can get some more." Tim responded, feeling sorry.

"No, I don't need any more calories tonight. Besides, we should get going." Shannon buckled her seat belt. Tim did not secure his belt.

"Seat belt, Tim…" She gently urged him as she grabbed the gear shift lever, preparing to back out of the parking space. She moved it into "reverse."

"Yeah…in a second…" Tim whispered, almost inaudibly. Shannon looked to the right. A changing traffic light reflected off of Tim's cheek. A green wet streak turned to red. Shannon shifted the car back into "park." She opened her mouth, but paused. She tried again.

"It's about your father, honey?" Shannon's voice sounded very kind. Tim nodded, then cleared his throat.

"Um, uh, yeah. Not easy stuff." Tim said.

"I can imagine what just happened - that old man on the walker. There's a rough place in your heart that has never really healed." Shannon said gently.

"Yeah. Here I am in my thirties - deep into my thirties – and I still get caught up 'looking for daddy'." Tim cleared his throat again and sat up a bit.

"I've noticed. An older man sends some attention your way, and you feel like you need to…" Shannon stopped in mid-sentence. She put her hand over her mouth. Her eyebrows went up.

"Need to what?" Tim looked at his wife.

"Listen, I'm treading on a really tender place here. Maybe I shouldn't." Shannon sounded worried.

"Shannon, we're not newlyweds tiptoeing around each other anymore. I know you; you're not the 'step on someone's heart' kind of woman. You must have seen something. What is it?" Paul looked at the side of his wife's face, scanning her features.

"Grandpa Marino." Shannon offered.

"Grandpa Marino? What? You lost me." Tim shook his head.

"Remember how much he meant to you?"

"Of course I do. He still does, but I don't get it. We built a stone wall together. I responded to him paying attention to me. I know that. Hey, he bought me a lot of Mike and Ike boxes!" Tim managed a half smile.

Shannon reached into her purse and pulled out an opened box of the candies. Tim nodded as he recognized the product.

"Yes, and every time we buy some of these candies, what do you say?" Shannon asked.

"'Thank you, Grandpa'!" Tim nodded.

"Now, let's try another one." Shannon sounded more confident.

"Another what?" Tim shook his head.

"Bear with me. Think back. Remember that manager you had about seven years ago? The one who meant a lot to you?"

"Sure - that was Pat. He knew how to run a fair and honest shop. He cared about the people who worked for him. He taught me a lot."

"Remember how you helped him build a sprinkler system at his house one week in that hot summer – just before we bought your old Jeep?" Shannon asked.

"Sure. I'm not following you. I'm not building a sprinkler system..." Tim stopped as he became aware of where the conversation was going. His eyebrows went up. Shannon nodded.

"Uh-huh. Yes. There it is. There's 'the look'. You know where this is going. The sprinkler system is..." Shannon gestured for Tim to finish the thought.

"...the boat engine." Tim whispered.

185

"Exactly."

"You got all that from an old man using a walker and tapping on our license plate?"

"It wasn't the old man - it was the look in your face. That look told me everything about what was going on. I've learned how to read your expressions too well, my friend."

"Oh, wow. This isn't about how we communicate, or about you being afraid of the ocean. We communicate pretty well, then."

"Well, it's still about those things, but the big engine that's powering the emotions in this boat is, well..." Shannon stopped.

"...is my need to have a daddy in my life." Tim nodded.

"I don't want to go out on the ocean. If you don't go, you risk losing this new father figure; his name is Paul."

"So, it is about me choosing you or choosing him." Tim continued.

"Yes, and you don't want to deal with that choice."

"I don't..." Tim repeated.

"We have to find a way through this somehow." Shannon responded.

"Strange - Paul has a similar choice. He feels like he has to choose between Meredith and the boat."

"I saw that, yes. How do you think they'll resolve that?" Shannon asked.

"He told me. He'll sell the boat."

"What? So why should you go out to Catalina? There's no point." Shannon asked.

"Yes, there is. It's about Grandpa Marino."

"What? How does he work into this?" Shannon smiled.

"I'm not sure if you picked up on it or not. When Paul was a kid, he went on a camping trip with Grandpa Marino to a place called Parson's Landing."

"Okay, I remember hearing something about that. So?" Shannon nodded.

"There was some kind of embarrassment there, and Grandpa Marino hid a box of something at the edge of some rocks in a campground there."

"Embarrassment? What do you mean?"

"Paul hasn't said much about it, but he's convinced there are some items from his childhood in a box at the northern tip of Catalina Island, and he feels like he needs to retrieve them." Tim explained.

"You're kidding me."

"No, I'm serious. I think he sees this as a way to make peace with his dad. I guess his dad left those things there and didn't mean to. I guess it's sort of a way to make some old wound right. We've talked about his dad and I think he sees Grandpa Marino differently now."

"Maybe you DO have to go with him." Shannon said with an air of certainty in her voice.

187

"What makes you say that?"

"Maybe you'll learn how to move forward – about your own issue. That's just a guess. My sense is that you learned a lot about life this weekend – not just about a boat." Shannon said.

"What about you? What will you do? I know you won't be on the boat."

"Nope, I am still not going out of the harbor. Maybe Meredith and I can hang out. Maybe I can explore the hidden issues with my mother…" Shannon smiled as she shrugged.

"Oh, no! Issues with your mother! Shannon! The kids! Remember? Look at the time!" Tim exclaimed. Shannon sat up.

"Oh, good Lord! Buckle your seat belt." Shannon nodded toward her husband.

"What about the mega-calorie-chili-chipotle-burger thing?" Tim asked as he pointed down at the box between them. Shannon nodded toward the exit of the parking lot.

"How can a company sell a product that has a name that no one can properly remember? What the heck is it really called?" Shannon shook her head as she steered to the right.

"Got me…" Tim responded as he picked up the wrappers from their impromptu meal.

"There - a drive-up trash can. That's where it belongs anyway." Shannon pointed.

As they drove toward the exit Tim noticed the lady in the drive-through window. Next to her, in a large window, was a sign advertising the very burger he had just eaten a part of.

"Okay, now I know. That's a mouthful! The sign calls it an 'Ole's Chili-Bacon-Potato-Fries-Chipotle-Chicken Maximum Double Cheese Burger, on a Sesame Seed Bun'."

"Otherwise known as an 'everything-we-could-find-in-the-back-thrown-into-a-bun' kitchen sink burger. Yeah, keep that in mind for when you want to come back for another one." Shannon said sarcastically as she steered the car on to the highway.

The two rode quietly for a few minutes as Shannon turned the car on to the freeway on-ramp. A minor bump surprised both of them.

"Oops. Didn't see that pothole. Sorry." Shannon said.

"Ugh..." Tim groaned.

"Are you okay?" Shannon quickly glanced at her husband.

"Uh. I think my stomach is telling me that kitchen sink burger might be coming back to haunt me later..." Tim burped.

"Oh?" Shannon slowed the car down and shot a glance at Tim.

"Oh, no, don't worry. Not urgent. Just worried about an hour or two from now, after we're home..." Tim looked out the window.

"Well, traffic's light…or we could stop again." Shannon added. She pointed at the next off-ramp.

"Just get us home and I'll be fine." Tim said quietly.

Chapter 20

"Tim! Can you get the phone! I've got my hands deep into the washer! Somebody's underwear got tangled around the agitator again!" Shannon called out as the phone rang a second time.

"What?" Tim called out.

"Why she doesn't use a delicates bag is beyond me…" Shannon whispered.

"Shannon? What?

"Get the phone! I'm busy!" Shannon yelled.

"But I'm holding a hot plate here! Remember, I'm doing dinner?" Tim responded as he pulled something from the microwave with his hands covered with unmatched kitchen mitts.

"Tim! I'm soaked!" Shannon replied.

"Joey! Annie!" Tim called out. There was no response.

"Tim! Get it! They're down the street!" Shannon called out.

"Damn…" Tim gently cursed under his breath. The phone rang yet again. He looked around the counter.

"I heard that..." Shannon said from the other room.

"Yeah, I know. Okay, okay...hold on..." Tim hastily put the plate on the counter and tugged at the oven mitts as he stepped toward the telephone. He picked it up in the middle of a ring as he threw down the mitts.

"I really can't get it..." Shannon added.

"Hello?" Tim asked with a rush in his voice.

"Hi, Tim! This is Paul..." A male voice said. Tim immediately recognized the voice and closed his eyes.

"Hey, Paul! Sorry, you caught me busy in the kitchen. My turn to make dinner!"

"So, what are we having?" The voice teased.

"'Tim's cheese quesadillas'! I have my own salsa that I mix into the cheese. Bits of tomatoes, onion, cilantro, stuff like that. Oh, and my secret ingredient - black beans." Tim smiled.

"Hey, wait, that actually sounds pretty good! You can cook!" Paul responded.

"Of course it's good. What did you think?" Tim feigned being upset.

"Oh, I'm just amazed! You're a multi-talented guy! You can work with engines, supervise crews and make killer quesadillas!"

"Well, thanks. They'll have less digestive impact than the final meal I ate in your area, last Sunday." Tim sighed.

"What? Something Merrie made that was bad?" Paul asked. Tim recoiled emotionally.

"Oh, no, no! That's not what I meant. Her cooking is fine! Great, actually..."

"So, you meant...um, what?" Paul asked.

"We stopped at an Ole's Burgers near your place as we were leaving."

"Oh, Tim, you could have waited for dinner with us. We had planned on you being there."

"No, really, we just stopped to, uh, get a drink, and I ended up with a mega-something burger." Tim backpedaled.

"You're kidding? You got that sloppy thing? What is it? A chipotle potato chili burger? We saw some neighborhood kids eating them once..."

"I didn't order it. Really, it was a mistake."

"Hah! Sure! I know how you like to chow down..." Paul teased.

"No one believes me." Tim shook his head.

"Hah! I'll have to try one. Once." Paul offered.

"Oh, no. Take my word for it - don't do it, Paul. I won't even try to remember what it's really called. We used to call it the 'kitchen sink burger'. Now we named it after another device, one in the bathroom." Tim smiled.

"Bad experience, huh?"

"Let's just say it was NOT worth missing a day of work for..."

"Ouch! That's a bad experience..." Paul whistled.

"Oh, yeah." Tim sighed.

"Glad you're okay now..." Paul trailed off.

"So, you've softened me up. What are you selling tonight?" Tim said with a smile as he changed the subject.

"Oh, no, no, not selling! Just wondering if this coming weekend will work for you? Remember, our little excursion out on to the great Pacific?" Paul asked.

"This weekend?" Tim sighed. Shannon walked out of the laundry room, dangling a shredded-looking pink undergarment.

"If you're free..." Paul responded.

"Hold on a minute..." Tim covered the mouthpiece of the phone and turned toward Shannon.

"That was messing the washing machine up? What is it?" He whispered to Shannon.

"Well, when it was alive it was called a 'bra'."

"What happened to it?"

"This is what happens when one does not use a delicates bag..." Shannon sighed.

"Why didn't you use one?" Tim asked. Shannon turned and stared at him.

"Tim! Not ME! There is another female in the house." Shannon shook her head and walked by. Tim felt the rush of blood come into his face. He turned back to his phone.

"Sorry, Paul. Minor emergency in the laundry room. Resolved now."

"Oh, I know about those!"

"Can I call you back? Shannon's on her way back to the laundry room and I can ask her about this weekend."

"Sure, I understand. The three weekends after that are not good for us, so I wanted to see if this weekend works. I got all the parts and service done." Paul said.

"Hey, that's great! Yeah, let me call you back. Here she comes..."

"Don't forget about the quesadillas! Talk to you soon!" Paul responded. Tim shook his head as he looked at the food on the plate. He knew he'd have to re-heat it, and he hated re-heated quesadillas.

"Right – in an hour or so..." Tim hung up the phone.

"Well, are we ready to eat? I called the kids, but I'm not sure where they are..." Shannon shook her head as she sat down.

"I guess so. The quesadillas are warm..." Tim said as he picked up the plate of food and walked to the table. Shannon was dishing out salad from a bowl.

"They'll be fine, Tim. And let the kids re-heat their food when they come in." She said as she reached for a bottle of salad dressing. Tim sat at his usual place at the table.

"So, Paul called." Tim started as he reached for the bowl of corn next to his salad plate.

"Oh, yeah, the phone. What's going on?" Shannon asked as she reached for and then bit into a triangular shaped quesadilla.

"He wants to do the maiden voyage boat thing this weekend. I guess the next couple of weekends are bad for him." Paul pulled his own slice of the large quesadilla on to his plate.

"This weekend? There's no way I can get someone to hang out with the kids, and you remember what happened the last time we left them alone overnight..." Shannon shook her head.

"Yeah, who'd have thought so many teens could get so many messed up haircuts and hair colorings in a matter of 18 hours." Tim sighed.

"...and the dog." Shannon added, reaching for a drink.

"Why? Why a lime green dog? I'll never figure that party out as long as I may live." Tim bit into another quesadilla wedge.

"Hey, leave some for me..." Shannon smiled.

"Oops. Sorry." Tim nodded.

"So, I'd have to stay here with the kids if you went this weekend."

"Yeah, but I figure I could drive down on Friday after work, we'd get up on Saturday, do the boat thing, and I could probably get back on Saturday night. So it wouldn't be the whole weekend." Tim sat back.

"How long should it take, I mean how long would you be on the boat?" Shannon asked. Tim paused, deciding on whether or not to bring up the idea of her going along on the boat ride. The kids could go to Huntington, too, he thought. He knew it would be an uphill battle and decided to leave it alone.

"Paul said if we can get out of the harbor by six in the morning we can easily be back by dinner." Tim reached for the salad bowl.

"So there is still a problem with someone watching the kids."

"What about your mom?" Tim sprinkled pepper all over his salad. He took a bite.

"She's going with her girlfriends to Las Vegas, remember?" Shannon responded. Tim stopped chewing.

"Oh...I thought we could count on her anytime."

"She does have her own life, Tim." Shannon shook her head as she reached for another piece of the quesadilla. Tim nodded.

A sound came from the front door. A number of people walked in, talking loudly.

"Hey! Joey, Annie! Whoa – we're eating dinner here!" Tim said as he turned around. He noticed a number of other teens behind his son and daughter.

"Oh, hey, sorry. We're all going to go down to Ole's Burgers – Shawna said they have some cool new mega burger there!" Joey said.

"Joey, your dad made dinner here..." Shannon said in a matter-of-fact voice as she pointed at the table.

"Has Shawna actually eaten one of those burgers?" Tim asked.

"She did!" Anne answered. A girl with bright orange hair nodded enthusiastically.

"It was great! Has French fries right in it! And chili!" The teens all started talking at once.

"Yeah, I know..." Tim said, under his breath.

"What?" Joey asked.

"Hey, enjoy the burger..." Tim said while waving his hand and shaking his head. The teens rushed out the front door, except for Joey.

"Yeah, uh, so, do you think you could loan me like a twenty or something?" Joey asked his father. Tim looked over at his son.

"Is the weed whacking done?" Tim asked.

"Yeah...just about." Joey looked uncomfortable.

"Just about?"

"Like ninety percent." Joey sounded more confident.

"Well, let's see. Ninety percent of twenty is..." Tim started.

"Eighteen dollars!" Joey finished. Tim reached for his wallet and pulled out a ten and a five.

"All I have is fifteen..."

"We can make that work!" Joey grabbed the money and ran out. Tim turned and looked at Shannon. She had her brows down low over her eyes. Too low, he thought.

"Why, Tim? Why do you cave like that?" Shannon shook her head.

"I don't deal well with confrontation. You know that..." Tim looked down.

"I know. We'll work on this next time." Shannon sighed as she shook her head.

"Can I get the lemonade?" Tim asked as he pointed across the table. Shannon handed the pitcher to him.

"Back to this weekend. What do you think?" Shannon asked.

"Like I said, I'll go down Friday evening and come back Saturday night. So, is that okay?" Tim poured a cup of lemonade.

"I guess." Shannon answered as Tim stood up and walked to the phone on the counter. He stopped and looked at her, studying her expression. "I guess" was not on the list of statements Shannon used often.

"Shannon, let's be sure..."

"Look, I don't like the idea of you going out there."

"Shannon, it's not like to Tonga or someplace on the other side of the planet or something. It's to Catalina. 26 miles and back."

"Tonga? Where did you get that?" Shannon looked surprised.

"Get what?"

"Tonga. You've actually heard about the country named 'Tonga'?"

"Hey, I know stuff! They have a flag with a red cross on it!"

"No way. You are making this up."

"I am not. I know stuff." Tim protested.

"Okay, smart man, what's the capital of Tonga?" Shannon asked as Tim stopped walking.

"Uh…"

"See, I got you! You're making this up!"

"It's something like 'Noo Koo'. 'Noo Koo All Over'." Tim looked confused.

"Oh, come on."

"Wanna bet?" Tim turned toward his wife.

"Why not? Where's my cell phone? I'll look it up." Shannon looked around. Tim grabbed Shannon's phone and held it behind his back.

"Wait, wait. What'll we bet?" Tim asked.

"Whoever is wrong does the next two loads of laundry that I have to do today." Shannon offered.

"Wait. If I win I get nothing. You were going to do the laundry anyway. What kind of bet is that?"

"What do you want? Besides THAT!" Shannon smiled, seeming to read her husband's mind. He blushed.

"How about the dinner dishes? I did dinner tonight, so if I win, you take care of the dishes. I usually do them the nights that I cook." Tim pointed at the sink.

"Deal. Give me the phone."

"I get to watch..." Tim handed the phone over. Shannon swiped the front and then went to her favorite internet search engine.

"Tonga. Oh, you are kidding me. A red cross on a flag!" Shannon exclaimed.

"Yep."

"But you had no idea about the capital. Let me look that up..."

"Go ahead.

"This is ridiculous! You said 'Noo Koo All Over'."

"Yeah..."

"I just do not believe this. 'Nuku'alofa'. Noo Koo Al Ofa!" Shannon trailed off, almost to a whisper. Tim grinned.

"I told you. I know stuff." Tim put his thumbs into his pockets and stood up straight. Shannon's eyes got smaller as she squinted at her husband.

"So, what grade were you in when you did a report on this place?" Shannon said sarcastically.

"Sixth. Mr. Edwards' class. It was fun. You know, I had to color that flag. I used a whole red crayon." Tim leaned over and pointed at the cell phone.

"Unbelievable..." Shannon whispered.

"I believe these are your dishes...?" Tim smiled again as he pointed at the sink.

- - -

"Hey, Paul!" Tim said as he held the phone close to his ear.

"Done with dinner?" Paul asked.

"Oh, yeah, and the dishes are taken care of, too." Tim smiled as Shannon turned from the sink full of plates and scowled.

"Really? That was quick. So, what about this weekend?"

"One question. Are you sure we can get there and back by dark on Saturday?"

"Oh, absolutely. Done it before on my buddy's boat. It's actually not that hard to do, if we can get out early." Paul reassured.

"Well, Shannon will stay here...can't get anyone to watch the teens. You know how dangerous that is. If that's okay, then let's do this." Tim answered.

"Oh, sorry to hear about Shannon, but I do understand about the kid issue. Will you have any problems with what stuff to bring?" Paul asked.

"Oh, no, I'll just throw everything into a duffel bag and I'll be good." Tim sounded sure of himself. He grimaced as he realized he had forgotten to look at the email message that Paul had sent the previous week.

"I didn't think it would be a problem. There is one thing you forgot, however." Paul mentioned in a serious tone.

"I did? What?" Tim was confused.

"You didn't scan and email the rest of my dad's journal..." Paul sounded disappointed. Tim realized he was right.

"Oh, yeah. I am so sorry. Maybe I can, uh..." Tim fumbled. He was at a loss for words. He looked at his wife. Shannon turned and looked at him with a quizzical look. Tim covered the mouthpiece.

"Forgot to scan his dad's journal. Where is it?" He whispered. Shannon put a soapy hand over her mouth and raised her eyebrows.

"I'll tell you what – don't stress it. We're busy this week anyway. Can you just bring the rest along when you come down on Friday night?" Paul asked.

"Oh, yes. Definitely. I'll put it into my bag tonight and I will NOT forget it. Promise." Tim said, solemnly.

"Great! I'll see you this weekend!"

Chapter 21

"Hey, Tim! In your office! Your cellphone's ringing!" A woman holding a stack of files called out from the nearby doorway.

"Okay...coming..." Tim answered as he picked up his pace on the way back to his office. He went through the doorway and reached for the cellphone. He noticed it was his wife.

"So, what's up, Shannon?" Tim smiled as he greeted her.

"Did I catch you at a bad time? I can call back later." Shannon asked.

"Oh, no, not a bad time..." Tim paused and looked out through the window in his office. A large man was pushing a transmission assembly on a wheeled cart across the shop work floor.

Tim waved at the man, who noticed, turned and stopped. The man pointed at himself – and Tim nodded. Tim pointed at his own lower back and then at the worker, signaling to be careful with straining himself.

"That's good. So, you're on target for getting off of work a bit early, then?" Shannon continued.

"I think so. Things are looking pretty normal for a Friday afternoon here. There's only one project hanging, and I'm not too worried about it."

"Will you be able to have dinner with us before heading south to Huntington Harbor? I'm getting started in the kitchen now. You sound congested. Are your allergies acting up?"

"Allergies? Yeah, about the same. And that's my plan – home for dinner. I know you're fixing pasta primavera, so it's a priority!" Tim smiled again.

"You may have the chance for seconds. Annie may want to stay at Jenny's house tonight. A sleepover thing."

"Jenny's house? Really? That's not like her. What's that all about?" Tim asked.

"I guess 'everyone' is going to be there. It's Jenny's birthday. She has moved into 'that' age group – where social image is everything."

"Man, I remember that. I also remembering that I couldn't keep up with other kids, so I thought, why bother trying?" Tim sighed as he shook his head.

"We were both in that place. I remember my friend Lisa having all kinds of clothes, and a new car. Heck, I had to find someone to fix my old bicycle or I was stranded."

"Um, that was me..." Tim said with a smile.

"Oh, yeah...I remember that time you came over to adjust my chain..." Shannon giggled. Tim anxiously shifted his weight back and forth.

"Um, uh, we don't have to bring up all of the old memories...especially at work..." Tim smiled as he fumbled. Shannon laughed gently.

"Oh right. Sorry!" She replied.

"Well, I'm just wrapping up a few things before I get on the road home. Hold on a minute..." Tim said as a man wearing greasy overalls entered his office. He was holding a large power tool.

"Sure..." Shannon answered.

"Hey, Tim, we've got a real problem with this transmission here. You know, on the rebuild of the '75 Jeep CJ5?" The man pointed over his shoulder.

"What's going on?" Tim asked.

"The bell housing does not fit that engine at all. No way, no how."

"Shannon? I'll have to call you back."

"I understand. I know I will just glaze over listening to that conversation!" Shannon said.

"Thanks..." Tim replied

"I'll let you go. Are you sure you don't have a runny nose? Sounds like it to me..." Shannon said.

"I'll take something for allergies, I guess. I'll talk to you soon. Got to go." Tim ended the call and put the phone in his pocket. He turned toward his mechanic.

"How is that possible? It's a 232 I-6 engine. The transmission Billy ordered was the right one. I checked it myself this morning." Tim walked toward his office door.

"I don't think it's a 232, boss." The man in the coveralls replied.

"What? I dropped that engine in myself a couple of months ago, in that last phase of the rebuild." Tim stopped and looked at his employee.

"I'm telling you, it is not a 232." Tim walked out and across the shop floor to the Jeep at the far end of the facility. He looked into the engine compartment.

"What the…?" Tim took a deep breath and stared. Another man, wearing glasses and an old Los Angeles Dodgers hat, walked up.

"I know what you're thinking, Tim, and you're right." The man said as he wiped his hands on an old rag.

"If you mean that I broke my own policy to actually see a car before ordering a major new part for it, you are damned right." Tim swore. He raised his hands and shook his head.

"Well, uh, I didn't mean you had, uh, you know…done something wrong…" The man with the Dodgers hat stumbled on his words and squirmed.

"Don't worry about it, Hank. It's not you. I do NOT understand what is going on here. That is not the 232 engine I installed in June. It was June, right?" Tim asked. The two mechanics nodded in agreement.

"I know it was before I left for my Fourth of July vacation, so yeah, that's right." Hank responded.

"Let me see the file…" Tim leaned over and extended his arm. Hank reached on to the counter and grabbed a file.

"Yep, you put a 232 in there." Hank said as he handed the opened file to his boss.

"What the hell? I put in one heck of great engine in there. What happened? Where did this oddball power plant and tranny combo come from?" Tim said as he looked over the paperwork, then over the engine area.

"I have no idea, but this new transmission will not work."

"Just put it aside for now. I have to make a call. See what you can do with the Mustang we have to start on Monday..." Tim trailed off as he walked toward his office.

- - -

"Hello, Mr. Schroeder? This is Tim down at Bouquet Canyon Custom Auto..." Tim started.

"Tim! Great to hear from you! I suppose this is about my baby! How's Jerry doing?" The voice on the other end of the phone asked in a sing-song voice.

"Jerry? Huh?" Tim was confused.

"Oh, you know Jerry. Jeremiah Jeep! He's sitting in your shop today!" The voice continued. Tim rolled his eyes, his memory having been restored. This was one of "those" customers who named their cars.

"Well, we started work on her today, but we ran into a snag."

"A snag? What do you mean?"

"Well, to be honest, I'm confused. Do you remember when I swapped out the engine in June?" Tim asked.

"Sure do. I think you called the engine a '232' or something." The man responded.

"Right, yes! That's it. What's confusing me is that the engine and transmission in the Jeep today are not the ones we put in the car in June."

"Oh, that's right. I was at a Jeep collector's rally and someone saw it there. He offered me a lot of money for that '232'. Couldn't resist. I knew it would finish paying for the rest of my restoration work in the engine compartment!" The man sounded proud. Tim was unable to speak.

"Huh?" Tim mumbled.

"Tim? Are you there?"

"Uh, yeah, Mr. Schroeder. I'm sorry – I'm a bit in shock. That engine was a prime piece of metal. I found it knowing it would take care of you. Remember when we talked?" Tim asked.

"Yes, I understand, but he offered me double what we paid for it." The man sounded a bit sheepish.

"And I was able to get it at a discount from a contact. It was one of a kind."

"Oh. Well, now, how about you guys go ahead and put in the new transmission and let's see how that works. I'm sure it will be fine."

"Well, no, it's not like that. We have a real problem here. Someone put in a completely different engine - and a completely different transmission. We need a 232 engine to use the tranny we have sitting here in the crate."

"Oh...what? Transmission? No, no, it was only the engine that we switched. You must be mistaken." The man on the phone responded.

"Did you watch them make the engine swap?" Tim asked.

"Of course not – I am so clueless about engines and stuff like that. That's why I always go to you." The other man said. Tim felt like cursing, but held his tongue.

"Well, let's get to where we are right now. They did swap the tranny, and no one told you." Tim said, carefully measuring his words.

"I am in shock." The voice said, quietly.

"I understand, but we're left with some confusion. That's why I am calling." Tim said.

"And how do we work through this?" The voice asked.

"Well, to install this new transmission, the one I ordered for you, you need to buy a new 232 engine. Or we can leave this engine and transmission as it is and I can return the new tranny. I just need to get your decision as to which way to go. Should I order an engine or just leave the Jeep – I mean Jeremiah - as it is now?"

"What do you advise me to do?"

"To be honest, the current engine leaks. It's got problems and I think it was poorly installed. I know this sounds terrible, but I think we need to pull the engine and the tranny and put in new ones."

"That does not sound cheap."

"Uh, no." Tim took a deep breath while shaking his head.

"How soon can you get a new engine? How much?"

"I can check on that and get back to you, but it will not be as inexpensive as the first one. That was a really good find. To be honest, Mr. Schroeder, I feel like someone took advantage of you. You're a good customer, so I feel protective."

"No one took me. Let's just see if we can get the new engine, and go from there." The other man said.

"I understand, but I just hate the idea that you got ripped off and you'll pay again." Tim was trying to sound as conciliatory and possible.

"I'll just pay. If you can get me a rough estimate today, I can approve it." The man's voice sounded icy. Tim paused.

"I can do that. I'll call you back as soon as possible." Tim shook his head.

"Tim, I'm sorry. I'll be honest with you..." The man sounded a bit troubled.

"Honest? You've been a customer for years now. I want you to be honest!"

"It was my brother. You remember how I got this Jeep a couple of years ago?"

"Yes..."

"I thought it would be a good way for us to get closer. He's into Jeeps and off-roading."

"Okay, so far I understand."

"When he saw the new engine I think he got, well, kind of jealous." The man's voice was quieter.

"What?" Tim asked, uncomfortably.

"I thought, well, I don't know." The man continued.

"I'm sorry, I'm not following you." Tim said, using a kind voice. He could tell his client was uncomfortable.

"Look, I've never had a good relationship with him. I thought by my doing that, you know, letting him have the engine...I guess I was wrong. He had his Jeep guy do the job."

"I see..." Tim nodded.

"Tim, I guess I am old enough to know that you can't buy love – with money or Jeep parts. Well, I should have known that. I'm sorry." The old man trailed off. Tim took a deep breath.

"I see. I can understand how you felt. I've been down that kind of road myself a time or two. I'm not really good with relationships. I like to think I am, but, well, you know what I mean..." Tim fumbled a bit.

"Sadly, yes. I'm sorry to say that nothing has changed. Now I find out he took my transmission, too. That's uncomfortable. It helps me see that there is not much between us to work with. I think I value the relationship more than he does." The man on the phone responded.

"You've been a good friend. I didn't mean to make you feel like you messed up. We can fix this." Tim said quietly.

"I know you can, and yes, I know it will cost me more. Tim, I grew up in a really broken family…" The voice on the phone paused.

"Welcome to my world…" Tim interjected.

"I am sorry to hear that."

"What can you do? It was a long time ago." Tim responded.

"You do what you can, with whatever you have to work with. My little brother and I grew up inside the same four walls but we had no emotional connection. I guess we still don't."

"It sounds like it." Tim answered.

"He went one way, and I went the other. Now, we can't connect on a lot of things, like politics, or kids, or religion. I don't blame him, and I hope he doesn't think I'm the cause of the problem. Our parents left us with a pile of relationship sewage. So you do stupid things, like give him a good engine, hoping that will make things a bit better."

"That's a lesson I've had to learn the hard way, too, so don't be too hard on yourself." Tim said in a kind voice.

"Thanks. I'm trying to not be so hard. It's not easy."

"I wish I didn't understand, Mr. Schroeder. I had a situation, well, I was used. It wasn't about an engine. I had a friend once who I tried to buy with money and things. He used me." Tim's feelings were bubbling up.

"Sadly, it seems to be a common experience. I paid with an engine."

"Someone died because of my stupidity..." Tim whispered.

"Died?" The older man said softly, and sounded confused. Tim took a deep breath.

"I know this sounds out there, but the guy ended up killing a man who I saw as my grandfather. So, you lost an engine. Isaiah, that was his name, took away the only real grandfather I ever knew." Tim cleared his throat.

"Oh, my..."

"Yeah. I'll never forget that. We do some strange things when we want to be loved." Tim was struggling to speak. He coughed.

"You're pretty wise for a man a lot younger than I am, my friend."

"Thanks, but if wisdom like this comes from all of this pain, sometimes I'd rather be a fool." Tim said, half joking.

"Don't we all? Can I ask a question, Tim, and, yes, I know you have to go and order an engine?"

"Sure, why not..."

"I don't want to tread on your feelings…"

"No, go ahead."

"Do you blame yourself for your grandfather's death?" The older man asked. Tim turned away from his shop window.

"Um…" Tim started, then took a breath.

"I'm sorry. I can tell this is hard…" The older man whispered.

"Uh, um, yeah. Let me see about getting an engine…" Tim cleared his throat.

"Good idea. And, Tim?"

"Yeah?"

"You're not responsible…"

"Thanks. I'll call you back today. Thanks for listening."

"Thank you for listening, too, my friend." The older man said.

"I'll be back in touch soon…" Tim said emphatically.

- - -

Tim hesitated as he looked over his cell phone. He hated calling his wife about coming home late. He pushed two buttons and raised the phone to his ear.

"Hello, Tim?" Shannon's voice was clear.

"Hi, honey! I just wanted to let you know that something came up here. I'm going to be a little later than I thought. It's a long story, but it involves a new engine I installed in July, a guy replacing that without us knowing, and Isaiah." Tim sighed.

"What? Isaiah? From Pine Mountain? What are you talking about? He's there?" Shannon sounded shocked.

"Oh, no. Someone talked about his brother and I mentioned Isaiah…"

"You met Isaiah's brother?" Shannon asked.

"Uh, no. It's not like that. The guy gave his brother an engine…" Tim started.

"It was Isaiah's engine?" Shannon asked, sounding more confused.

"No, no. Listen, it's hard to explain – I didn't meet anyone who knew Isaiah. Let's just drop it. I may be late for dinner. If you have to, go ahead and eat and I can re-heat the primavera when I get home."

"But you have to get to Paul and Meredith's place tonight…" Shannon said.

"I know. I'll be late, but I'll get there."

"And you have an early morning…"

"I know, I know. Not much I can do. I'll call you just before I leave." Tim said.

"I guess I understand. Well, some of this."

"I'm sorry. I'll get out of here as soon as I can…and I'll clear up the connection with Isaiah. It's complicated, but don't worry, he's nowhere around." Tim tried to sound reassuring.

"Okay. I should let you go. Love you!" Shannon said as Tim ended the call. He sat down and stared out of the window into the parking lot.

"What is it about people cheating others out of perfectly good engines?" Tim whispered to himself as he reached into his right rear pocket. A piece of paper followed the pulling of a handkerchief and fell on the floor. He tried, unsuccessfully, to catch it. As he leaned over to pick it up he noticed a small hand-drawn red heart.

My dearest Tim,

I know this will be a hard weekend, but I know we can get through it.

I love you,
Shannon

"Allergies! Hah! Now I have a runny nose, Shannon…" Tim whispered as he smiled.

Chapter 22

"Hey, Shannon, I'm home." Tim announced as he slid his car keys into his pocket. He closed the front door; silence filled the house. He turned and looked at the old clock on the mantle - it was ticking, as it always does.

"Shannon? Anybody here?" Tim called out again as he gently lowered his briefcase on to a chair near the front door. He walked slowly across the living room, listening for any signs of life in the house. It was unusually quiet. A voice from the kitchen compelled him to start walking in that direction.

As he entered the room Shannon waved and then signaled with her finger for him to be quiet. He noticed that she wore a very intense look, so he decided to stay out of whatever was going on. Tim shrugged and walked over to the stove; to the left was a half-consumed casserole dish.

"Ahh, Shannon's 'Pasta Primavera!'" Tim whispered with a smile. He walked over to the sink and ran water to wash his hands.

"Honey, it's only a pair of socks. Yes, I understand that. Yes, Marybeth is very popular. Don't you have another..." Shannon started. She stopped with her mouth open and started nodding. She put her hand over the mouthpiece and turned toward Tim.

"Tim! Dish some out...go ahead. Get some for me, too." Shannon whispered, then returned to her phone call. Tim reached for two bowls and a serving spoon; he ladled a portion into a bowl then stopped before serving more. He felt confused.

"Only a pair of socks? What?" Tim asked as he turned and looked at Shannon. She started shaking her head and rolling her eyes. She gave him the signal to be quiet – again – as she started to speak.

"Yes, I'll do that. No, I'll need about a half an hour. Where are the other ones?" Shannon asked. Tim moved two bowls of pasta primavera top the kitchen table. He noticed slices of French bread in a basket, and some steamed broccoli with lemons as he stepped over to the refrigerator. He grabbed a soda before sitting down in front of his dinner.

"I'm sure this 'sock saga' will be good…" Tim whispered to himself. He signaled to Shannon that dinner was "on the table", and she nodded.

"Listen, sweetheart, wouldn't it be better if I got off of the phone and got moving? The sooner I get going the sooner I'll be there and this nightmare will be over." Shannon said.

"A sock nightmare? What the heck is that?" Tim mumbled under his breath. Shannon frowned at him as she nodded at the phone. Shannon signaled to her husband to start eating. Tim shrugged and picked up a fork.

"Lord, for what I am about to eat, please make me truly grateful. And please put an end to the 'sock nightmare'…" Tim whispered in a mock reverent fashion. Shannon scowled as she put her hand over the phone's mouthpiece.

"Timothy Johnston!" She said in a strained whisper. Tim knew, deep down inside, that she'd rather have said it much louder, if it weren't for whichever family member was on the other end of the phone conversation. Tim put his hands up, in a surrendering fashion, and nodded.

Sorry..."

"Okay, honey, I'll be there in about a half an hour. Yes, I know where to look. No, I won't look in that drawer." Shannon nodded and hung the phone up.

"Man! That sounded serious. Was that Annie? What is going on?" Tim asked as he raised his fork to his mouth.

"First of all, sir, please try to use a little less humor in your prayer before dinner."

"Oh, come on, Shannon. God's got a sense of humor. He created us with one. Well, most of us." Tim smiled a big, fake smile. Shannon rolled her eyes.

"Yes, that was Annie. She's at that slumber party – they call it a 'sock party'."

"And she forgot her socks?" Tim reached for a piece of bread as Shannon sat before her bowl of pasta. She picked up her fork, paused and closed her eyes. Tim put the bread down and lowered his gaze. He knew when he had pushed his wife a bit too far. He was guilty this time.

"Lord, thank you for providing for our needs, for being there through all of our trials and tribulations, and for being with our loved ones when we can't be there." Shannon took a breath and paused. Tim looked up and noticed that Shannon had a tear coming down her cheek.

"Shannon..." He whispered. His wife did not respond.

"God, give my husband peace. Please bring peace to my children. Please, give me peace as well. Amen." Shannon's voice trailed off, ending in a whisper.

"Shannon...it's going to be okay. I presume this sock thing will blow over. You know how kids are..." Tim said with a soothing tone. Shannon jumped in.

"It's not about the socks. That's a teenage girl thing, Tim. They're supposed to wear strange, bright socks. They walk around in them." Shannon's voice was trembling.

"I see." Tim said, softly.

"Maybe you do. Maybe you don't. We went down to the store today and she bought some crazy socks." Shannon was agitated. She took a breath. Tim put the slice of bread down.

"Maybe...maybe I don't get it." Tim said in the same soft tone.

"...and minutes after arriving at the party she was mortified to discover that a girl named Anna was wearing the same socks! Almost the same name, with the same socks! That is what is wrong!" Shannon was almost shouting. Tim reached out and touched his wife's arm.

Shannon threw her fork down. It tumbled across the table and on to the floor. She put her hands across her face and sobbed. Tim pulled his arm back. He stood up and walked over to a chair next to his wife, then sat down.

"There's more going on here than socks, Shannon." Tim said quietly.

"It's not about the stupid socks. That's the little issue I can actually do something about. It's our son who doesn't like pasta primavera and would rather have a garbage-rubbish-trash-bacon-chipotle-vomit cheeseburger than my food!" Shannon lowered her hands. Tim was quick, but not fast enough to hide the smile that had crept on to his face.

"Sorry…" Tim struggled to not laugh.

"What in the hell is that about?" Shannon was upset again.

"Your description of the cheeseburger. I'm sorry, and I really mean that, but your choice of words was, well, um, kind of funny. You're hurting, and I can understand why. I really am sorry." Tim was able to wipe the smile off of his face. Shannon stopped and looked down. For a moment it was quiet.

"Ha…bacon-chipotle-vomit." She managed a slight smile.

"Now there's a taste sensation!" Tim contributed with a chuckle.

"I guess I over-reacted. I'm sorry." Shannon frowned. Tim touched his wife's arm again.

"I don't think you over-reacted. I'm sure this isn't about socks or cheeseburgers. Annie has always stressed out over parties, and Joey, or J.J., or Jehoshaphat, or whatever name he decided he has this week, has always been like this. He's a fast food addict." Tim said gently.

"Yeah, I suppose problems with socks and cheeseburgers are just a part of life."

"A part of life when you have teenagers. It doesn't stay this way forever." Tim offered.

"I know, but I wonder. I just cannot see these kids making it to adulthood. I cannot understand them sometimes." Shannon started. Tim decided to just listen.

"I won't argue with you on that issue…" Tim nodded.

"That stupid cheeseburger thing isn't food!" Shannon seemed to be pleading with her husband.

"Believe you me, no one knows that better than I do!" Tim shook his head. Shannon smiled lightly then continued. There was something in her look, or in her tone, that got Tim's attention. He wondered if she was going somewhere else with this.

"And who cares if your socks look like another girl's whose name just happens to be like yours? Our daughter worries about crappy little stuff like that?"

"Yes, she does." Tim agreed.

"These two kids will never survive in the real world! One will have a nervous breakdown over socks and the other will die from malnutrition!" Shannon said, her voice trembling. Tim took a deep breath and looked at the ceiling.

"Shannon, it's hard to believe, but I think they'll be okay. Really. Think about it. We survived - somehow." Tim said.

"I don't know how." Shannon shook her head.

"Do you remember the time you came over to my house and I was fixing lunch?"

"Which time?" Shannon asked.

"Let me describe the menu. Frozen packaged burritos warmed slightly, not but not hot..." Tim started.

"Oh, good Lord, I remember. You used to say you liked them 'crunchy cool'."

"And what did I put on them?" Tim asked.

"Peanut butter and jelly! You smeared that all over the burrito! Why? Because you couldn't decide if you wanted a peanut butter and jelly sandwich or a burrito!" Shannon shook her head and smiled.

"I can't believe I used to eat that." Tim smiled back.

"That's nothing compared to the chipotle-kitchen-sink-whatever-it-is-called burger." Shannon shook her head.

"And someday, somewhere, his wife will remind him he used to do that." Tim rubbed his wife's shoulder.

"Haha! Now that's an image I look forward to seeing!" Shannon smiled.

"They can change. We did. Someone else you know did." Tim said softly.

"Someone else?"

"Do you remember back then, when we were teens on Pine Mountain, and your mother, well, do you know what I'm talking about?" Tim looked into his wife's eyes.

"When we found out I was pregnant?" Shannon asked, but her tone of voice indicated she knew what Tim was describing.

"Yeah...and how she screamed at Grandpa Marino..." Tim sighed and stopped.

"Oh, yeah, was she pissed at us." Shannon nodded.

"And what do we have to deal with now?" Tim asked.

"'When can I come and see my babies!'" Shannon mimicked her mother's voice and gestures. She broke out in a big smile. Tim leaned over and picked up the fork on the floor, setting it on the counter next to the table.

"Somehow, we have to find the faith that this will work out. Sadly, neither of us has had a lot of experience in this faith idea." Tim said as he returned to his place at the table and picked up his fork.

"Or hope. I hope our kids will turn out okay..."

"Oh, yeah. Hope. I was always waiting for the other shoe to drop when I grew up. If something good happened, I was always looking over my shoulder, waiting for the bad thing that always snuck right up after the good thing and caught you when you were feeling better." Tim sighed.

"We both know about that." Shannon nodded.

"Joey and Annie are good kids. They've never been in any trouble. Yeah, they give us lip and storm out from time to time, but I think they're doing better than we did at those ages…"

"You got that straight." Shannon agreed.

"But these things aren't what's eating at you deep inside." Tim suggested.

"What do you mean?"

"My allergies told me what's going on. They hit me after we hung up the phone this afternoon." Tim smiled as he picked up a piece of bread again.

"Oh?" Shannon said sheepishly.

"Yes. I got your note." Tim softly said as he pulled a piece of paper from his shirt pocket and gently placed it on the table.

"I just, well, tried what Grandma Marino did…" Shannon looked away. She appeared to be embarrassed.

"We have to believe it won't be a hard weekend, honey." Tim touched his wife's arm.

"I want to believe that."

"But we're scared."

"You, too?"

"Me, too." Tim said as Shannon's phone rang. They looked at each other for a long time; Shannon picked up the phone.

"Oh, no. It's Annie. I lost track of time..." Shannon answered the call.

"We both did!" Tim looked up at the clock. It was after seven. He had hoped to be in Huntington Beach by this time.

"Hi, honey! I'm leaving right now...yes, the bright green socks...not the ones in the third drawer, no..." Shannon rose from the table while listening to her daughter. She walked toward the bedrooms. Tim took a large bite of pasta primavera, shook his head and took his plate to the sink.

"That boy would give this up for a mega-junk-chipotle-sink burger?" Tim shook his head.

- - -

"Shannon, I'm ready to go. I really have to get to Paul and Meredith's house - it's late." Tim called out from the front door as he zipped up his windbreaker. It was turning cold outside. Shannon ran to the front door, carrying her purse, her phone and a pair of bright green socks.

"Do you have your duffel bag?" Shannon asked. Tim looked at his wife. She had tears streaming down her face.

"Yeah...do you have your car keys? You'll be okay driving to that sock party?"

"Yes...and, yes." Shannon said, with difficulty. Tim instinctively turned off the entry light, after years of habit. They stood for a long minute, looking at each other in the near dark, not knowing what to say. The streetlight down the block bathed the couple on their porch. Shannon reached out for her husband, and he pulled her toward him.

"Not so different from back on Pine Mountain, huh?" Tim said, with difficulty.

"I thought when we got married we'd never have to say goodbye..." Shannon whispered as she pressed her cheek against her husband's chest.

"Then let's, uh, not. It's, um, just one day." Tim stumbled in his words.

"No...not goodbye. But it's the Pacific Ocean." Shannon was crying. She was close to him, and he could feel her sobs. Tim took a breath. He decided to make a stab at humor.

"Well, a 'good buy' is something on sale, right?" Tim asked. Shannon looked up at him, obviously confused.

"Um, uh, yeah..."

"So, let's say, 'on sale' when we mean 'goodbye'. So, 'on sale', Shannon!" Tim managed a weak smile.

"You're trying to be funny, huh?" Shannon looked up and smiled back, even if it was just with a faint smirk.

"It's not working, is it?" Tim asked. He stroked his wife's hair. She put her head back on his chest.

"Maybe if you try again?" Shannon closed her eyes.

"Sorry, that's all I've got in the humor department tonight. Maybe, uh, I don't know, how does 'I love you' feel instead?" Tim asked. He squeezed his wife.

"Just about right. I love you…" Shannon said in a barely audible voice.

Tim locked the door.

PART TWO

The Hope

Chapter 23

As the boat slowly pulled away from the dock the light on the house grew more and more diffracted, more blurry, and less intense. Dark fog filled the space growing between the house on firm ground and the drifting boat gently gliding on the waters of the harbor. The bow sliced through the waters quietly. Occasionally a new light would seemingly drift by, at a distance. It, too, would fade and diminish.

Beyond the low-pitched rumble of the hidden engine, the sounds from the dock, once so clear, became more and more muffled. The boat seemed to be entering a world only known to the two men on the ship at that moment. Before long the sounds and lights were further and further behind the ship. More and more the lights blurred into a distant glow, ever dimming. The darkness seemed to partner with the fog to surround the ship.

"Tim…" Paul called out.

"Huh?" Tim responded softly.

"Tim, are you awake?" Paul gently adjusted the helm.

"What?"

"Wake up…I need your help. We'll be going under the Pacific Coast Highway bridge any time now. I could use all eyes and ears on deck…" Paul turned the ship's wheel a bit.

"A bridge?" Tim was groggy.

"I think you'd better take another big gulp of Joe, my friend. I'm not sure you're completely with me yet!" Paul shook his head.

"Joe?" Tim asked.

"Coffee, man. Get another cup if that one's cold!" Paul pointed at Tim's right arm. Tim looked down at his hand, which felt warm, then brought the cup to his mouth and took a sip. The hot liquid surprised him and he pushed the cup away.

"Whoa...hot..." Tim exclaimed.

"Well, at least you're making some sense now!"

"Sorry. I'm not used to getting up and around at whatever time this is..." Tim mumbled.

"It's five in the morning. I'll bet you don't even remember getting out of bed an hour ago!" Paul chuckled.

"You mean I'm not still in bed?" Tim looked at Paul and pretended to study him. "I guess not. You don't look like Shannon." Tim managed a half-smile.

"Fog and darkness do that to sailors, Tim, so you're not alone. Funny things happen to a man out on the open sea." Paul squinted into the darkness before him, as if he were searching for something.

"Hey, then I'm not doing too poorly. I thought the open ocean would be choppier than this. Shannon gave me some seasickness medicine, but I'll probably not need it. I think." Tim took another sip of his coffee. He enjoyed the taste and

231

feel of warm liquid on a cold, damp morning – or what would be morning sometime soon.

"Hah! I hate to break it to you, but we're not on the open ocean yet." Paul said as the ship slid beneath a bridge.

"What?" Tim rubbed his eye.

"We're in Anaheim Bay. We just passed under the highway, so we still have a bit of distance to go. Believe me, you'll know it when we get there." Paul slightly turned the wheel again.

"Oh?" Tim started to worry.

"Yep. And, if I were you, I'd take one of those pills now." Paul added; Tim was already searching through his duffel bag. He found a pill bottle.

"Is it called something like 'dramamine'?" Tim asked.

"It's exactly like that. But it takes a little time to kick in. You, uh, don't get car sick or anything like that, do you?"

"Uh, only if I'm not driving the car. Sometimes I get an upset stomach when Shannon's driving…" Tim whispered as he struggled to get a pill out of the bottle.

"Um, you'd really better take a pill, then." Paul sounded serious. Tim was shaking as he tried to remove a pill. His anxiety was rising.

"Okay…" He said, nervously.

"Tim, whoa, slow down. Take it easy. You're going to spill them all over the place. Here, wait…" Paul pulled back on the throttle, and the boat slowed. He put a strap on the ship's wheel.

"Huh?" Tim looked up.

"Let me have the bottle. I'll get the right dosage out for you..." Paul leaned over and Tim handed him the container.

"Paul, the boat..." Tim pointed at the ship's wheel.

"Not to worry. I locked into position, and our speed is almost nothing. Here, take this..." Paul handed a pill to Tim, who popped it into his mouth. He took a swig of coffee to wash it down. Paul returned to the controls and looked over at his friend.

"It's down..." Tim nodded.

"Now, take a breath. Calm down a bit. It won't be as rough as you're thinking. The weather shows a storm coming in tomorrow, but things should be calm today."

"You're sure?" Tim took another sip of coffee.

"We usually don't get a lot of fog when a storm's coming in, so this is a good sign."

"One of those 'red sky at morning...sailor take warning' kinds of things?" Tim asked.

"Well, sort of. Let me show you a trick I learned a few years ago, before we pick up speed. Here, come up to the area that looks like a dashboard in front of us..." Paul gestured. Tim stood up and walked forward.

"Yeah? Here?"

"Yep, that will work. I found a way to minimize the effects of a bouncing boat as it's traveling through the water. Now, hold on to that board, yes, that one, with one hand and just keep looking ahead. Try not to look around much. That helped me a while ago. Maybe it'll help you."

"It will?"

"I can't guarantee anything, but it's worth a try." Paul shrugged.

"I guess so..." Tim sounded anxious again.

"Also, move your legs apart a bit more, giving yourself a more stable base. And position one leg a bit further back. Yeah, that's it." Paul pointed down. Tim nodded as he followed the older man's suggestion.

"Okay, let's get out on to the Pacific." Paul said in a quiet tone. He revved the engine up and removed the strap on the wheel. The boat responded strongly to the command of the throttle. The rear of the boat seemed to drop a bit as the front end rose. The ship pushed forward strongly.

"Wow...that engine does have some pick-up!" Tim exclaimed.

"Wait until we get out on to open water. She's not at half throttle yet! We have a speed limit in the harbor, you know!" Paul smiled.

"Hah! A speed limit – what a weird idea. Like the freeway!" Tim said nervously.

"Yep. We want to avoid sending big waves across people's docks and boats. And, Tim?" Paul asked.

"Huh? Yeah?" Tim was trembling.

"We'll be fine. Believe me." Paul used a calm, clear voice.

"Yeah, we will." Tim nodded, though he was far from convinced. He wondered if he shouldn't have listened to Shannon and her "Pacifica-phobia," as she once called it.

"So, changing the subject, did you bring the rest of my dad's journal along?" Paul asked.

"Journal? Oh, yeah, I did. It's in my duffel bag; Shannon put it into a plastic bag to protect it from getting wet. She thinks of stuff like that."

"I can tell. I remember my father telling me about her after, uh, well, you know when." Paul looked down at a compass.

"Yeah, back then. So, what did he say about me?" Tim asked, afraid of the answer.

"Wait. Do you feel that?" Paul asked.

"What? Feel what?" Tim felt more anxious but continued to stare straight ahead.

"Nothing to worry about. The water. Does it feel different?"

"Is it choppier? It seems rougher..." Tim trailed off, still staring.

"Exactly! Welcome to the Pacific Ocean, my friend! We're clear of the harbor now."

"That is so cool! I'm on the Pacific Ocean! I have to call Shannon!" Tim reached into his jacket's pocket to get his cell phone.

"Um, that's probably not a good idea, Tim."

"Why not?"

"Does Shannon usually get up before five thirty in the morning?" Paul laughed.

"Oh, no, she's not like that…"

"You can call her when we get to Avalon. Maybe in a couple of hours?"

"Yeah, maybe she'll be up and around by then."

"Until then, just enjoy the ride."

"Wait. You said we were going to someplace called 'Parson's Beach' or something." Tim asked. He turned to look at Paul and immediately started feeling queasy. He started to make some unpleasant sounds.

"Tim! Eyes front." Paul barked. Tim complied; his stomach started feeling a little better.

"Uh, yeah…"

"It's called Parsons Landing, and it's on the north shore. We'll go to Avalon first, the big city on Catalina. Remember, 'big' is a relative term. There's a little bistro in town that has some great cinnamon rolls." Paul said.

"Ugh…no rolls…" Tim sighed.

"Oh, sorry, um, we'll stop and get some gas."

"Uh, no gas, either…" Tim said with a hint of laughter.

"How about we'll stop and walk on some dry land for a bit?" Paul chuckled.

"Now THAT's something I can look forward to!" Tim smiled.

"Seriously, I like to stop in Avalon. It's a great town; always wished I could live there. I think you'll like it. Call it a temporary diversion from our mission." Paul said as he pushed the throttle higher.

"Whoa…she's still got some power in her!" Tim exclaimed.

"Now that the fog is lifting, I'll open her up for a minute. The sun should be coming up behind us. I'm able to see a glow on the horizon…but DO NOT TURN AND LOOK!" Paul said emphatically.

"Not trying that again any time soon. I'll just have to believe you on that." Tim whispered.

"Do that." Paul nodded.

"Hey, the windshield is getting a bit lighter. I can see that." Tim put his head down.

"Barely. That's what's doing it – the Sun's on its way. Are you taking deep breaths, Tim? Try to relax."

"Working on it. Can we talk about something besides…boats…right now?"

"Great idea. You were asking about my dad, and what he thought about Shannon."

"Oh, yeah. What he thought…" Tim started breathing erratically and rapidly.

"Tim. Breathe. Just slow down." Paul pulled the throttle back a bit, slowing the boat.

"…about…" Tim tried to continue. He was able to take a bigger breath.

"Breathing now? Is slower better?" Paul asked. Tim nodded and started breathing more regularly.

"…me?" Tim nodded as he finished. He felt more relaxed as the boat slowed.

"I thought you'd ask that next!" Paul smiled.

"Well, he meant a lot to me."

"Our talk on my dock a couple of weeks ago helped me understand why. I remember him telling me how hard you worked on that wall. He told me how you and he talked about Shannon's situation…" Paul stopped talking suddenly. He glanced over at Tim.

"Do you mean how she was going to have a baby?" Tim looked over at Paul. He immediately regretted it. He turned forward again. The feeling in his stomach started to subside again.

"Hey, this may not be the best conversation topic for your first sea voyage…" Paul sounded apologetic.

"I'm not sure what would be a good topic..." Tim forced a smile.

"Probably true. I remember my first trip out on to the old Pacific. And that trip is connected to this one." There was a long pause. The sound of the engine running filled many moments. Tim just practiced slow, easy breathing.

"Yeah, I want to know more about why we're going to that Parson's place." Tim took another deep breath. He could tell the sun was definitely rising and the fog was lifting. That helped his stomach a lot. As he looked forward the ocean appeared, more and more, as a steel blue plane spreading out to the horizon. Directly ahead was what appeared to be a hill, a mountain.

"We'll talk about Parson's Landing in a bit. Can you see Catalina?" Paul pointed. Tim nodded.

"You mean that mountain there?"

"Sailors call mountains in the ocean by another name." Paul chuckled.

"What do they call them?" Tim's question blurted out; he was unable to focus his mind. Paul let out a small guffaw.

"Tim, it's a joke. They call them 'islands'..." Paul smiled.

"Oh, yeah..." Tim felt a blush rising on his neck. He smiled. The sun made the sky glow. Daylight was brushing the waters. Once again, the hum of the engine filled a number of silent moments. In a calm voice Paul broke the quiet after taking a deep breath.

"Tim, my dad thought highly of you. I think you meant about as much to him as he meant to you. That's my guess."

"You think so?"

"Of course. He worried about your future, but I can tell that's not a problem now. I wish he could see how well you've done for yourself, for Shannon and for your kids. I know he'd be proud of you." Paul said as he adjusted the ship's course.

"I've done what I could." Tim nodded.

"You've done just fine. You seem really worried about what he thought about you."

"I never had anyone say they were proud of me. Well, except for Shannon. I guess knowing your dad felt that way was important to me. I just felt guilty..." Tim started then immediately closed his mouth.

"Guilty? About what? I don't know about anything you should feel that way about, I mean about back then, when you helped him build the wall. Do you mean about Shannon being pregnant?"

"No, well, maybe a little, but all that is okay now."

"Of course it is. You guys are almost done with raising two kids – in a couple of years you'll see them off into their new worlds. You're succeeding, Tim. They're doing better with your kids than how you grew up."

"Oh, yeah, that's true. But..." Tim nodded.

"Look – there's Avalon. Almost there!" Paul sounded proud as he pointed. Tim squinted as sunlight started to reflect off of a building.

"Hey! We're going to make it!" Tim exclaimed. His stomach started to feel a lot better.

"I told you we would, oh 'ye of little faith'!"

"Sorry I doubted you!" Tim smiled as he turned to look at Paul. The queasiness arose yet again.

"Take a breath...tell yourself you made it. No guilt in doubting." Paul used a calm voice.

"No, not like the guilt I felt about Isaiah..." Tim felt giddy but immediately stopped talking. He wished he could retract those words – as soon as he realized what he had just said.

"Isaiah? What?" Paul's tone turned to one of a very business-like nature.

"Nothing...forget it..." Tim said under his breath.

"Tim, that's the guy who murdered my father."

"I'm sorry - it slipped out. I'm not feeling too good..." Tim started. Paul eased back on the throttle again.

"We'll be coming in to port soon. Maybe we need to clear the air on this Isaiah character here. I know my dad worried about how you hung around him..." Paul said. Tim interrupted with strong emotion.

"Listen, I hate what happened back then. I mean I HATE IT! I will never forget that day. I hate myself for hanging around that bastard. I don't understand why I...uh...um..." Tim turned away from Paul - he felt like his head was spinning. He grabbed on to a railing and pulled himself to the side of the boat.

"Tim, take another breath! Look forward..." Paul yelled as he pulled way back on the throttle. The boat was barely moving in the water. It was too late. Paul watched as Tim heaved what little was in his stomach over the side of the boat.

"Ugh..." Tim mumbled.

"And you almost made it the entire way! Look how close you got, Tim! We're here!" Paul pointed.

Tim looked up and saw three men. They looked, to Tim, like they had spent a lifetime on or around boats and they were staring at him. One was flashing an almost toothless grin and pointing – right at Tim.

"Hello, Avalon..." Tim said meekly as he waved. Paul edged the boat closer to the dock.

"Whoa..." Paul, sounding surprised, said under his breath. Tim looked at his friend.

"What?" He asked, working hard to catch his breath.

"I wonder...no, it can't be." Paul whispered.

"Who? What?" Tim stood up straighter.

"The old guy – to the right. Could it be him...? No..." Paul nodded his head toward the dock.

"Do you mean the 'Peg Leg' guy you met years ago?" Tim asked. Paul nodded. The old man turned and walked quickly away from the dock.

"It's him. Look at the walk..." Paul whispered and nodded.

Chapter 24

"Let's sit here, Tim." Paul pointed at a tidy little bistro table on the terrace of a small restaurant. Tim lowered his duffel bag on to one of the chairs.

"Nice place..." Tim said as he looked around. His eyes were drawn to the ocean, past the harbor.

"It is. Right over there is where my family stayed when we came back that second time. You know, with the box of books for that kid?" Paul pointed to his right.

"Oh, yeah. Has it changed much?" Tim asked.

"I think they've spruced things up a bit, but not much."

"It's not too bad here..." Tim added.

"Like I said, Avalon's a great little town."

"Seems like it." Tim said. Paul took a deep breath.

"You feeling any better? I'm hoping a little break in our journey will get you back on an even keel."

"Keel...is that one of those nautical terms?" Tim smiled gently.

"Actually, it is, yes. You must be doing better if you can crack jokes. But we'll have to work on the material. Pretty corny, my friend!" Paul reached out and squeezed his friend's arm. He looked directly into Tim's eyes. Tim nodded.

"I'm doing a lot better, thanks, in other ways, too." Tim looked down and found his chair. Paul did the same. Both men leaned back and looked away, out to the sea from whence they had come.

"Are you two here for breakfast? We have our 'everything omelet' on sale this week." A pretty voice said from behind Paul. Tim turned and found a smiling waitress holding a small notepad.

"Everything omelet?" Tim turned and asked with a pained accent in his voice. Paul looked at his friend.

"Well, it has avocado, bacon, cheese, onion and chipotle sauce. Really yummy!" The waitress said as Tim looked down.

"Miss? Is it Kathleen?" Paul asked.

"Yes, it's Kathleen! Right here on my badge!" She smiled as she pointed.

"Right! Well, how about if we start out with some ice water, coffee and toast? Just wheat toast, lightly buttered? Then we could take a breath and look over the menu for a few minutes." Paul smiled and ordered.

"I can do that!" The young lady responded then walked away. Tim leaned over toward Paul.

"What is it about dumping everything you have in the kitchen into one meal nowadays? Wait until I tell Shannon about this." Tim smiled.

"Oh, right. You had that mega-bacon-chipotle-kitchen-sink cheeseburger thing!" Paul laughed.

"Not willingly!" Tim shook his head.

"And that is how I feel about your friendship with Isaiah." Paul said, in a quiet tone.

"What do you mean?"

"Tim, you were young and foolish, just like I was young and foolish. I think that's why my father told me about you. But what teenage boy isn't? We all have guilt. We all have regrets."

"Yeah, but mine got your father...uh..." Tim pulled back.

"Shot? Yes, I know what happened, but you didn't do it."

"If I had just stayed away from him..."

"Tim, Isaiah killed my father, not you. I was there at the trial, remember?" Paul leaned toward Tim.

"Oh, yes, I remember..."

"And I remember how Isaiah's lawyer kept trying to implicate you, and Shannon, and, heck, anyone else in the room, it seemed. But Isaiah did it, pure and simple."

"I know." Tim nodded.

"I have a similar problem – a haunting, if you will. Do you remember my story about how my dad and I drove that old Woody across the country?"

"Sure."

"For all of these years, when I see an Ohio license plate I cringe inside."

"Ohio? Why Ohio?" Tim asked.

"I snuck out of our hotel room early in the morning, before my dad woke up, and fiddled with our car's engine. I thought the car was making weird noises and it could do a lot better."

"So?"

"Do you remember what happened in Wyoming?" Paul asked.

"I think so. The fire?"

"Yep. Guess what they found after they got the flames out?"

"Wait, it had something to do with the carburetor..."

"Oh, yeah. They said something about how the engine was burning fuel too fast or too hot or something." Paul sat back and sighed.

"I see. You were messing with the engine..." Tim started.

"...starting in Ohio, and not telling my dad..." Paul continued.

"...and that destroyed the car." Tim finished.

"Yeah...I don't care about the car, Tim. Do you know how close both of us were to dying that day?" Paul leaned forward.

"I can imagine..."

"One of the cops on the scene that day said we were on fire, they guessed, for a few miles. We left a trail and a streak behind us."

"Now I understand why you wanted me to look at the boat's engine..." Tim smiled gently.

"Oh, yeah. I learned that the more complex the mechanical device, the more I need professional help. Lesson learned, the hard way. I wish I understood engines, but I think I do not get along with them at all."

The waitress walked up with a tray just as Paul finished.

"Here we are! Toast, water and coffee for two!" She gently placed the cups on the table.

"Great! Thanks!" Paul said as he reached for his cup of coffee.

"So, anything else?" Kathleen asked.

"Maybe we'd better go light. How about we order your fruit cup and some oatmeal? Does that sound okay, Tim?" Paul looked at his friend.

"I think I can handle that..." Tim nodded as he sipped his ice water.

"Okay, two bowls of oatmeal and some fruit." She turned to walk away.

"Wait...miss?" Paul called out. She turned back.

"Did I forget something? Cream? Sugar?"

"Oh, no. I wonder if I'm seeing things. Did you change your name tag? You were Kathleen. Now it says, 'K.P.'" Paul asked. Tim turned to look.

"Oh, that, yeah. Long story. I forgot my badge, and my boyfriend just dropped it off. Sorry."

"So, who is Kathleen? The other badge?" Paul shook his head.

"Me. But we have two Kathleens here. So we decided that she's 'Kathleen' and I am 'K.P.'. She started working here before me, so I had to pick another name for my badge."

"I'm lost..." Paul shook his head.

"I go by my initials. I borrow her badge if I forget mine. She always leaves it here when she's off. And I like my nickname because my boyfriend told me that 'K.P.' in the Army is like being a waitress! Kitchen patrol!" She turned to go back inside. Tim looked at Paul and both men shook their heads.

- - -

"Hi, Shannon! Guess where I am!" Tim was excited to be able to talk to his wife.

"Tim! I've been waiting since before dawn to hear your voice! Are you at Parson's Cove?" Shannon answered.

"Before dawn? Ugh…" Tim sighed.

"What's wrong?"

"I really wanted to call you out on the ocean, but Paul wondered if you'd be awake. It was like dawn. But I felt like I knew you, like you'd want a call. Oh, well…"

"It's okay now. Just hearing your voice helps."

"I feel the same way…" Tim said quietly as he looked down.

"So, you're at Parson's Cove?"

"Not yet, no. And it's called Parson's 'Landing,' not cove. But we are definitely on Catalina Island! We just had breakfast at a neat little restaurant in Avalon. I know you would love the place. It was like some sort of a bistro or something, with stone floors and iron tables!"

"Oh, sounds nice! Did you eat?"

"Yeah, just some oatmeal and fruit. Oh, and toast. It was good! Paul paid for it…" Tim answered.

"That was nice of him."

"Something on the menu made me think of you!" Tim smiled.

"On the menu?"

"Yep. They had an 'everything omelet' with avocado - and more!"

"Oh, no. Not another 'kitchen sink' meal!" Shannon laughed.

"Oh, yeah. I avoided that!"

"Glad to hear that! So, what are you doing next? How will you get to the Parsons place?"

"We're on our way to a hardware store. Paul forgot a shovel and he thinks we'll need it. We'll take the boat from here."

"You need a shovel on a boat?" Shannon sounded confused.

"No, no. It has something to do with whatever he's trying to find on the north side of the island. We may have to dig."

"Dig? I'm still confused about the Parson's Landing connection. Have you found out anything more about what he hopes to find? This sounds like one of those 'pirates-looking-for-buried-treasure" kind of trips."

"Haven't found out much yet, but I'll bet I will soon. I know he's looking for a blue box of some kind. I don't know much about this being a pirate trip, but I did see one guy on the dock who looked like he's been here since there were pirates." Tim laughed.

"An old guy?"

"Paul thinks it's that 'Peg Leg' guy."

"No way! After all this time?" Shannon was surprised.

"Yes, way! I saw 'the walk'!"

"Whoa…"

"It looked like what Paul described. He swung one foot kind of wide."

"So, I have to ask the one hidden question…" Shannon paused.

"'Hidden?' What do you mean?" Tim was confused.

"Well, honey, did you get seasick?" Shannon asked. There was silence for a moment.

"Oh, come on, why would I get seasick? Not possible." Tim bit his lip.

"Because I know you, like when I drive. And I know Paul was driving." Shannon verbally poked her husband. Tim took a deep breath.

"I can honestly say that I did not get seasick on the Pacific Ocean." Tim was adamant.

"Okay. Where did you get sick then?" Shannon continued her questioning. Tim exhaled.

"In Avalon Harbor. Right by the dock." Tim shook his head as Shannon gently laughed.

"In the harbor! Oh, my! I hope it landed IN the harbor - not on the boat." Shannon was giggling.

"Oh, yeah, right in front of Mister Peg Leg himself. I humiliated myself before I'd even stepped foot on the island." Tim smiled.

Chapter 25

Tim took a deep breath as he looked at the boat before him. A big part of him would rather stay on solid ground.

Maybe, he thought whimsically, he could get used to living on an island, and, just maybe, he could find a way to get Shannon to cross the ocean to be with him. And maybe he could find a job working on custom cars here. Just then a golf cart whizzed by.

"Can you believe how many golf carts people drive around here, Tim?" Paul interrupted Tim's daydream.

"Huh? Oh, yeah - I did notice."

"There wouldn't be much work for someone like you here..." Paul smiled. Tim looked at his friend, wondering. How did Paul know what he was thinking?

"I guess I'd have to learn how to work on golf carts. How did you know?" Tim asked.

"How did I know what?" Paul frowned as he pulled a few items out of a shopping bag.

"Oh, nothing. I was thinking about how much I like it here in Avalon."

"We all kick around schemes to be able to live someplace like this. Avalon is where I wanted to live, way back when. So, I got as far as Huntington Harbor. I think I did okay." Paul shrugged.

"Shannon and I dream like that from time to time - still."

"By the look on your face I guessed you were trying to build some kind of daydream about not getting back on the boat..." Paul smiled as he pulled on the rope that held the boat to the dock.

"Huh?"

"That's how I felt the first time I came out here, so I figured we aren't so different."

"You?"

"Me. I tease you but actually you made it closer to Avalon then I did." Paul shrugged as he tossed a bag on to the boat.

"Closer to Avalon?"

"Yeah. Heaving at the dock. I was about five miles out. And four miles. And three miles. You know, feeding the seagulls? Hint, hint?" Paul smiled.

"Feeding the seagulls?" Tim was confused but came to understand as Paul pointed at a few gulls picking at the remains of an old pile of French fries on the dock.

"Ugh. Okay, I get it. You mean when I showed my digestive talents to Mister Peg Leg."

"Hah! Good old Peg Leg. If it is him, he's been here a long time. You'll be able to meet him in a bit, when we get some gas. It seems he has spent his whole life on that dock. Don't worry, I'm sure he's seen a lot of folks lose their cookies in the harbor."

"Do you know anything about him?"

"Oh, not much. The rumor is he ran away from home when he was in high school, found his way here and never left. He hasn't aged well. I don't think he's much older than I am, as I said back home."

"Wow. Do they really call him 'Peg Leg' around here? Or was that you and your dad?"

"Yeah, we called him that. But the locals did, too - that's where we got it. When you see him again, check his left foot – when we pulled in I noticed that he is missing a couple of toes. It's him. There's a story there, but I don't know much about it."

"Did your dad, or you, ever ask him?" Tim wondered.

"Oh, no. He's not much of a talker. He'll shy away from you if you try to get close. I think he has a better relationship with the duct tape he carries everywhere than any human being."

"Really? Huh..."

"The rumor says he has never left Catalina. He's so afraid of people that he can't walk up to a counter and buy a ticket to the mainland. Of course, all of this is just rumor and hearsay."

"Makes me wonder what happened in his childhood, looking back at my own." Tim said quietly.

"I believe there are a lot of hidden childhood stories out there, my friend, stories that we think are in the past but aren't. I'll bet there are lots of people who continue to battle the demons from their childhoods. I remember the last trip over here – Peg Leg helped me climb off of the boat. I was wearing a Chicago Cubs baseball hat. When he looked up and saw it, he started breathing hard. He turned and walked away quickly."

"What? Over a hat?"

"Yeah. He mumbled something about he thought he was done seeing that hat. He kept looking back over his shoulder at me, and picked up speed. Think about it. For me, it was just one in my collection. Yeah, I like the Cubs, but it was just a hat. What old pain was rattling around in his mind that day, from a long time before?"

"I have no idea." Tim shrugged.

"So, you didn't bring a Cubs hat today, did you?" Paul asked as he stepped on to the boat. He nodded toward an ice chest and Tim got the signal.

"No, no Cubs hat. Aye, aye, with the ice chest, captain!" He said as he lifted the box and handed it to Paul.

"Since we don't have a Cubs hats, Peg Leg will probably be easy to deal with. I think he helps out around the gas station – our next stop." Paul pointed down the dock as he walked over to the control panel. He turned the key to start the engine; it easily roared to life. Tim looked down the dock. Peg Leg was standing next to a gas pump, looking at a paper.

"She sounds pretty good!" Tim smiled as he pointed at the engine compartment.

"I have a good mechanic!" Paul said loudly as he checked the sides of the boat.

"What should I do?" Tim asked as he stepped, gingerly, on to the boat.

"Cast off the lines. Start with the stern." Paul checked his compass and other gauges.

"Stern is the back, right?" Tim asked as Paul smiled and nodded.

"You're catching on!"

"Line cast off! Tim called out.

"Cast off bow line." Paul said loudly. Tim walked to the front of the boat and pulled on the ropes.

"Line cast off!" Tim repeated himself. He smiled – he was thinking this boat stuff was kind of fun, as long as his stomach agreed.

"Let's get some gas and head north!" Paul said as he steered the boat down the dock.

"Hey, wait. It's not that long of a trip out here. Does this thing get poor mileage?" Tim was confused.

"Well, no. You see, it's like this…um…to be honest, I didn't plan. I forgot to fill the tank yesterday…" Paul shrugged.

"So I'm not the only one who does that…" Tim smiled.

"And now you know the real reason we're in Avalon. I screwed up." Paul shook his head. Tim reached over and squeezed Paul's arm.

"No guilt. It all worked out – it was a good stop. Let's call it an 'adventure'. That's what Shannon and I did with the kids when we went camping once. The car got a flat tire. She took them over to look at a creek – an adventure – while I cursed the stupid spare that was flat."

"You did that, too, huh? Looking after my spare tire was never one of my strong points. But you're a car guy!" Paul smiled.

"Oh, man, sometimes we mechanics are the worst people with our own cars! Just ask Shannon. On second thought, don't…" Tim and Paul chuckled together.

"Well, here's the gas station…" Paul pulled back on the throttle.

"I'll get the bow line." Tim responded.

"Good man. We're becoming quite the crew!"

"It's easy with a good captain!" Tim smiled.

Chapter 26

"What do you mean, Peg Leg? Is there a problem?" Paul asked. Tim reached into the ice chest and pulled out a bottle of soda. He unscrewed the top.

"Do you know me?" The man on the dock asked nervously and stepped back. Paul threw a look at Tim – raising one eyebrow. He turned back to Peg Leg.

"A little bit, my friend. We've met a couple of times. I came through here a few times, back when I was a kid." Paul sounded like he was trying to reassure the man. He tightened the bow line as he spoke.

"You kind of look like I know you..." Peg Leg said. Tim half-smiled as he turned his head away. He considered reminding Peg Leg about a certain Chicago Cubs hat, then quickly decided against it.

"Oh, sure. A lot of years ago I came with my dad. I wonder if you remember him. He gave you a box once; it had a lot of paperback novels in it." Paul asked.

"What! The man with the box?" Peg Leg exclaimed.

"Well, he was a man with a box, yes."

"No, no, no. Not a man. He was the man!" Peg Leg said reverently.

"So you do remember him. That was my father..." Paul said.

"Remember him? Oh, yes, yes, yes! He is Mr. Marino! Yes, yes! I still have every book he gave me! He used to call me by my name!" Peg Leg, without saying any more, immediately turned around and ran off.

"Wait! Peg...!" Paul called out. Peg Leg turned a corner and was gone.

"Used to call him by his name?" Tim asked.

"I have no idea what his real name is. But, wow, he remembers my father. I can't wait to tell Merrie." Paul shook his head. A mechanic, working on a nearby open metal utility box, wiped his hands with a rag and walked over.

"Sorry, sir. Peg gets like this, but he'll be back. He's a bit odd, but he's really a good guy. Helps out around here. What he meant was we're waiting for a pump unit for the gas system. Can't sell you any gas yet. Should be about twenty minutes. Maybe a half an hour."

"Oh, that's the problem. Anything you could help with, Tim?" Paul asked.

"I doubt it – I'll bet these guys have the know-how with these pumps. Me? I'd take an hour just to figure out how it works." Tim shook his head.

"I suggest you just sit back and wait it out, unless you don't need the gas so much. Take it from a mechanic." The man said.

"Uh, we need the gas. I forgot to fill up on the mainland – only got about an eighth of a tank."

"Cutting her pretty close, huh?" The mechanic smiled and shook his head. He walked back toward the utility box. Paul glared at the man. Tim could see his muscles tense and relax in his neck and face.

"I'll bet that idiot runs out of gas on every trip." Paul whispered angrily.

"Don't worry about him, Paul. If it helps any, I wouldn't hire him in my shop."

"Why not?" Paul looked at Tim.

"I can tell a lot about mechanics by how they dress. A professional knows that his clothes are like his tools, too. You store tools on a belt or in special pockets. If you don't have the right clothing, you lose tools. This guy's wearing an old pair of slacks, with wrenches shoved in the back pocket." Tim gestured toward the mechanic. Just then a wrench slipped out, bounced on the deck and fell into the water. The mechanic started cursing.

"Whoa, Tim. You're amazing."

"Can I call it or what?" Tim smiled.

"Well, hand me a drink. I suppose we should just sit this one out. Don't have many other viable options."

"I think you're right." Tim agreed.

"Over the course of my life I've learned that there are times when doing nothing is your only option. I hate those days, but what can you do?" Paul said as Tim reached into the ice chest and pulled out another soda. He handed it his friend. The two men plopped down on seat cushions under the canopy shade.

"I'm slowly learning that myself." Tim nodded as he sipped his soda.

"It strange being here. I can still see my dad walking along the dock, looking at a map. He always traveled with maps. Hah. My dad's paperback, you know the one I told you about, was on that board right over there…" Paul gestured as he opened the bottle of soda. Paul's voice grew quieter. He scanned the items on the dock and the building to one side.

"Maps, huh? Reminds me of his son." Tim reached over and tapped on the nearby nautical chart.

"And you, my friend, remind me of the first trip my father and I took to Catalina." Paul smiled.

"How is that?"

"At first he was as big a land lubber as you are! Maybe bigger! Hand me that chart. The first trip we made here started with us looking at a map. It was not a pleasant situation, however." Paul fully opened the chart – and a piece of paper fell out.

"Hey, a note..." Tim pointed. Paul picked it up.

"Oh, wow! It's from Merrie." Paul began to read out loud, softly.

Dear Paul,

I know why you have to make this trip. Please believe that I'm behind you. I admit that I was upset when you said you needed to keep the boat a bit longer, but when you explained why I completely understood. I'm thankful that you have Tim with you, someone who can fix the boat if there is a problem. Besides, you shouldn't be alone to deal with this. Tim's the right crew member for this voyage.

Shannon and I talked all week about the trip, and we're here for each other. Don't worry about us. Don't tell Tim, but Shannon has some notes for him, too. Sort of a throwback to your Mom, I suppose!

Love,
Merrie

"You know, Paul, your mother sure had a long reach. Now she has her daughter-in-law writing notes. And I have to search for something from Shannon!" Tim smiled, shook his head and took a drink.

"It looks like it..." Paul sighed as he looked away.

"What's going on?" Tim asked.

"It all started with a map. Like this chart. It was a long time ago, on our kitchen table. Want to hear that story?" Paul sat back and looked toward the horizon.

"Of course..."

"Imagine my mother, with a map spread across a kitchen table..." Paul began to erase the distance of time.

Chapter 27

"Joseph!" Anne called out, half turning toward the doorway to the living room.

"Coming! I had to change…" Joseph answered as he walked into the kitchen while zipping his pants. He stopped when he noticed that Paul and Anne were looking at a large map on the kitchen table.

"Paul has been telling me about this year's Boy Scout trip to Catalina." Anne said.

"Yeah, I know about it. What do you need?" Joseph responded brusquely.

"This is the third year his troop has gone to Parson's Landing, and I think he should do it this time." Anne took a deep breath.

"Well, there are issues. It's not that simple."

"What issues?" Anne asked.

"Well, the big one is money." Joseph answered. Anne reached into the cookie jar on the counter next to her and pulled out a wad of money.

"Not this year. I've been putting a few dollars away all year. What else is blocking it?"

"What…?" Joseph stared at the cash.

"And I know you're off that week, so time is not an issue." Anne sounded stern.

"You don't understand. It's, uh, not that simple." Joseph stammered.

"It's the boat problem, isn't it?" Anne's voice softened. Joseph stared at his wife, unable to speak. He nodded.

"Look, here, at the map. Catalina is 26 miles off of the coast. It's not more than like two hours to get there. I know you can do it."

"It's not that simple..." Joseph whispered. Anne turned toward her son.

"Paul, why don't you go back to work on your bike? Dad and I will talk this out." Paul stalled for a moment. Anne nodded toward the living room and gave him a look. Paul walked away slowly. Anne kept looking at the map.

"Joseph, was it what happened in Chocolate Chip Creek? Anne rubbed her husband's arm. Joseph nodded.

"That hurt more than I can say..." Joseph looked out of the window.

"You did not hurt that kitten, honey. You've been blaming yourself for decades." Anne said softly.

"Things don't work out well when I get into a boat."

"Okay, yes, there was the time when the canoe capsized on the lake in Maine, but I'm okay, right?" Anne asked. Joseph nodded.

"Yeah..."

"Maybe it's time we face this demon and knock it down? You used to like boats and being near the water..."

Chapter 28

"So, you stood outside the kitchen and listened to your parents arguing about the trip?" Tim asked. Paul nodded.

"They weren't really arguing. I rarely saw that happen. My mother's kindness always seemed to melt my father's crust."

"I saw that." Tim nodded.

"Well, my mother wasn't happy when she found me hiding behind the chair, right outside the kitchen. But she got my father to agree to go. That was one of the first times in my life that I noticed that my dad had fears. Those fears were not so different from my own." Paul took another sip of his soda and adjusted the sun shade on the boat.

"What happened next?" Tim asked.

"Can you promise something to me?" Paul asked.

"Like what?"

"Keep this private? Only my wife knows."

"Sure. One of those childhood things, huh?"

"Yeah. Sometimes the neighborhood kids, well, they called me a nickname. I didn't like it."

"What was it?"

"Polliwog. You know, sounds like Paul. I was an anxious kid, and I think the other kids knew that. I got picked on a lot." Paul took a deep breath.

"I know the feeling. Some kids called me 'Timid' back then…" Tim whispered.

"Well, let's go back into time again. Dad did pretty poorly crossing over, as I told you. We left here in mid-morning, kind of like now, and were just getting into Parson's Landing. The scoutmaster was organizing the campsite - barking orders left and right." Paul began.

Chapter 29

"Dads, you'll be over there, by those cliffs. Boys, you set up camp near the creek, there." The old man announced as he pointed. Groups of people started to break apart, sons from fathers, then re-organize and pick up equipment. There was obvious respect for this impeccably dressed Scoutmaster.

"He was a beach master in World War II. He runs these camps like we're the Iwo Jima United States Marines or something." Another dad leaned over and whispered to Joseph, who had his hand on Paul's shoulder. Paul looked over at the Scoutmaster.

"Wow. World War II…" Paul whispered.

"Oh, and troopers, don't forget your ammo cans! Company dismissed!" The scoutmaster barked and then blew a whistle. Joseph turned toward his son.

"Paul? Where's your ammo can?" Joseph leaned over and whispered.

Paul looked around and was unable to find his ammo box. He looked back at one of the rubber landing boats moored nearby. A lanky, older, tall boy, named Mark, was carrying a bright blue ammo can, as well as another one, one that was far more beat-up looking. He waved the blue can around.

"Hey, look what I found! It's Polliwog's freshly painted ammo can!" Mark laughed as he lifted it high. Paul ran over and tried to grab it from Mark. Paul was not tall enough to reach it.

"That's mine!"

"Sure is. And boy, I'll bet it has some pretty stuff inside! Why'd you paint it blue, Polliwog? Should have been pink!" Mark laughed as he worked to open the box. A few boys came closer to watch what would happen. Paul, in an obvious panic, jumped at Mark and knocked him over. A fight started.

Two of the dads, including Joseph, ran over and broke the boys apart. As they stood back, Paul leaned over and picked up his ammo box. He was on the verge of tears.

"Polliwog's going to cry..." Mark taunted the younger boy. The Scoutmaster walked up.

"Jefferson, if we had a way, I'd ship you back to the mainland for this behavior. Do I need to remind you about our agreement before leaving?" The Scoutmaster was very stern.

"No, sir." Mark brushed himself off as he glared at Paul.

"Boys, Scouting is about fair play and respect. Now, I want you two to shake hands, and start things fresh. Am I clear?"

"Yes, sir…" Both boys said, almost in unison. Paul gingerly pushed out his arm. Mark looked at it for a long time and then met the shake.

"Good. Now, let's get back to the job at hand. We have to establish a beach head here! We've got equipment to unload, and a mess tent to set up! Let's go! We're burning daylight!" The Scoutmaster pulled the two fathers away and walked toward the stacks of equipment. Mark continued to glare at Paul.

"Watch out, wimp. I'm putting the word out. I'll pay five dollars to anybody who can get the stuff out of your pretty, newly painted ammo can." Mark smiled in a sick way.

"Why can't you just leave me alone?"

"Because you're a wimp. You were too scared to go here the last two years, and now you're here just because your dad forced you. Wimp!" Mark whispered.

"He did not…it was…" Paul stopped talking. He didn't know what to say.

"Let me guess. It was 'Superman', right?" Mark pointed at the crudely painted "S" logo on the can. He chuckled.

Paul pulled his ammo can closer, turned and walked toward the camp area.

"Five dollars for the pretty can, Polliwog!" Mark laughed.

Chapter 30

The laughter from decades ago faded; Paul looked away from Tim. He took a deep breath as the boat bobbed beneath him. Tim leaned back.

"Mark, that idiot, was in prison the last time I heard." Paul said.

"Sounds like someone else I once knew." Tim responded.

"Isaiah?" Paul turned toward Tim.

"Yeah. He would hurt animals. He'd do things to people just because he liked seeing them in pain. Now that I look back, he was really sick."

"That was Mark, too. I have a hunch how he got like that. His father was one of the meanest, cold-hearted people I've ever met. If he just looked at you he gave you the creeps." Paul added.

"From what I remember of Isaiah's father, Mark's father and Isaiah's dad might have been related…"

"Sounds like it. You know, these talks are helping me to see things differently. Maybe my image of Joseph Marino was, well, incomplete." Paul said.

"Isn't that true with most of our relationships?" Tim asked. Paul nodded. A larger boat passed by, at a higher speed than was allowed.

"Someone can read the speed limit signs." Paul grumbled.

"Whoa…really pushing us around!" Tim grabbed the side of the boat.

"That's why they have speed limits in harbors!" Paul shouted at the nearby boat.

"I guess…"

"IDIOT!" Paul stood up. Tim noticed his friend was trembling.

"It's alright, Paul. Really, there was no harm done. I think the waves from the first time you were here are hitting you harder than these."

"Yeah, probably true. That was a long day, and a tough night. Those kinds of memories stay with you." Paul said as he shook his head. Tim turned and looked toward the building. Someone was walking toward the dock.

"I think I see things a little clearer now, about how this trip has to do with that blue ammo can." Tim said. Paul nodded.

"I'd go on, but it seems our friend Peg Leg is back."
Paul pointed. Peg Leg was carrying an old box.

"With a cardboard box. No way!" Tim added.

"Oh, wow. It's not possible!" Paul said under his
breath.

"What?" Tim asked.

"I'll bet you ten boxes of Mike and Ike! That box has to
be the one from my dad! I know we'll find the name 'Marino'
on it."

"No way...and you're on with that bet." Tim whispered
as Peg leg began to speak.

"See, I told you. Every book he ever gave me. I think
I've read each one maybe five times. Or maybe six." Peg Leg
lowered the box to the dock, next to the boat. Paul and Tim
stood up and looked inside.

Paul tapped Tim on the shoulder, then nodded toward
a corner of the box. There, in faded black lettering, was
written the word "MARINO."

"My father did give that to you – there's our name. I
remember him handing it to you, right here on this dock."
Paul said.

"Yep, that's his name. I call this my Marino box. I don't
take it out for just anyone to see, you know." Peg Leg
sounded proud.

"And I appreciate you showing it to us, my friend." Paul
said softly.

"So, is Mister Marino with you on this trip?" Peg Leg looked past the two men on the boat. He seemed to be looking over every inch of the deck. He even walked up the dock and looked into the windows, shielding his eyes from the sun.

"Oh, no, Peg, I'm sorry. My dad, he, uh, he passed away a few years ago. You're stuck with his son now – me. But I was there that day." Paul said as he pointed at the box.

"Oh..." Peg Leg stood looking into the boat, quietly nodding.

"I'm really sorry..." Paul repeated as Peg-Leg gently lowered the box to the dock.

"He even gave me a note. It says, 'I believe in you, Christian.' I kept it here in my wallet all this time. Peg Leg pulled an old, worn wallet from his back pocket, then extracted a very tattered piece of paper. Paul gasped.

"Oh, my..." Paul whispered as he reached for the paper. Peg Leg pulled it back.

"Just look. Can't touch. No one touches it. It's mine." Peg Leg scowled. Tim walked over to the edge of the boat to get a closer look, next to Paul. They studied the note carefully – the writing was very much like what they'd been seeing in Joseph's journal.

"I understand. We'll just look." Paul said.

"Oh, wow. That is grandpa's writing!" Tim said quietly as he extended his arm toward the slip of paper. Peg Leg pulled the note away.

"It's really important to me. I touch it; no one else touches it." Peg Leg whispered.

"I understand. Can I call you Christian, like my father did?" Paul pointed at the note. Peg Leg nodded.

"He did call me by my real name. If you are his son, you can call me Christian." Peg Leg looked over at Tim.

"No sorry, he was not my father. I guess I'll have to stay with 'Peg Leg'." Tim said. Paul leaned over and grabbed Tim's shoulder.

"My dad was Tim's grandfather, Christian." Paul said. Peg Leg stared at Tim, who was looking at Paul.

"Then he can call me 'Christian', too." Peg Leg, now renamed, announced. Just then the mechanic working on the utility box returned.

"Peg, can you get over to the hardware store? They called and said the part's in. I can't leave the dock. I'll pay you five dollars..." The mechanic asked.

"Five dollars! You bet!" Peg Leg picked up his box, turned and ran behind the same building he had come out of with the box.

"We'll see you, Christian..." Paul called out, but got no response.

"You guys related to him? Not many know his real name. I only found out like a year ago, by accident."

"My father knew him, it seems." Paul answered.

"What? Was he the famous Mr. Marino? He talks about that guy all the time. I saw him bring out the box, the one no one else can touch. He's pretty easy-going, but if you mess with his box, watch out. Your dad made a difference with that tough case."

"That was my dad, yes. I'm sorry to say that he's gone now."

"Oh, that's too bad. I'll bet that would hit Peg hard. Anyway, we should be up and running about fifteen minutes after he gets back with the parts." The mechanic shuffled off.

"That reminds me, Paul. Your dad's journal. We should read a bit more of it while we're waiting."

"Why not? Can't think of a more appropriate place!"

"To be honest, I think we have a bunch of time. Have you noticed that we keep getting twenty minutes re-sets? Twenty minutes. Then twenty more. It'll be an hour and a half by the time we're done, if you ask me." Tim sat back down and reached for his duffel bag.

"Unbelievable. My dad meant everything to that guy." Paul whispered.

"He helped a lot of kids, Paul." Tim said as he pulled a notebook, encased in a plastic bag, from his duffel bag. He opened it up. An envelope fell out.

Chapter 31

"Well, look here. I got a letter." Tim smiled as he held up a flowered envelope.

"Gee, what a shock - or not! I'll bet this one sounds like Merrie's letter and I'll bet she coordinated this 'literary effort'." Paul smiled as he sat back. Tim was reading the note to himself.

"Huh..." Tim whispered.

"Aren't you going to read it? Come on, man. We're sailing buddies. We don't hold stuff like that back." Paul reached for another soda from the ice chest.

"I suppose. After what just happened it's kind of eerie..." Tim whispered.

"Oh?"

"Yeah, and it's, well, kind of personal."

"More personal than my story about being called 'Polliwog'?"

"Yeah, you're right..."

Dear Tim,

I've been talking to Meredith this week and she's shown me that going to Catalina is important to both of you. I keep thinking about how you have been searching for your father all of your life. Remember the parking lot at

Ole's Burgers? I know how much Paul means to you.
Merrie told me that Paul is looking for something there,
but now I see you are, too.

Somehow, I hope you find your father there.

Love,
Shannon

"That kind of hit hard…" Tim said softly.

"It sounded nice. What made it eerie?" Paul asked.

"What you just did with Peg Leg, I mean Christian."

"What did I do?" Paul put his drink down and leaned forward.

"You introduced me as your father's grandson." Tim said softly.

"Well, you called him 'grandpa', so I figure it worked."

"He accepted it. He believed you."

"That's a positive thing. It's all good. Everybody's happy." Paul nodded.

"Think about it."

"I'm not following you." Paul said in a quiet voice.

"That makes me your son…" Tim whispered. Paul put his drink down and looked out at the harbor.

"I see what you mean." There was an uneasy quiet on the ship for a moment.

"Hey, I shouldn't be dumping my issue on you, Paul." Tim hurriedly folded Shannon's note and placed it back into the envelope. He was embarrassed. Paul reached across and stopped him.

"Tim, I see nothing wrong with what you said. What you've been through, in your childhood, no one should have to deal with that for life. I'll ask just for one favor."

"What's that?" Tim asked in a very quiet voice. A tear was running down his cheek. He could not look up. Paul touched Tim's chin, which lifted his head.

"Just keep calling me 'Paul'..." Paul nodded and smiled.

"It's a deal..." Tim nodded as he answered. Paul gently squeezed Tim's shoulder as he stood up to stretch.

"Come on, where's the gas?" Paul sounded tired.

"Well, here's the next part of your dad's journal. Shannon put a little sticky note in here, near where she thinks we left off. Should I read?"

"Hey, why not? Sure..." Paul walked toward the stern of the ship.

"Well, here goes. I think this is the place." Tim cleared his throat.

MONDAY, ABOUT A WEEK LATER, I GUESS

Hi, Anne. I've been busy dealing with the teens. Sorry if I'm not writing as much. I had to post some rules, like respect each other, no smoking or swearing, and to put the tools back. I'd forgotten what it was like dealing with teens – I guess I've been retired too long. I feel like two of the kids, Shannon and Tim, are figuring things out but I don't know about that Isaiah. He is quite a piece of work, if you ask me.

"Oh, man, your father called it right on Isaiah, Paul."

"As the years have gone by I've come to see that he knew more than I ever gave him credit for." Paul sighed. Tim continued to read.

What bothers me is how they don't know much about proper meals – and I thought I was bad! I'm trying to teach them about regular meals and a balanced diet. Yeah, I know; don't laugh too hard. I can see you up there on Heaven's Chocolate Chip Creek, pointing at me and telling everyone, "Who is HE to teach kids how to eat?" Everyone's getting a big belly laugh right now, aren't they?

"Oh, wow - Chocolate Chip Creek. That kept getting mentioned in our house. It's even weirder since my mother, just before we left for Catalina back then, talked about some incident on that creek – something about a kitten. Remember, that was one of the things that kept him from coming over here." Paul said.

"Did you ever find out what happened with the kitten?" Tim asked.

"Never. There are a lot of questions when parents pass that go unanswered, I've learned. There's no way to figure out what pieces of information you really need like twenty years later. This is one of those..." Paul shrugged.

"Well, here's more..." Tim cleared his throat again.

THURSDAY

It was cold out as I went to work on the wall, Annie. I slipped my medium work coat on and guess what I found in the pocket? Well, you know what I found – another note. I can't quite describe the feeling I get whenever I find one of these pink envelopes, but I want to try.

First I feel a lump in my throat; it's like I am able to touch you once again. Second, I take a deep breath and build up the courage to open it. I know you'd never put anything mean in these notes, and it's not really that. I'm not sure if I have the nerve to read what you write. I don't need a bourbon and lemonade any more, but I do have to sit down and take another breath.

This note was short, but it hit hard. Don't worry about not climbing Pine Mountain with me. In fact, I'll tell you what – I'll climb it with Tim and Shannon. Isaiah, well, I can't seem to find a way to reach him, but I have some hope for the other two. When we get the wall finished we'll do it. I promise.

"Those notes again! Man, my mother was something…" Paul smiled and shook his head.

"I'm sorry we did climb that mountain. Maybe what happened…?" Tim stopped.

"Tim, it happened. We can't change the past. We have to let go - both of us…" Paul said. Tim nodded.

"Well, hold on. The next part is about you…"

Climbing Pine Mountain was easy to deal with but then you mentioned Paul, and how I called him that one day. Hard, hard, hard. That's a goal that I really want to work for – being able to reach him, being able to express myself in the way that I'd like to.

You know how I struggle to tell him that I love him, because of everything that has happened, and because of my own crappy background. I want to find a way to give him some hope that I do love him. Hope – there's the word. If he could find something to hold on to, something

to cling to, maybe that could carry us until I figure this out.
I've decided that I want to find a way for him to believe
that I do care. I can't give up, even if it feels like I'm trying
to stop the waves from hitting the beach.

"Wow. Now I'm the one who feels eerie." Paul sat up.

"What was eerie in that passage?" Tim asked.

"Trying to stop the waves from hitting the beach. Tim, think about where we are going."

"Oh, yeah..."

"I don't believe in magic, but that is pretty bizarre." Paul nodded.

My father, and you know this, was a hard man to get any
expression of love from. It has always troubled me that I
can't figure out how to show love to my children – at least
not in a way that truly shows it. I just wish I knew how to
do this. I hope I can get there.

"It was only after he passed away that I noticed that he had this problem. He had no idea how to show love to me. I'm seeing that he did it the best way he knew how. Maybe this journal was his best." Paul pointed at the papers that Tim held.

"It's pretty darn good, if you ask me." Tim responded.

281

Paul and Tim noticed a commotion. Peg Leg had returned with a box of parts. The mechanic, with Peg Leg's help, was installing the new pump parts. The mechanic turned a switch and an electric motor began to hum.

"Hey, you guys on the boat! Ready to buy some gas?" The mechanic yelled.

"Absolutely!" Paul rose and walked to the dock side of the boat.

"Peg Leg! Get me the clipboard. Let's get this ship gassed up. This ship..." The mechanic stared at the stern of the boat.

"Is there a problem?" Paul asked.

"What kind of name is that? Your boat is called the H-N-L-J-U?" The mechanic asked. Paul rolled his eyes.

"Yep, that's it. The strangest boat name in the Pacific, and proud of it!"

"What's it mean? Is it a word, or is it like one of those word puzzles? You know, like each letter means a word?"

"It means...well, whatever you want it to mean." Paul threw his arms up and smiled.

"Okay, how about *'he's not leaving Jimmy's ungassed'*." The mechanic said. Paul look confused – until the mechanic pointed at his work shirt. In greasy letters there was his name on a patch - Jimmy.

"You know, that's the best one we've heard so far. We'll go with that. Fill 'er up, Jimmy!" Paul smiled. Jimmy moved over to the pumping station. Peg Leg approached the boat.

"Thanks for showing us your book box, and the note from my dad, Christian." Paul said in a kind voice.

"I wish I could see him again." Christian replied.

"I do, too, my friend. You know, seeing that box, and the note, gave me some happiness." Paul said.

"Will you come back?"

"We'll be back tonight. Sure - I'll come by and see you, if you're here."

"I'll be here. There's a storm coming. I'm worried." Christian said.

"I heard, but it's not supposed to be here until Monday night. We'll be back in plenty of time. Don't worry." Paul looked over at the gas pump. The mechanic was running a fuel line toward the boat.

"Tim, can you hook up the fuel line?" Paul pointed. Tim stepped toward the dock and nodded.

"Will you bring a book when you come back?" Christian asked. Paul smiled.

"Absolutely. We will make darned sure you have some new books! I know my father would be happy about that." Paul saluted from the bill of his cap and then pointed at Christian.

"Your dad used to point at me like that! Come back! Then I'll be happy!" Christian smiled.

Paul stared at Christian. Tim noticed that Paul was biting his lip.

"The tank is full, Captain! Ready when you are!" Tim called out.

"Tim..." Paul said.

"Yeah?" Tim turned and noticed something in Paul's hand.

"Let's put my dad's Swedish flag up on the radio mast. Let's go into Parson's Landing flying his colors." Paul handed the cloth to Tim.

Chapter 32

"That's Two Harbors off the port side, Tim. We're only a few miles from Parson's Landing now."

"Port. That's the left side, huh?" Tim asked, half-jokingly. He was looking at the small village as Paul announced it. Tim looked up and watched the pretty blue and yellow Swedish flag flapping in the breeze.

"Oh, yeah. I'm going to make you a proper sailor on this trip. On the starboard, well, that's called the Pacific." Paul smiled.

"Nice that the waters are smoother than they were early this morning." Tim said.

"Well, they aren't much smoother. I think you're getting your 'sea legs'." Paul said as he adjusted the ship's wheel a bit to the left.

"Come on, that's just a story…"

"Nope. It's true. Each sailor learns how to ride in a boat. We each learn at our own pace. You've done well."

"Huh. Just feels smoother to me."

"There's the Cherry Valley Boy Scout Camp. I don't think it was here a few decades ago."

"It sounds like you know this area." Tim shielded his eyes.

"Maybe only a little. I study the maps."

"Charts, right?" Tim teased.

"Hah – you got me. Yes, charts."

"Have you ever tried to look for this blue box on your own?"

"There was always some reason we couldn't make it work – mostly because kids needed to get to a soccer game, or we were only on Catalina for the day and we had other things to do. Life is like that…" Paul sighed and shook his head.

"What's that called?" Tim pointed.

"Arrow Point! Wow. What a trip back in time. It looks so familiar. I must have really been absorbing everything back then. I remember the Scoutmaster telling us how it looked like an arrowhead. I kind of saw it. Well, I think I did."

"I think I can see it…" Tim looked up from a paper. Paul noticed he had been reading.

"So, you can read while we're plowing through the Pacific, Tim?" Paul smiled.

"Not really well, but I want to finish this one page."

"My dad's journal, huh?"

"Yeah. I can read it out loud…" Tim offered.

"Do it. But if you feel seasick…"

"Not going to happen again!" Tim smiled.

"Then read. We'll be at Parson's Landing soon." Paul adjusted the throttle.

"Here's the rest of that page…" Tim started.

A STORMY SUNDAY, AND I DON'T KNOW HOW MANY WEEKS LATER

I hope you don't mind, Annie, but I'm going to switch to writing to Paul for a little bit. I realized after I re-read that last entry that maybe I could write some things down, like a script, and maybe, just maybe, I could make sure he hears these words. Maybe is the best I can do. Perhaps this is just a set of desperate scribblings by a broken man who doesn't know how else to do this, but what do I have to lose? I'm just going to do it.

Dear Paul,

Before I write much about anything, I want to ask that you forgive me. I know I've been distant. I know I've not been able to fully understand you, and I see I have been the one who lost out because of that. I'm not going to make any excuses, but I will say that I want you to know that I am a man who has struggled with some nasty demons all of his life. Maybe, at your age now, you understand this.

"I wish I didn't understand that, Dad. I'm about to be a grandfather, and I wish you were here now..." Paul said softly.

"Really? A grandfather?" Tim asked. Paul nodded.

"We're passing Strawberry Cove now, Tim. Parson's Landing should be on the left in a couple of minutes."

"I've got that lesson down now, Captain. It's not the left, it's the port side!" Tim smiled at his friend. Paul nodded and smiled in return.

Chapter 33

"It's just like I remember it, Tim. This place has not changed a bit!" Paul exclaimed as he pulled back on the ship's throttle. Tim shielded his eyes from the mid-day sun. A pretty cove with rocks and a sandy beach was in view.

"Looks a little rocky, Paul. How are we going to get the boat in there?"

"We're not. Look in the cabin – we have an inflatable raft. We'll anchor about fifty yards out and go in on the raft. Hold on. I want to get a better angle on the cove…" Paul said as he turned the boat into the slight harbor. They were moving slowly.

"Yep, I think this is it." Tim pulled out a rolled up rubber craft. Paul nodded.

"It sure is. Let's get anchored and I'll show you how to pop that thing open!" Paul said.

"Will do. Uh, wait. What should I do?"

"There's an anchor up front. We'll put down a second one from the rear, but let's get the big one down in front first." Paul pointed.

"That will hold us?" Tim asked.

"Oh, yeah. The anchor has these flukes on it, kind of like wings. As it drags along those flukes dig into the sea bed. A second anchor insures we're good and tight."

"Aye-aye!" Tim responded and went forward.

- - -

"So, we're anchored, and the raft is ready to go. What do you say we get to shore?" Paul rubbed his hands together.

"Are you sure about this thing? It, uh, looks like it, uh, bobs around a lot." Tim studied the small craft.

"Not as much as you think. It'll have your weight and mine on it – and we have that little outboard motor. We'll be fine. Take my word for it, Tim. Besides, look how close the shore is. We'll be there in about a minute and a half." Paul pointed as Tim wiped his mouth.

"Kind of hungry…maybe we could wait a bit…?"

"No, Tim. The food is on the raft. Hey, if it'll help, I brought some really great chow for lunch. Just like what we Scouts had all those years ago. Come on – you can do this."

"Yeah, what kind of food?"

"Got to find out on shore!" Paul laughed. Tim watched as Paul slid over the side of the boat and planted himself squarely on the raft. Tim noticed that the bobbing did diminish once Paul's weight was on it. It seemed clear to Tim that Paul had experience doing this.

Tim slid over the rail, just as Paul did, and extended his leg, imitating his friend. At that moment a swell of the ocean pushed the raft up, then dropped it. Tim's foot missed its intended target just as he let go of the railing; he tumbled into the ocean.

"Gah!" He yelled. Tim slowly gained his composure and started treading water.

"Got to learn how to read the surface, Tim! But that wasn't a bad way to fall into the Pacific, I must say! You had style!" Paul had a huge grin on his face.

"What the…" Tim started, but a splash of water hit him in the mouth.

"Hold on. Here…" Paul picked up and threw a rope with a life-saving ring on its end. Tim reached out and grabbed it.

"Thanks…" Tim was pulling the ring closer.

"Anything hurt?" Paul asked.

"I think I twisted my wrist. And my phone is either gone or totally soaked now. What do I do?" Tim asked.

"Glad to hear you didn't break anything. The easiest thing to do might be to just hold on to the ring. I'll get us closer to shore. You'll be able to walk soon - on the ocean bottom."

"Whatever works – get us over there…" Tim was stressed. Paul started the small outboard motor and pointed the raft toward the shore.

"Casting off!" Paul called out. The lines to the ship were disconnected, and the raft moved toward land. In less than two minutes Tim was able to start walking on the bottom. Paul beached the raft between two rocks, and Tim walked up beside the small boat.

"That's one heck of a lousy way to make a landing…" Tim grumbled.

"Any landing you can walk away from it is a good landing! And you're walking, my friend!"

"Hey, I used to work on jet engines, remember? That saying's for airplanes!" Tim shook his head as he tried to push and squeeze water from his clothing.

"Works here, too..." Paul shrugged. Tim was searching through his pockets.

"Crap."

"Something wrong?" Paul asked.

"My phone. It is gone."

- - -

"The tent's up, and the gear's laid out. Deck chairs. Check. Ice chest. Check. Tools, check. Sleeping bags, first aid kit. All good. You have your duffel and I have mine." Paul looked around.

"Still don't get why we brought sleeping bags." Tim shook his head.

"Always prepared. You never know what to expect when you hit the beach, my boy."

"Playing the old World War II Scoutmaster, huh?" Tim teased.

"Where do you think I learned it?" Paul nodded.

"So, about that lunch you promised?" Tim asked.

"Good point. We deserve it! Let's dig into that ice chest!" Paul walked over, opened the chest and extracted two large sandwiches.

"Whoa..." Tim exclaimed.

"So, you like submarine sandwiches, huh?" Paul chuckled.

"Oh, yeah!" Tim leaned over and took one.

"You didn't get the joke…"

"Joke?"

"Submarine – the ocean. Submarine sandwiches?" Paul smiled. Tim shook his head and suppressed a smile.

"That's beyond lame, Paul." Tim answered.

"Hey, you taking a dive into the ocean made it even funnier! Get it? Submarine? Dive?" Paul unwrapped his food.

"Being on an island does something weird to you!" Tim smiled.

"I'm a kid again…" Paul took a bite and started chewing. He slowly scanned the hills and rocks around him.

"While we're taking a break, want to hear more from your dad?"

"That would be interesting. I heard from him here, all those years ago. You know, it just hit me – you were probably not even born when he and I camped here."

"Maybe." Tim replied. Paul stopped chewing and shook his head.

"On second thought, let's not count the years…" Paul shook his head.

"Well, here's more from the great author…"

"Uh, don't spill mustard on the papers." Paul pointed.

You remember Grandpa, my father, and how cold he was. I remember trying to do anything that would get him to hug me, or smile at me, or praise me. I never learned how to be a dad, my son, except by trial and lots of errors.

It breaks my heart that you may have seen me in a way similar to how I saw my father. I hope I was a little better. I see that you are better with your children, so I think, just maybe, I was a bit better than my dad. Well, I hope. There's that word again.

Sometimes when we have little else, we can find some way to hope for something better. That's why I write this. I can say that I love you, and I do, but I am praying for a way, some sort of a sign that will take you beyond hope, to a knowing deep in your heart, with certainty.

I hope there is something in any of these meanderings, somehow, that you can point at and say, "Now I believe." If I could know you felt that way, I would feel something deep inside myself, and we could share love, the true love between a father and his son. Maybe I don't make any sense at all.

I kind of figured that I'd write this down just in case I can't get it done. I've fallen short too many times. At least I wrote down that I love you with all of my heart, even if I had a hard time spitting the words out of my mouth.

One last request – just blurt out "I love you" when you see your own son next time. Break this stupid multi-generational chain…please.

To P.M. from Daddy. (Can you remember when I called you that decades ago?)

Paul slowly stopped chewing. Tim picked up a small bag of chips and opened them.

"I kind of understand how you're feeling, Paul. Reading this stuff makes me miss him, too." Tim said softly.

"I understand what he means – now. I feel the same way about my own kids. I can only hope they know that I love them. I don't know much about how to show it either."

"Maybe being here again, finding your blue box, will help? After all, the last time he was here it was with you, and that box." Tim said.

"No."

"No? What do you mean?" Tim asked.

"Remember when we came back as a family, and he was gone all day?"

"Yeah…"

"Where do you think he went?" Paul asked.

"Here? He came here - alone?"

"He did. I got a hint back then and didn't know it."

"What do you mean – a hint?" Tim asked.

"Ever see something and not really understand what you were looking at until decades later?"

"Maybe. I'm not sure."

"He dropped his jacket that night, on the hotel room floor. My mom asked me to hang it up for him, and I did. Inside the pocket was an invoice - sticking out. It said 'Parson's Landing' on it. I didn't think about it much then, but I did know the words and what they meant. I asked to go back that second trip, but my father had shut that down."

"Okay. So, when did it hit you?" Tim asked.

"Decades later – during a phone call with my mom, just before she died. She reminded me about that trip, the one we took as a family. She asked me if I remember him coming back from being gone. Of course I connected the image of the invoice in my mind as she spoke."

"Then I guess he didn't find the blue box, since we're here now."

"No, he didn't. He never even told me, directly, that he came back here alone. I think he was ashamed that he didn't find it."

"Hold on a minute. Something dawned on me. We might have a big problem, Paul." Tim put his hand up and stopped chewing his sandwich. He swallowed.

"A problem?" Paul asked.

"Yeah. What makes you think that you can find that box now, all these years later?" Tim worried that the odds were against them.

"Well, if he had just asked me, back then, I could have given him a map that I drew to remember where it would be." Paul reached into his duffel and pulled out a plastic envelope. Inside of that was a yellowed piece of paper.

"No way! A real treasure map!" Tim leaned over to look closely.

"Well, it depends on how you define treasure." Paul responded.

"That brings up a question, Paul. I still don't know what's in there, what is so important to drag us on this trip."

Paul paused and looked at the map for a long time. He took a deep breath. Tim wondered if he had heard him.

"Paul?"

"Can you trust me on this? It's a little embarrassing. When we find it, I'll tell you. It's hard for me to explain. I'm not sure you'd understand the mind of a twelve year old."

"It's not the mind of a twelve year old that has been pushing us this far." Tim commented.

"In some ways, it is the twelve year old in me that is doing this, yes." Paul looked down.

"Well, I guess we've come this far. Might as well see what we can find."

"That's the spirit!" Paul perked up.

"After all this time and travel I have to find out whatever this is that's driving you." Tim said as Paul stood up and pointed.

"So, do you see those two rocks there, next to the cliffs?"

"Yeah."

"When I saw them I knew I could find the box. Here, look…" Paul flattened the old paper on the top of the duffel bag. Tim saw two round objects next to a curve of the bay. There was a line that went up the cliffs between them. Near the top were two other large rocks.

"That line?" Tim asked.

"That little dry creek – right there." Paul pointed again.

"And that 'x'?" Tim gestured.

"As the old pirates used to say, 'x marks the spot'!" Paul nodded.

"Oh, I see where you mean. Yeah, it looks right. But, I have to ask…" Tim stopped.

"I know what you're thinking. Is it still there?" Paul responded.

"The question is definitely bouncing around in my mind, yes."

"Tim, I'm going on hope here. There's no guarantee, but I buried that sucker really well. I mean, there was no way that Mark or his stupid friends would be able to get at it."

"You were determined…" Tim nodded.

"Oh, yeah. I'm not sure if it was this way when you were a boy, but, to me, they were the 'big boys.' There always seemed to be some older guys who were determined to make life miserable for the younger ones."

"Believe me - that did NOT change with my generation!" Tim was emphatic.

"So, I had to be tougher than they were. I had to be smarter and to dig deeper than they would be willing to go." The two men looked back up the slope leading between the two rocks.

"It sounds like you were a smart kid. I guess we'll see if those smarts paid off all this time later." Tim said.

"It's weird. All these years, I've wondered if it is still there. Is what's inside still okay?"

"Well, there's only one way to find out. We have to hike up there with a shovel." Tim said.

"I piled a ton of rocks up there. It has to be there. It just has to be…"

"That's strange. I piled stones for your dad…"

"So now you'll tear some down for me. We'll do it together." Paul smiled.

"Don't forget that I work for Mike and Ike candies!" Tim responded. Paul reached into his duffel bag and pulled out a new box.

"Like these?" He smiled.

Chapter 34

"I know it's here. It's between these two big rocks, under a pile of stones. I remember there was a big dark red stone..." Paul said as he scrambled across the slope, digging with his gloved hands. Tim straightened up, leaning on the shovel he was holding.

"Paul, you keep saying that! We've been digging for two hours. Look at your map again. You got something wrong." Tim said with an agitated tone. Paul, breathing hard, stopped and slumped down on a rock. He stared at Tim as he pulled out his ancient hand-drawn map.

"Two big rocks. Wait. I show...a third rock here, above...the two big ones." Paul spoke with difficulty as he looked around. He was trying to catch his breath. Tim pointed further up the slope.

"Maybe that one?" Tim asked.

"Could...be..." Paul leaned back.

"Hey, wait. How could you have hidden your box when the whole camp down there could have seen you?" Tim asked while wiping the sweat from his brow.

"I did it at night. Alone."

"You're kidding me. Then how could you remember these stones?" Tim asked.

"I planned it out before dark, then drew the map. I knew where I would put it."

"How soon before dark?" Tim wondered.

"It was really late." Paul took a deep breath – finally.

"So, could a shadow have looked like a rock to you back then? Which way would the sun have come from then?"

"The west." Paul pointed.

"I wonder if we should wait until the sun starts getting lower and we can see where the shadows fall." Tim said.

"That's a brilliant idea! That long rock on the map might be a shadow." Paul exclaimed. Tim paused in wiping his head.

"Wait. That's not so brilliant. How will we get back to Avalon tonight?"

"I'm up for camping overnight. We brought the equipment." Paul answered.

"Let's try to get out earlier. I think Shannon will freak out if we're missing. There's no cell service here. My phone went into the drink and yours has no bars."

"I'll tell you what. Let's go back down to camp and watch as the shadows grow. As soon as I get a bearing, we'll come back."

"Agreed. I could use a break anyway." Tim started down the slope. Paul followed. As they clambered down Paul reached out to steady himself. His hand missed the rock he was reaching for, and he tumbled. He landed on his back and slid halfway to the valley below.

"ARGH... Help!" He screamed as he skidded to a stop.

"Paul!" Tim shouted

"Uh. Can't...get...up..." Paul said with pain.

"Don't move. Hold on - I'm coming." Tim huffed as he worked his way across the slope toward the injured man. Small stones tumbled from under his shoes.

"Slow. Don't get hurt...loose...rocks..." Paul called back to Tim. As Tim got closer he noticed that Paul's left arm and shoulder looked odd. He closed his eyes – he wasn't good with injuries involving broken bones or blood, and this looked like it was one of those situations. Paul's leg looked bloody, too.

"I've got to get you down." Tim gently pulled on the older man's right side.

"I can't get up..." It was obvious that Paul was in serious pain. Tim worked to create a handle in Paul's shirt by folding the cloth.

"I'm going to use your shirt to pull you down. Just try to relax..." Bit by bit Tim edged Paul closer to the beach. As they made it to the sand, Tim rolled over and tried to catch his breath.

"My left arm feels numb, Tim. What's going on?" Paul tried to sit up.

"Stay there!" Tim pointed and shouted. Paul sat back again.

"Is it…is it broken?"

"I think so. I don't know. I'm going to move the tent over here. I'm not going to try and drag you across the sand, and the way your leg looks I don't think you should be walking."

"No, I can't. I think we have some pain killer in the first aid kit. I need it…my leg burns." Tim sat up and looked at Paul's leg – there were a number of shallow scrapes bleeding into the sand.

"Looks like some scrapes. I'll get the kit. You stay right here and, I don't know, maybe watch the shadows on the hill…" Tim worked to find something that would distract Paul from his injuries. As he stood up he noticed Paul was already watching the shadows. Tim scanned the area around them as he walked, trying to find help, but they were alone on the beach.

"My stupid luck. Nobody around." Tim mumbled.

Tim pulled the tent over to Paul, and then went back for the rest of the equipment. Over the next half an hour he re-established their shelter and lined up the equipment around his injured friend.

"Tim, you have to check our raft. Make sure it's secure. The tide may be changing soon." Paul said.

Tim glanced over and noticed that the water was pushing the raft back and forth. He ran over and pulled it up further on to the shore, then tied it off on a large rock. He stumbled into camp, exhausted.

"I think we're set for now, but we have a big problem, my friend. We have to get you some medical help."

"Tim, there's ice in the cooler. On my arm…that will help." Paul suggested. Tim pulled out a plastic bag and filled it with ice.

"Less than that – we have to make this last." Paul said. Tim nodded and poured some of the ice back.

"Understood." Tim then took a rag and cleaned off the worst scrape on Paul's leg. It wasn't as bad as Tim had feared. He sat down under a lean-to he had erected; he was exhausted. The two men sat in silence for a long time.

"Tim! The shadow! I see the shadow! Look!" Paul struggled to sit up.

"Where?" Tim turned over. He followed Paul's extended finger. It was difficult for Paul to raise his arm.

"The point of the shadow!" Paul's voice was trembling.

"You mean next to that rock on the side of where we were digging?" Tim asked.

"Yes! You were right! I was fooled by the shadows!" Paul started breathing hard.

"Calm down…hold on. You'll go into shock." Tim gently pulled Paul back down to a lying position. He pulled a blanket from the tent.

"No, I'm okay, really. You have to do this. Go up there and I can signal you. Please, Tim!" Paul looked up at Tim.

"Paul, your health…." Tim said; Paul glared in return.

"Damn it. I've come this far. I can climb up there myself…" Paul tried to stand up. Tim reached out and held Paul down.

"No! You are in no condition." Tim commanded.

"Tim, I am so close…" Paul argued. Tim was startled to see that Paul was crying.

"I get that, but you're hurt." Tim's tone of voice softened.

"I don't know how much more clearly I can put this. I am going up there. I will not argue about it." Paul sounded adamant. Tim stared at his friend for a moment, looked up at the slope and then back at his friend.

"Let's make a deal. I'll make one try for it - no more."

"That's all I ask. I know we can find it." Paul nodded.

"No. You will stay here. I'll go up, but not you. I can't drag you back down again. My arm really hurts."

"I understand, and I agree."

"You really have no choice. Look at your arm. Your leg…" Tim said as Paul looked down and nodded.

"You're right." Paul whispered. An uncomfortable silence filled the moment.

"You know, you're asking a lot of a man who you told back in Avalon that he could not call you 'dad'." Tim shook his head and chuckled nervously. It was either laugh or cry, he thought.

"Tim, if you find that box, you can call me whatever you want. Damn it, you could call me 'grandma'!" Paul slowed his crying and managed a small smile. Tim nodded.

The younger man stood up, took a few steps up the slope and looked back at Paul. He looked past the camp. There was the HNLJU, bobbing on the water, with the blue and yellow cross flag still fluttering in the late afternoon breeze.

"Let's give it a try, then."

"Yes...try. I'll signal you, left or right. Keep going. Get the shovel!" Paul said as Tim found the shovel, right where he had dropped it.

"Okay..." Tim said as he started climbing.

"Go up. Left. Further left. Yes..." Paul directed Tim with his one hand. Every five or six steps, Tim looked back, moving according to Paul's instructions.

"How much further?" Tim called out.

"Almost on top of it! To the right just a bit. Are there red stones there?" Paul asked. Tim looked down and found a number of large red stones.

"Yes, to my right!" Tim shouted.

"Are the big rocks down here like what the map looked like?" Paul asked.

"Yes, I think so!"

"Tim! You're there. DIG!" Paul shouted to the best of his ability.

"Okay, just sit back. Don't get up! Stay in the shade!" Tim responded. He put on his gloves and picked up the shovel.

Tim dug and pulled at rocks. Some he pushed away; others he dug at with the shovel. He looked for something blue, but found nothing but gray sand, red and brown rocks - and a piece of rusty green metal.

"No blue box, Paul!" Tim shouted.

"It has to be there! It just has to be! What do you see?"

"Sand. Red and brown rocks, and a rusty green thing." Tim was breathing hard. He felt dizzy as he looked up and noticed the sun. It was getting very low on the horizon. It was then and there that he realized there was no way he could get Paul to the boat and get back to Avalon, let alone Huntington Harbor.

"TIM! TIM! THAT'S IT! You found it!" Paul screamed as he tried to stand.

"Paul, STOP! I will not do any more until you sit down!" Tim yelled angrily as he pointed at the older man. Paul appeared startled, then slowly returned to his place under the lean-to.

"Tim, that's it..." Paul's voice was quieter.

"It's not a blue box! That's it. Look! The sun is going down!" Tim yelled as he pointed. He turned as if to go back to camp.

"Tim, STOP! Listen to me. Please, just listen. Think about it. I painted it blue – my dad had some old tractor enamel paint. If the paint wore off, underneath it would be Army green, like olive drab. Does it look like that?"

"Damn it." Tim stopped and cursed under his breath as he looked down.

"I'll see how big this metal thing is. Then it's over. Do you understand? I am dog tired." Tim barked. Paul nodded.

Using his gloved hands, Tim pulled stones and sand away from the object. He got enough of it exposed to see the corner, then sat down. A gentle breeze buffeted his hat.

"Tim?" Paul called out. Tim barely heard his name – the wind seemed to carry it away.

"Holy unbelievable crap. It IS Army green - and it's metal." Tim whispered to himself.

"Tim! Can you hear me?" Paul shouted. His voice trembled a bit.

"Yes, I can hear you!" Tim shouted back as he brushed dirt from the box.

"What is it?

"It's metal! It's a rusted box and it is mostly Army green!" Tim shouted.

"Oh! Oh my God! You found it! Tim, you did it." Paul shouted. Tim could hear his friend crying, the tears slowly turning to laughter.

"Not yet – I have to get it out of here and down the hill. Whatever little kid buried this really didn't want it found!" Tim teased. Paul laughed from below.

"All these years later and here it is." Tim shook his head as he whispered to himself. He finished digging and extracted the battered box.

Chapter 35

"Well, 'dad', is this what you were looking for?" Tim asked as he approached the camp. He had a big grin on his face. He was holding a shovel and a beat-up, rusted, corroded Army green metal ammunition can.

"Oh, Tim! That has to be it...it has to..." Paul was crying gently.

"I hope so! You didn't bury two or three out here, did you?" Tim chuckled.

"No, no. But if you happen to find Mark's box, I'll happily dump it overboard on the trip back!" Paul smiled.

"Sorry, only one box per customer. This is yours, the one you get." Tim said as Paul reached out.

"Look there – I can still see flecks of blue paint near the rim!" Paul said as Tim handed the beaten object to him. Tim turned to watch the sun sink below the crest of the hill. He looked the other way and watched as the last rays of the sun streamed across the small valley that surrounded them.

"I absolutely know it's yours, Paul. You neglected to tell me that you scratched the letters "P.M." under the handle." Tim smiled.

"That's right. I did."

"I'll get a lantern fired up. It'll be dark soon." Tim went into the tent and returned with a portable light.

"I'm too nervous, Tim, and my arm hurts like the dickens. Can you open it for me? I hope the stuff inside isn't ruined. I have to know. There are a couple of items that mean everything…" Paul stopped talking quickly.

"Yeah, I'll open it. Now I really have to know what's inside." Tim nodded as he sat down in the sand. He pulled the battered box closer.

"Yes…" Paul nodded.

"I'm going to have to use the claw end of the hammer – the lid may be corroded shut." Tim reached for the tool box and pulled out a hammer. He positioned the claw under the front of the lid and pulled. The lid moved a bit. He kept working around the edge of the box, inch by inch, until the hinge, aged with rust, gave way.

"Well?" Paul asked.

"Almost there. Just…pulling…" At that moment the top of the box popped up.

"You got it!" Paul shouted.

"Here, I'll let you do the honors. Take a look inside." Tim slid the opened box to Paul, who anxiously tugged on it. He leaned over and looked inside.

"Yes, better than I had hoped!" Paul smiled.

"So, can you let me in on the secret now?" Tim asked as he pulled a soda from the ice chest.

"I am more than happy to do that. I can't believe we did it. You did it…" Paul praised his friend.

"We did it. We both made this happen, 'dad'." Tim smiled.

"Okay, 'son' – there, I said it!" Paul returned the smile, then reached into the box.

"So, it just looks like worn cloth on top…" Tim noticed.

"A lot of this stuff is like extra underwear and a pair of socks. I worried about things like that back then."

"We made this trip for old underwear? Heck, I would have stopped at the store and just bought you a package if I'd had known that!" Tim shook his head and smiled.

"No, no. Hold on. Look! My Boy Scout manual is here."

"We could have picked that up for you, too. There's a BSA store near us."

"…and some papers. Just some of my poems. I used to write poems. I think they're ruined, though…" Paul shook his head.

"Okay, now I understand why you were afraid of that Mark character getting into the box. That would be embarrassing." Tim took a sip of his drink and smiled.

"…a little yellow Matchbox Jeep. Yes, there it is. One of my favorite toys when I was a kid."

"Really? Okay, now I'm interested!" Tim looked closely at the toy.

"…a little crucifix from my bedroom. I used to take it with me whenever we travelled."

"Okay. Understandable there. I don't see anything too weird about this stuff, Paul. Well, maybe the underwear." Tim looked in and only saw what appeared to be an old rag, wrapped tightly.

"There is one more thing."

"Oh?" Tim asked as Paul gently unwrapped the old rag. There was another piece of cloth inside - Tim noticed it looked like a woman's handkerchief. Paul gently unwrapped that, too.

"Shannon has a handkerchief like that. She said it was a lady's handkerchief or something."

"That's what it is. From my mother." Paul whispered. He touched it lovingly as he unfolded it carefully.

"They're...they're here..." Paul's voice was almost inaudible. He began to cry quietly as he clutched the objects in his hand. He pulled his hand to his chest. Tim stayed silent.

"What are they? I didn't see..." Tim leaned over. He turned on the small light as the sun was almost gone below the horizon. Paul was bathed in the rays from the light. Heavy shadows covered him where his arm blocked the rays.

Paul slowly opened his hand. He was breathing hard.

"My mother's pearl earrings. They're with me again, after all this time." Paul was unabashedly crying.

"You mean, like the pearl necklace?" Tim whispered.

"Yes, yes. My mother made these earrings from some of the pearls my father gave her over the years, you know, the ones from her birthdays. These two were for my sister and me." Paul started to cry. Tim stood up and helped his friend adjust to a better position. He pulled a sleeping bag from the tent and put it next to Paul.

Paul would not let go of the pearls. He held them up to admire their glow in the dim light but it was obvious he was struggling to stay upright and awake.

Chapter 36

Tim sat quietly next to the tent, looking up at the billions of stars above him. The glow of the dim lantern allowed him to check on his friend every few minutes. As he glanced at the older man for what must have been the fiftieth time he noticed Paul was stirring.

"How are you doing now?" Tim asked. Paul looked around as if he were confused. He stared at a campfire burning nearby.

"You're on Catalina. It's night. I lit a fire – I hope it'll keep any wild animals away. It sure is dark out here." Tim was trying to be helpful.

"Yeah..." Paul mumbled.

"How's the shoulder?" Tim asked. Paul sat up quickly and looked around.

"The pearls..."

"Got them right here. You were really out. I put them in this plastic bag. They're fine." Tim handed the bag to his friend.

"I owe you, Tim. I can't tell you what this means to me."

"Maybe you can try?" Tim asked. Paul took a deep breath.

"I should do that. I'm sorry."

"No apologies necessary. I can tell there's more behind this than I know."

"Oh, yes. Yes. I wanted to come here for camp, but I have to admit that I was scared, too. I guess I was kind of a momma's boy. My mother knew I needed to get out on my own more, so she wanted my dad and me to go to camp."

"Okay so far." Tim nodded.

"As we were leaving, I told her how scared I was. I'm sure she could tell. Mom immediately pulled these off of her ears. She told me I could borrow them, and when I got back, I would return them. She wrapped them in her kerchief and gave them to me just before we drove off early that morning. It was so dark." Paul paused and looked up at the night sky.

"I get it. You'd have something of your mother's to 'hold on to'."

"Yes. I'm not proud of that. I hope you can understand."

"Strangely, I do. We all do that, each in our own way. Kind of like 'Peg Leg' and your dad's letter." Tim nodded.

"Nobody, especially a guy, wants to admit they're weak like this. We just learn how to cover it deeper and deeper as we get older." Paul said.

"You speak the truth, my friend." Tim agreed.

"There's more."

"Oh?"

"My dad buried the box for me – the first time."

"The first time? What?"

"Yes. It was over there…" Paul pointed into the dark, in the opposite direction from where the box had been found.

"I'll be…"

"He decided he was 'helping' me, I think. He found out what was going on, with the older boys, but I noticed that the older boys saw him hide it. It wasn't rally buried, but he thought it was. He just hid it behind some rocks."

"Okay, I get it."

"So, I snuck out that night and buried it, only in a new place. I worked quietly, and I think I was up there half the night. Just before he died we talked about it, and he was shocked that I had done that. Our communications were so bad that this could have all been easily fixed years ago."

"Yeah, I'd say so!" Tim nodded.

"And what's weirder is that I let the kids tease me about being afraid of camping on Catalina. I didn't want them to know that my father had the real fear of boats. A boy wants to be proud of his dad. He saw them ripping me up for being afraid, and he couldn't admit his fear, so he decided to help me by hiding the box. It was his way of defending me, even if it was weak."

"We dads do strange things sometimes..." Tim whispered; Paul nodded.

Chapter 37

Tim noticed that Paul was shaking, and he knew it what it meant. He had seen enough injuries in his years running an engine shop to know when shock was setting in. Every now and then Paul had a pained expression on his face as he touched his injured arm or leg

"It'll be getting cold tonight, Paul. You really should get into the tent. I think you'd be better off." Paul nodded as Tim stood up and walked toward the injured man.

"Yeah. I'm pretty cold..." Paul's voice was uneven. Tim picked up a blanket and put it over Pau's shoulder.

"Here. Can you grab my arm?" Tim held out his hand as he assisted Paul in standing. Paul was unsteady but was able to rise. They walked slowly into the tent. Tim turned on a small flashlight then helped Paul to lie down.

"Good. Let's get you into the sleeping bag." Tim said as Paul helped as best he could.

"See? The bags came in handy. Scouts are prepared..." Paul said. Tim nodded.

Tim crawled back outside and looked toward the ocean. He could barely make out the outline of the HNLJU, anchored in the small bay.

"Good night, whatever your name is..." Tim saluted toward the boat. He gathered a number of other pieces of equipment, including the other sleeping bag and both of their duffels, and dragged them into the tent. After he zipped up the fly of the tent up he turned on a second flashlight.

"Not too bad, Tim..." Paul said. His voice sounded a bit more relaxed now.

"Yeah. The perfect little camp, with all the comforts of home!"

"Sorry, Tim, but not quite. Merrie would make it perfect!" Paul smiled. Tim nodded with a half-smile.

"Yeah, I get it. You're no match for Shannon, you know."

"So, we'll call this 'Camp Bachelor'." Paul announced.

"You got that right..." Tim said as he settled down into his own sleeping bag. His joints and muscles hurt; he massaged his left wrist.

"Still got my father's journal?" Paul asked.

"Not sure I feel much like reading, to be honest."

"I'll do it. You're read enough." Paul offered. Tim nodded as he reached into his duffel. He pulled out the notebook.

"Here you go." Tim rolled on to his other side.

"Well, this is rich. Get a load of how this starts..." Paul began.

MONDAY

Well, Annie, we found another note, in the first aid box. How did you know I'd need that sooner or later? I got hurt and Shannon helped me out. She's been such a great helper. That's why I said that "we" found the note.

"First aid box! And look at you now!" Tim laughed gently.

317

Recently I've been kind of down, and feeling lost. Maybe I sound upbeat (I don't know), but I have some down times. I wish they would leave me alone. When I read your words – the ones in which you remembered why you married me – I felt like I had a life raft to cling to. Your notes have done that for me.

"Okay, that's too weird. A life raft?" Tim asked. Paul shrugged.

You worried that I needed to forgive you. I cannot find anything you did that I should forgive you for. I mean that, but I know how this goes, though. We need to hear that we are forgiven, no matter what.

Anne, I completely forgive you for ANYTHING you want me to forgive you for, but I honestly feel no grievance against you. Your notes, these bits of love wrapped in pink, have more than covered anything you've said or done for our entire lives. I mean that.

WEDNESDAY

Well, Anne, I just had to let you know that I got a box of chocolate chip cookies from Maine! The note apologized to you for them being late, but I didn't care. Hey, look how

screwed up my journaling system is! The cookies were
great but what is really important is that someone has to
teach Tim how to not eat and talk at the same time!

"Oh, man, I remember those cookies from Maine! They
were good! I wish I had some now!" Tim interjected.

"They were good. We used to get them every time we
went back there, when I was a kid." Paul added.

The two men were startled by the sound of the wind
picking up. The tent twisted back and forth. Both took a deep
breath at once.

"My mom ordered them every year. We got them in the
mail." Paul said in a monotone. The wind picked up again.

"Now I'm hungry." Tim whispered as he stared at the entry
flap.

"It's just the wind, Tim. No need to worry."

"No, not the wind. I mean it - I'm hungry. What's in the ice
chest?" Tim sat up and reached for the box. The wind died
down.

"Pull something out. I'll keep reading."

SATURDAY

Hey, Anne, can you see the stone wall? Check out these
muscles! I'm really built now! Yep, I feel strong enough
to climb Pine Mountain. That old man has been laughing

at me - still. I think it won't be long before I take him down a notch or two…

"Well, this mountain on Catalina took ME down a notch or two…" Paul chuckled.

"Or I took you down from a notch on this mountain." Tim responded with a smile. The wind picked up for another moment, and the two men looked at the entry flap again.

"So, what do we have to eat?" Paul leaned over and squinted.

"On tonight's menu you have a choice. Would you prefer a frozen burrito that's thawed or some cereal from a little box or a raw hot dog in a bun? We have raisins, too."

"Oh?" Paul looked at Tim.

"Or we could have a burrito-cereal-hot dog-raisin sandwich, if that's appealing! But no cheese or chipotle or chili!" Tim smiled.

"Uh, I think I'll go simple." Paul smiled weakly. He looked at the entrance to the tent. Tim started shaking his head.

"Nope, no, no way. I know what you're thinking. I am not going out there to the fire…" Tim shook his head.

"Thawed burrito, then." Paul said with a sigh.

"An excellent choice. The chef's special tonight…" Tim pulled two soggy burritos out of the water in the ice chest. He pulled out an old pocket knife.

"Was that my father's pocket knife?" Paul pointed.

"Yeah, it was in the orange box. Thought it would come in handy." Tim answered.

"I think it will. How are we doing for ice?" Paul asked.

"We can maybe make one more ice pack, then all we've got is the ibuprofen in the first aid kit." Tim said quietly. A gust of wind made Tim turn quickly toward the tent flap.

"I hate the wind…" Paul whispered.

- - -

Paul finished the last of his burrito, then leaned back. Tim was staring into the ice chest again.

"Hoping there's a black bean quesadilla in there, Tim?" Paul smiled.

"Oh, yeah. Or some of Shannon's pasta primavera. Either one would be great right about now."

"Well, we've got slim pickings there. Are considering a hot dog?" Paul asked.

"Yeah, I guess. A man gets hungry looking for old ammo boxes on Catalina Island." Tim pointed at the end of the tent, toward the box.

"Ugh." Paul shook his head.

"I take that to mean you don't want a hot dog, huh?" Tim smiled. Paul shook his head.

"You eat – I'll read. Not sure I can stomach much more raw food."

TUESDAY

This is it, Annie. Tomorrow I'm attacking that old Pine Mountain. He has irritated me enough all of these years. Tim and Shannon will go with me, and I will make it to the top – I promise you. That crazy mountain will feel differently about me after this trip! I'll fill you in on how it goes after I get home.

I have to admit something to you. Like a man totally obsessed, I've looked all over this building for more of your pink notes. I feel like there's got to be one more there, somewhere. Where did you put it? I can't believe it is in this house. I've looked in just about every cranny. Maybe after I get back I'll find it.

I also have to admit that I never told you something. I would say that I forgot, but we've known each other too long. I didn't want to tell you, but maybe you already knew. Somebody stole your pearl necklace. I haven't forgotten, and I will get it back. I am pretty sure I know who has them.

Never forget that Joey loves Annie. And Paul, and Sarah. I love all of you, in my own, broken way. I hope you can hear this…

"Hey, did you ever find any more notes from your mom, you know, maybe ones that your dad never found?" Tim asked.

"Just that one that Shannon, you and I found at the end of the stone wall years ago. I think my dad tore the house apart looking for more. He had a nice stack of them."

"Hah! He missed it! Tore the house apart but missed the one in the pile of rocks!"

"Yeah. We think we look everywhere, but we always miss one spot." Paul nodded.

The wind blew, a bit more quietly, and the flap sounds became more rhythmic. The two men just stared at the point of light from the flashlight, shining on the roof of the tent.

"Going to read more…?" Tim asked.

"Huh?"

"Read?" Tim whispered. The tent grew silent, except for the faint sound of the wind in the distance. He leaned over and noticed that Paul's eyes were closed. His hands were still holding his father's journal. Tim leaned over to check Paul's breathing; he noticed his chest was rising and falling. Tim pulled the blanket up over Paul's shoulder.

"Good night…" He whispered.

Chapter 38

Tim was awakened by a strange, distant gurgling sound. He opened his eyes as he tossed and turned. He noticed that the orange tent was glowing on one side - it was after sunrise. Tim pulled up his wrist and looked at his watch.

"Almost eight o'clock. Whoa." He whispered. He heard the distant sound again, but from another direction.

"Harrg..." Paul was snoring.

"Well, I suppose snoring is a good sign, medically speaking." Tim took a deep breath. He propped his pillow and re-settled himself back into his sleeping bag. He decided to let Paul get more sleep. It was very quiet, and very still. Even the wind was minimal.

"BRAAA-HAAP!" A loud, mechanical sound screamed through the tent.

"What the HELL was that?" Tim sat up screaming.

"Huh? What? What was that? Tim? What happened?" Paul struggled to sit up.

"Lie back, I'll go check!" Tim yelled as he scrambled to the end of the tent. He was shaking as he looked around for something to protect himself with. He grabbed a hunting knife from the corner of the tent. As he exited he had to immediately shield his eyes from the bright sun. He thrust the knife out in front of him.

"HEY! BACK OFF!" Tim yelled in confusion, hoping he looked fierce. As he looked around he noticed there was no one nearby. All he saw was the large rock in front of him, and the slope where they had found the box. Then it happened again.

"BRAAA-HAAP!" Tim jumped again, turning toward the ocean. He stared out to the small cove. Next to the HNLJU was a large white ship, sporting a large reddish-orange and blue stripe on its side.

"Calm down...got to calm down..." Tim gasped for air.

"Tim! What's going on?" Paul had managed to get to the flaps of the tent.

"A ship, next to yours. Much bigger, with a blue and orange stripe on it." Tim was breathing hard as he pointed with the hunting knife. As Tim looked around he realized that the rocks hid the tent from a large part of the cove.

"The Coast Guard! YES! We're going to make it!" Paul shouted with laughter as he smiled. Tim turned to look at his friend.

"There was a doubt?" He managed to force a smile as he lowered the hunting knife.

"They're probably looking for us!"

"Hey, you told me the Coast Guard wouldn't be hunting us down!" Tim teased.

"Aren't you glad I was wrong? Go out and wave your shirt at them or something." Paul barked.

"Aye, aye, captain!" Tim yelled as he ran toward the cove.

- - -

"We'll have you on board in no time at all, Mr. Marino." The Coast Guard officer called out as two "coasties" lifted a stretcher. Tim watched as a coordinated lifting effort hoisted Paul safely to the deck of the big white ship.

"It seems you guys have done this sort of thing before!" Paul said nervously with a half-smile. He was gingerly holding his shoulder.

"I'll bet this isn't the first time this year." Tim smiled.

"Oh, we've had lots of practice. No problem at all." A "coastie" answered.

"Captain! Hoisting the gear!" Another man in uniform called out. Tim turned to look at the officer standing near him.

"Is that our gear he's talking about?" Tim asked.

"Oh, yes. We don't want to leave the beach full of litter."

"Tim! My box..." Paul called out suddenly from the stretcher. He sat up.

"No worries. Got it right here, Paul. Everything's inside." Tim lifted his duffel bag as another Coast Guard officer quickly approached Paul.

"Hold on, sir. Let me have a quick look at that shoulder..." He said. The officer held what looked like a medical emergency bag. Tim turned away and wiped his face.

"Oww…" Paul exclaimed as the man massaged and pulled on the joint. He also looked over Paul's leg.

"I don't think anything's broken, but I believe you've dislocated your shoulder. Captain…" The officer turned and called out to the man standing behind Tim. Tim turned to see who was in charge.

"Yes, ensign?" The captain was studying Paul's boat; he seemed to be perplexed.

"Sir, I believe he's ambulatory. It appears that he dislocated his shoulder. His leg has some minor scrapes, but nothing serious."

"Good report. Thanks. So, we have two forlorn sailors on board, and their gear."

"Correct." The ensign responded.

"All we have to arrange is a way to get their ship back to Avalon. The S.S. Huys will not sail itself." Tim turned suddenly when the captain spoke some sort of a name for Paul's ship. Paul looked over quickly.

"The S.S. what?" Paul asked.

"Sir, it's your ship. You don't know its name? And it's written on the stern?" The captain stared at Paul.

"We, uh, usually call it the Honiljoo, yeah, like it says on the back. Or we make up some meaning for the letters, like 'he's never leaving jeans unwashed'…" The captain, with a growing smile, turned toward Paul.

"The 'Honiljoo'? Oh, that's funny!" The captain chuckled.

"I'm sorry, I'm lost here." Paul shook his head.

"Captain!" The younger Coast Guard officer called out.

"What is it, Mister Boston?" He replied.

"All gear on board and stowed. Your orders for the civilian boat?"

"I believe that is the last issue, yes. Hold on…" The captain turned toward Tim.

"Well, Mr. Johnston, have you had much experience piloting a craft on the ocean? I don't believe Mr. Marino is up to the job, due to his injuries." The captain asked.

"Well, captain, um, realistically?" Tim looked uncomfortable.

"Oh, yes - we only deal with what's real out on the Pacific Ocean." The captain paused and looked Tim over.

"I'm okay with engines, but, I think I wouldn't know what to do with sailing it, to be honest." Tim said in a resigned tone.

"You're an honest man. I respect that. By the way, I'm Charles Monjian, Lieutenant, United States Coast Guard." The officer extended his hand as he looked over the now-small looking and properly named S.S. Huys. Tim shook his hand.

"Oh, yeah, well, thanks. Well, sir, I'm pretty green with boats."

"We don't need another rescue effort today. I'll have one of my people get her back."

I think you're right…" Tim agreed.

"Mister Boston!" The captain called out.

"Sir?" The captain turned so Paul, Tim and the other Coast Guard officer could hear.

"With your consent, the ensign here will bring the Huys back to Avalon, Mr. Marino. He'll have one of our best sailors along, so you won't have to worry about your boat."

"Of course, that would be great…but, the 'Huys?' How do you know it's said that way? Do you know the boat? Is it the way the letters look funny?" Paul asked. The captain smiled.

"I've never seen your ship before, Mister Marino. But I do read some Armenian. My grandparents were Armenian."

"Armenian? What?"

"Yes. 'Huys' is an Armenian word, and the lettering is in an Armenian font."

"Oh, wow. That makes sense. The man who sold me the boat had Armenian heritage. Said it had something to do with his mother."

"Well, maybe it was her name, but I doubt it." The captain replied.

"What does it mean?" Paul asked.

"In English, the Armenian word 'huys' means 'hope'." The captain replied. Paul turned and smiled at Tim.

"Man, were we wrong? We were so far off!" Paul said. Tim nodded.

"Maybe not so far off. Think about it, Paul." Tim looked over at his friend.

"What do you mean?"

"Hope brought you here." Tim pointed at the beach.

"Hope…" Paul nodded.

"And we'll get her back to Avalon, too." The captain added.

"Thanks…" Paul said softly.

"Mister Boston – take command of the 'Huys'!"

"Aye, aye, captain!"

Chapter 39

Tim held on to the rail as the Coast Guard ship plowed through the waves. He made his way to the captain's side.

"So, did Shannon call you guys? Just wondering why you started looking…" Tim asked.

"Yes, Mister Johnston, your wife called us in the wee hours of the night. She was pretty stressed. She told us you had promised to call. We got our crew and ship moving just before first light." The captain replied.

"But it doesn't take hours to get to Parson's Landing from Avalon on this thing." Tim answered.

"Nope, and we would have been here pretty quickly if we knew it was Parson's Landing. You were lucky we happened to be moored in Avalon last night. We usually operate out of the Los Angeles Harbor area."

"I guess we should buy a lottery ticket!" Paul smiled.

"Your wife was adamant about you two being at the Boy Scout camp. Around here that is Camp Cherry Valley. We did a search and, obviously, you weren't there. We did a scan of the ocean for debris and found nothing. We continued up the shoreline until we saw a Swedish vessel with an Armenian name!" The captain smiled.

"And then you blew the air horn!" Tim nodded.

"We knew that would get your attention. We found your ship unoccupied, and noticed a tent, but no sign of anyone about. We weren't sure where you were. I thought the air horn would save us some time scrambling around the shore. It did the job!"

"I really appreciated seeing you guys. Now I'm a huge Coast Guard fan!" Paul smiled.

"Well, we're about to dock, so I've got to handle some things. You guys will be on shore in a few minutes." The captain said as he turned toward Paul.

"That sounds really good to me!" Tim smiled.

"We're getting you to the hospital, Mister Marino. You should get an x-ray of that shoulder." Paul nodded at the captain's comments.

"Tim - don't forget the old box."

"Are you kidding? All this way just to lose it on a Coast Guard ship? Nope. Not going to happen." Tim smiled and tapped his duffel bag.

"Good man..." Paul nodded.

- - -

"Paul, look! It's 'Peg Leg'!" Tim pointed as the ship settled next to the dock.

"Let's call him Christian now, Tim." Paul looked troubled.

"You know Christian?" The captain asked.

"Well, not well. My dad kind of knew him. It was on that trip here decades ago, like I told you." Paul looked at the Coast Guard officer.

"Oh, wow, the son of the famous Mister Marino!" The captain smiled.

"What?" Tim asked.

"Everyone who comes through this dock has heard of your father."

"Amazing..." Paul whispered.

"Do you know anything about Christian?" Tim asked the captain.

"Hold on. Let's get it done right this time, boys."

"Aye, aye, sir." Two "coasties" answered.

"Not much. He's from Chicago. I heard he ran away from an alcoholic father, but no one really knows for sure. But he's a kind-hearted guy. Everybody sort of just looks out for him."

"That explains the Cubs hat." Paul mentioned.

"Cubs hat? How does that fit in?" The captain asked.

"I wore one here once, when I was a kid, and he ran from me – he seemed terrified. Mentioned he thought he was done with that place, or something like that."

"Paul..." Tim pointed. Christian noticed Paul and Tim on the ship.

"Oh, man. I promised him a book..." Paul whispered.

"A book?" The captain asked.

"Yeah. My dad used to bring them to him. I don't have one on me. Darn."

"I'll get one at the book store near that café while you're getting your arm checked." Tim said quietly.

"That'll work. I'd give you some money if I could get my wallet out."

"You can catch me on that later. Just get your arm checked..." Tim said as they walked off of the Coast Guard ship. The captain met them on the dock.

"I suggest you moor your boat here for a bit and find a way to come back for her. Take the Catalina Ferry home. Have someone pick you up."

"I think we'll do just that, captain. I don't know how to thank you." The men shook hands.

"Tim, let's meet at that clinic. You go get a book."

"What should I get?"

"I don't know. I always liked John Steinbeck – maybe find something by him?" Paul shook his head.

"Maybe we should meet here?" Tim asked.

"No. I don't know how long the clinic will take." Paul suggested. Tim nodded.

"First I have to make a phone call." Tim whispered.

"I'd better do that, too." Paul nodded.

Chapter 40

"I've never heard Shannon cry like that. She was so relieved." Tim shook his head as he walked alongside Paul, now sporting a sling around his arm.

"Merrie sounded a lot like that, but, boy, I got chewed out, too. It ended okay, after I told her it was just a dislocation." Paul smiled sheepishly. As they walked toward the dock they noticed Christian was staring at them, as if he had been waiting. Paul stopped suddenly.

"Tim. What book did you get him?" Paul asked quietly as he pointed at the bag that Tim was carrying.

"They had a Steinbeck novel in front, so I bought it."

"Which one?" Paul asked.

"'Travels with Charley'. About a guy and a dog." Tim answered.

"Hah! I know it well!" Paul chuckled again.

"Something funny?" Tim asked.

"What was the captain's name, on the Coast guard ship?"

"It was an Armenian name...no, wait..."

"Yep, you got it. Charles!" Paul smiled.

"Mister Marino! Your boat – it's out there!" Christian greeted the two men. Tim and Paul turned and looked at a line of ships. There was one that stood out – the only one flying a Swedish flag.

"Good to see you, my friend! We have something for you!" Paul looked at Tim who pulled a book from a paper bag.

"Oh! Another Marino book!" Christian smiled, turned and ran off around the building.

"Well, he's predictable!" Paul smiled.

Chapter 41

Paul pointed at two seats near a large window. Tim lowered his bags to the ground and nodded.

"So, do you want to be near the window or the aisle?" He asked.

"You take the window, Tim. You deserve it." Paul pointed.

"Well, this time let's just enjoy the ride!" Tim smiled as the two men settled into their comfortable chairs on the Catalina Ferry.

"I won't argue with that! I have the contents of my old ammo box, so no more worries on this trip." Paul sighed as he put his head back.

"Paul, we did find one more thing from your dad in the other box, the orange one in our garage. I wanted to give it to you on the island, but, well, you know how insane things went out there." Paul turned to look at Tim.

"Oh?"

"We didn't open it. It was sealed." Tim reached into his duffel bag and pulled out an envelope addressed to Paul.

"Can you open it for me?" Paul asked.

"Sure." Tim tore at the envelope. The pages inside were very different from the notebook paper of the journal. These pages were very clean and crisp – obviously a higher quality paper. He handed them to Paul who looked them over, one by one.

"Well, well. Some of this looks familiar. This one page, it looks different – here..." Paul scanned a page.

"That's the part about the trip to Catalina that we read you last month."

"Yeah...but he changed some of it." Paul read the passage silently.

"Oh, that's strange." Tim whispered.

"That would be an interesting study, wouldn't it?" Paul asked.

"Why don't you read it now?" Tim asked.

Chapter 42

Dear Paul,

The sun is sliding down the back side of Pine Mountain as I write this; the time of day I've come to hate is here - night. Ever since your mother passed away, nighttime has been hard on me. It's too quiet, too lonely and too dark. I know I'm strange for turning on too many lights as the sun goes down, but I feel compelled to do so.

I just hung up after our phone call. Well, actually I sat and stewed for a while before I decided to scribble down these thoughts. I stared out of the window, at the last shadows of the very mountain we were talking about. As the sun finally made its exit I decided I had a lot more to say. I'm just throwing words on to paper here - I don't know another way to get my ideas across. I know my emotions are getting in the way, too.

Son, I decided it is time that I tear down a stone wall. I built a physical one for your mother, but what I've never told you is that one day, as I was stacking the rocks higher and higher, she asked me to tear down another wall. I remember looking around for the other wall and then into her eyes. I knew what she meant.

She wanted me to tear it down more than she wanted me to stack the stones outside this house. In many ways, every word in this letter is like a stone from a certain wall you're familiar with. Like those physical stones, each word is being crafted (well, I tell myself that) for an effect, for a bigger picture. I'm trying to say something here, and I'm just not sure how to say it. I hope whatever I'm trying to say deep inside will come through these words.

What started me writing tonight was something you said. You mentioned I seem different since your mother died. I believe I am the same – but I think I'm trying, in my own flawed way, to live day-to-day being true to who I always wanted to be. That's what it looks like from my side of the wall. At my age, and considering my history, however, that is not an easy task and it probably looks like I'm sputtering and flailing a lot.

I'm just fighting with something inside, something older than you are, and it's impossible to talk about. That's why I'm writing.

Let's go back to that "lights on after dark" idea again. Maybe that's one little stone we can push aside first. I know you meant well when you told me that I don't need to turn so many on, but it makes me feel low to be lectured to like that. I'm guessing you'll be surprised to read that. You probably don't understand why I was so tense during our call. I suppose you hung up and told Meredith that you will never be able to understand me.

There - right there, that's my point. We find it almost impossible to understand each other. Sadly, most of the flaw, the problem, the issue, is on my side of the wall between us.

Ever since your mother left us, I've tried to be true to her heart, if that makes any sense whatsoever, and live as she knew I should live. She always told me to try to be more open about my feelings, and I feel like I failed miserably while she was with us. I was able to be open with her, but very few other people. Sadly, that means you and your sister, too.

This is really hard for me. Sorry – I smudged a few words here, and this is the third time I've tried to write this letter. To be honest, my hands are trembling. I'm looking into the darkest places of my soul right now, and I'm shining lights into places I don't want to see.

Oh, well - I'll just go on to the big stone lowest in our wall. Sadly, I know it belongs to me. It was in place there before you entered the world, Paul.

As I built the wall outside taller and taller, I noticed that harder-to-manage stones went lower. I saw that they supported what was higher up. Sadly, not all of the stones lower in the wall are helpful. Sometimes they crack, and pieces fall off. Sometimes their weaknesses allow stones higher up to fall – and the wall crumbles a bit.

Resting on the ground itself is a massive, crusty, ugly rock that I just can't seem to move. I call it my B.D.S. - "Big Demon Stone". At my age I see that I've battled some vicious demons almost every day of my life. Most of the time I did not even know they were there. How does one know the demons are haunting you when you've never known a time when they weren't there?

Sadly, the older we get the harder it is to dig out these demon stones and remove them. The irony is that I was too preoccupied when I was younger to do the job. I had to make a living. I had to drive kids to baseball practice. I figure you understand what I mean now that you are a dad.

These are not creatures with horns and tails. I wish they were made of flesh and bone – that would have been a whole lot easier to cope with. Sadly, they're not really stones, either. Heck, I would have found some dynamite to disintegrate my "Big Demon Stone".

That stone is the twisted remnant of ancient angry words (and sometimes fists) hurled at me by people I thought I could trust, and thrown at me at an age when I had no defense against them. Now it is a giant boulder, embedded in the very ground we walk on. I say "we" because I've seen it affects everyone around me in my life. I used to believe it didn't, and I was a fool for doing so.

How does a man explain to his son that he is afraid when all of his life he has been had it drilled into him that showing weakness means he is not a real man? I don't have what it takes to say it, face to face, but I figure I have little to lose, at my age, by writing it down here. Maybe, just maybe, it might help after I'm gone.

341

Son, I have spent a lifetime afraid. That fear has also brought shame. You can't feel good about yourself when you see others able to do things that would take a month of self-talk to work up to doing, and then fail. Here's an example - do you remember that time we took the camping trip to Catalina Island? That trip was one rock on top of the Big Demon Stone. Heck, a lot of rocks were on it.

I was terrified about riding in a boat. I postponed that trip, year after year, in spite of your mother's wishing to do it. Every year the YMCA group ran the trip, and every year I had an excuse about why we couldn't go. You were embarrassed with your friends. You were the only one who didn't go. Yeah, I remember. It's hard to forget.

It took me three years to be able to get up the guts to agree. There. I admitted it. Because I couldn't see it back then we had fights and arguments, and the wall got thicker and wider.

Strangely, your mother knew what was really going on. She had a gift like that. She could look down, lower in the stone wall, and see what rock was wobbly.

I think things got worse on that trip across the United States in my father's old car. You know how THAT ended. I hate how something inside of me created the rift that has grown between us.

I hate my own fear. Do you remember dealing with the motorcycle gang in the Midwest that one day? You got them mad. You were scared and I could tell you were looking to me for strength. Son, I was just as frightened as you were, and yet I had nowhere to hide. I had to be the rock you could hide behind, and I knew it. Sadly, my anger toward you for that moment added yet another stone to our wall.

Like your mother used to say every now and then, I go on too much sometimes. I think this is one of those occasions. There are many stones in this wall between us, and I don't need to address each one for you to get the message. It's my hope that you can peer through the wall now and see a bit of a light on the other side. I hope my showing you the "Big Demon Stone" helped.

There is one more thing, one more stone – and this one's not mine. One day you and I dug up a stone on Mom's wall, the day you worked with me. Do you remember how that section of the wall wouldn't stay together? Do you remember how we found a rotten rock under the ground, long covered up? We had to dig it out and find a better stone. It took all day, but it was worth it in the end.

That hidden stone was my father. Son, when I was a teen he was horribly abusive. He was an alcoholic. The things he said to me, the things he did to me, are too difficult for me to write or say. Needless to say, when you are told that you are a failure, at age 10, or beaten because you tried to take his bottle of vodka when you are 14, it does something to a boy…and the man years later. I hope there's enough there for you to understand what I went through. There is the "Devil Stone" beneath the "Big Demon Stone," I suppose.

For years I used to think the problem was like something chemical – like it's just something about the mix of nitro and glycerin, if you will. I now see that as pretty superficial. There were times when I think we bonded. We had a few laughs on that drive across America, and there were moments when I was happy to be with you.

Paul, please, don't think I forgot about how we laughed that one time at the camp fire on Catalina. We sang some great camp songs. And I remember how embarrassed you were as we walked back to our tent. I never did tell you what I did with that box. I buried it by that big rock near the beach camp – the one you climbed on so much. I didn't actually intend on leaving it there – but we got so busy trying to get back home in that rainstorm two days later that I forgot to dig it up.

I thought I was helping you, but I remember how angry you were for years after that. Please know I didn't mean anything – I just got so busy that I forgot to go back again, after the second time. Someday, let's go back. If it is still there, it'll be under a weathered-looking reddish stone. Hah – another stone connection!

So, I'm off to climb Pine Mountain with Tim and Shannon tomorrow. I'm not sure if you remember how afraid of heights I am. My fears have run things too long. Whether I make it to the top or not, I will have won by trying, with all of my heart. In a way, I will crack that Big Demon Stone if I am able to look down and see our house and my Swedish flag.

I need to break that Big Demon Stone; it's my hope that this will tear down the wall between us.

I love you,
Dad

PART THREE

The Stones

EPILOGUE

The door opened; Meredith was standing on the inside, holding the handle, and smiling broadly. Tim and Shannon, each carrying a covered dish, greeted her.

"I'm so glad you could make it, Shannon! Oh, and you, too, Tim!" Meredith reached out and hugged the younger woman.

"We wouldn't have missed it! Tim wouldn't tell me what was in that box – he said Paul had the honors. This has been driving me crazy!" Shannon smiled.

"He has the right to have that honor! Besides, I think how he wanted to do this would have a much bigger impact." Tim added.

"I'm not sure how much impact it will have, but I thought we should get together anyway. Come on in!" Paul gestured.

"I see that your arm is a lot better!" Tim smiled.

"Almost like new, my friend." Paul flexed and moved his arm as he stepped aside.

- - -

"So? What was it? What was in the box?" Shannon asked as she placed her dinner dish on the table."

"It can't wait until after dinner?" Paul smiled.

"Oh, no, not after we had to call the Coast Guard on you two! And I'm the only one 'out of the loop'!" Shannon waved her finger at Paul.

"We?" Paul looked at Meredith.

"I told them not to tell you I called, too." Meredith tilted her head and smiled. Paul shook his head.

"Well, okay. We put something new in the hallway. Come see it." Paul gestured. Tim, Shannon and Meredith led the way. As the came to a small table Tim noticed two new picture frames on the wall. The bigger one had a bright display light shining on it.

"Your mother's necklace?" Shannon sounded confused.

"Yes, that's it..." Paul paused.

"But you had that when we were on Pine Mountain. How could that have been on the island?"

"It wasn't. Look again." Paul pointed as Shannon leaned forward.

"Pearl earrings!" She whispered.

"They match the necklace. Here they are, back from decades of being buried on Catalina!" Meredith added. She then pointed at the table top. There, neatly bound, was a black book titled "Joseph's Journal".

Paul looked at Tim and nodded toward the area above the frame. There on the wall was another frame with three items in it. In the middle was an old, well-loved crucifix. To the right was a piece of paper with a message neatly written in calligraphy.

Timothy Johnston can always call me Dad
Signed, Paul Marino

To the left was another well-crafted piece of calligraphy, with one word on the page.

Hope.

THE END

APPENDIX

JOSEPH'S JOURNAL

The Journal Of Joseph Marino, A Retired, Bald, Overweight Old Guy Who Is Supposed To Be Building A Stone Wall But Can't Find The Energy.

TUESDAY

There, this thing has a starting point. I guess I am supposed to call it a journal, but I'm not really sure what to write here.

For about two weeks now I've been staring at this sheet of paper, not exactly sure how to start writing. I can't believe that today I wrote something. Mostly I've just scratched the stubble of my beard and watched the mockingbird in the tree next door. But today we have a title! Yeah, I know the title probably sucks, but there it is.

You know what? Note to future editor, if anyone does that to these scribblings: I decided I want that title to stay just like it is. All I give permission to do is edit it in case I capitalized a word I wasn't supposed to capitalize. I decided I'm not going to spend any time trying to look those kinds of things up.

WEDNESDAY

Okay, so I didn't write a whole lot on my first day. To be honest, watching a mockingbird sends me into the emotional dump. Mockingbirds were Annie's favorite. I can remember her telling me about how those little things can imitate all kinds of things, like a lawn mower or a dog. Well, I'm not sure about the dog part, but yesterday Mocker (as I call him) imitated my neighbor's lawn mower really well!

I turned to call Annie, to have her come over to hear Mocker, and that ended my writing efforts for the day. And guess what? There's that bird again, trying to distract me from writing this thing. Hold on a minute while I close the window.

Yes, I know I'm wandering. Why in the heck would I write asking you, the reader, to "hold on" while I closed the window? Heck, will there ever be a "reader"? Like you were in this room with me? Shoot, if you were here I'd be kind of embarrassed. I'm not half the housekeeper Annie was. Heck, I'm not a housekeeper at all. I'm now an official "house messer."

Well, when I sat down today the choices presented to me boiled down to either writing about the mockingbird or describe in intimate detail how I suck down soda, or chips (or both), wondering why I would want to write anything. Who would want to read anything I would have to say?

I think I'm just going to quit for today. I caught myself just staring at on old family picture. At least I wrote a little more than I did yesterday.

THURSDAY

Okay, it's not much but at least now this journal idea is moving. Yeah, I've decided to call it a journal. I'll try to write every day, and I suppose that's how a journal works. I looked the word up in the dictionary. Comes from French – for "day". If nothing else, I'm learning something.

So, now we have a title, a bit about mockingbirds, and some sordid details about my inability to clean up my own messes, for what all of that is worth. I can now tell people that this thing isn't blank anymore. Just getting the title down seems to have started the engine. I have to thank Mary down at the post office. She was asking about what I was doing with my time, besides building the stone wall, and I, well, decided to kind of lie. I told her I was writing a book.

Isn't that what all old guys do? Don't we all write down our important thoughts and the wisdom gathered from having lived on this Earth for almost 80 years?

I've never written a journal before, and I'm really not sure where this is going, to tell you the truth. How are you supposed to do a journal? Who do you go to ask? Yeah, sure, I could call a retired English teacher friend of mine, but that's uncomfortable.

I can imagine THAT conversation. "Hey, Heather! How are you doing? Yeah, it's been years! Oh, Annie passed away. Yes, she was a nice lady. Thanks for saying that. By the way, can you give me some advice on how to write a journal?" Sure, I'd sound sane. Or not.

Okay, I'm done for today. That was not productive.

SATURDAY

I know I skipped Friday, but I really had nothing to write, to be honest. I sat for a while looking at the paper and nothing happened. I got angry – felt it's a waste of time to just sit and stare at paper when there are no words coming. I still don't know why I'm doing this. I mean, do I have some deep thoughts that will bring peace to the world, or change the course of human history? I don't think so. This old high school teacher knows that greater minds than his have busted many pencils and pens and crumpled millions of pieces of paper for a long time in those fields and come up empty-handed. So I went outside and stacked a few stones on the wall.

I guess I need to change the title of this journal now that I've started back on the wall. Nah, let's leave it like that. Did you read that, future editor? Don't change the title! It's how I want. I also decided that even if a word should or should not be capitalized, leave it just the way I wrote it. It's my writing. Leave it alone.

I figure I'll try to work on the wall for a while, then try to find some meaningful words to scribble here. Maybe if I write long enough something worthwhile might come out of it.

This is looking more and more like that old story about having a thousand monkeys working on typewriters for a thousand years – eventually they'll produce something like "The Grapes of Wrath" or another piece of real literature. But there's only one monkey and I'm not using a typewriter.

My apologies to John Steinbeck – he has always been one of my favorites. John, I'm sure a million monkeys in a million years could not create anything close to what you wrote. I think that was the iced bourbon and lemonade in me talking. I had three of them and I really need to stop for today.

SUNDAY

I did something really strange today, Anne. I walked over to that church behind the post office and went to a service. I don't exactly know why, but I had never done that before, so I figured, why not?

Even though it's not Catholic, the pastor or minister, or whatever he's called, was really good. He talked about being lonely, and he said something that I couldn't stop thinking about - he said everyone has to deal with that at some time in their lives. On the way out he hugged me.

A lady I didn't know hugged me. She said she knew you from the crafts store, and knew that you were still with me, in my heart, Annie.

The hugs were nice, but I couldn't stop thinking about what that lady said. Those words and hugs sounded like something you wrote to me in that letter you gave to Shannon. I ran (or what passes for running for someone of my age) home and dug out your note. Yes, I kept it. I put it in that old wooden box on my desk, the one right next to me that I got on a trip to Solvang. I remember how good the fudge was that used to be in the box!

There it was – your letter. You wrote, "I have wondered what it would be like to be alone after more than a half of a century. Perhaps, this is a way I can stay with you."

As soon as I saw your note, I knew you were still here with me. And then I found a reason to keep writing in this journal, or diary, or whatever it's called. I never answered your letter! Tomorrow I'm going to change that! I'll work on the wall and then write to you!

MONDAY

Dear Anne,

Yes, I got your note from Shannon. And yes, I remember getting up early and getting to work on the wall. I didn't know you were awake. Sorry if I woke you up. Strange, but I think a big part of what I'm struggling with over the time since you "went home to heaven," as you called it, is worrying about all the times I never apologized for stupid little things I did to hurt you – like that, waking you up. Guilt – my boogeyman.

The meatball sandwich was great, as it always was when you made them. Shannon did a pretty decent job putting it together. I can tell that you taught her!

I do remember seeing you sitting on the porch while I worked on the fence. I thought you were writing a diary, but, boy was I surprised when Shannon delivered the letter. But I still don't know what you mean by leaving letters around the house. I decided I didn't have the stomach to turn this place upside down looking for more. To be honest, I'm a little nervous about finding more. What in the world could you find to write about?

Well, now for the hard part. Yeah, it's been hard since you, well, passed. I have never found it easy to write or talk about well, that night – when you passed. I've tried the other ways of describing what happened that horrible night when I, uh, found you, but I am struggling to get myself to write those things down. I'm going to stop for right now. I think I need a stiff drink before I write any more about my feelings.

TUESDAY

No, it's not really a day later, Annie. It's just after midnight and yes, I'm sorry to say, I had two bourbon and lemonades, on ice. I've never been much of a drinker, but what I need to write now is a bit past my line of courage. I'm sorry, but somehow I know you'd understand.

The night you died – there, I wrote it just like it was – was one of the worst nights of my life. To feel the cold skin of someone you've lived with for a half a century is not something you'd wish for anyone. To be honest, what happened after that is a blur. I'm not sure why I can't remember much until I got home after your funeral. Everything from that night you left until I was home with our kids here is patchy. I guess it's what's called shock or trauma or something. I know it was bad because I needed two bourbons to be able to write this, and I can't remember much of it. I think I've written all I can about that night.

WEDNESDAY

Sorry, Annie. I decided I can't write much today. I'm going out to pile some stones. I think I need a distraction. I'll try again tomorrow.

THURSDAY

Well, I'm back, Annie. I jammed my thumb (and got a nasty gash to boot) trying to position a rock on the wall yesterday, so forgive my crappy handwriting today. Yes, I put some ice on it. Yes, I took two aspirin. Yes, I cleaned it with soap and water before putting a Band-Aid over the wound.

I'll make this short tonight – my hand does ache. In your letter you asked if I would finish the stone wall. The two drops of blood to the right of this paragraph are my answer. As I was putting the bandage on the cut two drops fell.

I've been staring at those two drops. Maybe I read too much into things, but they kind of remind me of us. They're connected by little strands, but they are definitely two distinct drops. Maybe it's a fitting answer to your question. As long as my heart pumps, I'll keep trying on that wall.

But you do know me. If there are times when I'm not up to it, I hope you'll forgive me. I am seeing that I have up and down days. I guess this isn't going to be a short one – the blood drops just, well, affected me.

I've not been too excited about that question you asked about loneliness, but yes, it has been hard since you left. Sorry, that is how I look at it. I can't get myself to "call it like it is" – maybe someday. When I stop and think of how the days stretch out ahead, without you, well, I, well…

I think I'll go take a shower and get some sleep now.

FRIDAY

Annie, I went into the post office again today and Mary asked, once again, how my writing was going. I was really excited to tell her all about my "book" – and I called it a journal. She smiled and asked me what format I was using. I stood there with my mouth open and shook my head. I said, "Um, I just write down whatever I want to."

Mary laughed and asked if I use daily headings and titles. She told me she has been keeping a journal since she was a teenager (and that was a while ago, but don't worry, I didn't say that to her). She then went on to tell me about how these things should be designed. Designed! Hah! Here I was, all proud of having written like 8 pages and now I have to go back and re-do everything. No, ma'am. Sorry, Annie. I'll just keep writing like this. I figure some high-powered editor can "format" all of this.

I did feel bad that I haven't been putting the actual dates on each entry, just the day, like today is "Friday", but then I thought, what does it matter? I don't think any of this will be used in any kind of legal document (note to any future lawyer: none of this is true, unless it would make me a lot of money, then every word is true).

Anyway, you went on to ask me about Tim and Shannon, about being "their parent". I'm not sure how to answer that one, Annie. I am trying to listen, as I know you've told me to do for decades, and to offer whatever advice I can, but I'm not sure how much else I can do.

You said I'm a warm and caring man, and you made me cry when I read that. No, it's not a bad thing. This is one of the reasons you mean so much to me, Annie. As you know, more than anyone else, when I was a kid I was always made fun of for being "too emotional."

When I think back to when we were first married, I can see how much the trials, pains, stresses and problems of life, and living as an imperfect man in an imperfect world that seems to want us to be perfect, changed me. I am not proud of how I became hardened, and you saw it more than anyone else. I sometimes wonder if every human being has like some sort of "pain storage system" and my "container" is smaller than what other people have. I don't know.

I remember how you told me that I learned how to not "feel" things sometimes because I could only take so much, like whenever Paul had a "boo-boo." I'm not proud of that, Annie.

I'm trying with Sarah and Paul. Tim and Shannon, too. That's all I can say, but right now I'm kind of raw about, well, you know. You aren't here now. I'll do what I can.

Sorry, but I have to get to bed. I always start writing these things with a lot of energy, but it runs out quickly. Of course, I'm not writing about baseball or world history –

this stuff kind of hits too close to home. Or way too close. When I read your mention of Chocolate Chip Creek it pushed me over the edge. So, is there one over there, in heaven?

Oh, and I flew a Swedish flag on my flagpole today, just for you. No, I didn't leave it up after dark. I wouldn't want to start an international incident!

Thanks for that note, Annie. It meant a lot to me and I just wish I could tell you.

SATURDAY

Not much to report today, Annie. I got the flu, or at least I think it was the flu. Pretty weak tonight. Yes, I drank lots of fluids and got lots of rest. All I could really keep down were some saltine crackers, but I'm feeling a little hungry now. Maybe I'll warm up a bit of soup to go along with the crackers. You know how much I like cheddar cheese on crackers, well, that's not real appetizing right now. THAT is how sick I am!

I'm feeling strong enough to get over to the desk and write this, so you can see that your "prescriptions" still work. I'll try to write more tomorrow.

SUNDAY

I'm sorry, Annie, but I'm still feeling a bit under the weather. I mostly slept through the day – that helped a lot. I have to make the drive to Bakersfield tomorrow. I didn't want to tell you this, but the teens got into a bit of trouble and I have to go to court. No, not Shannon. Tim and that jerk that hangs out with him, Isaiah. I swear, sometimes I wonder about Tim. Why would he hang out with Isaiah I will never understand – he is a real troublemaker. I hope that someday Tim will really step back and ask himself why he makes the decisions he does. Remember when we had a talk about why I made some bad choices? Yep. He needs that.

Strangely, I know what you'd want me to do in that courtroom. I'm just going to shut my mouth and let you do this your way. You know how hard THAT will be for me. I'll let you know what happens tomorrow, after court. I'm going to try to not bite my tongue too much.

MONDAY

Well, you got me again, Anne. I was getting ready to go to Bakersfield. I decided to look professional and wear a tie. On my way out I started to slip on my favorite coat, you know, the one with the patches on the sleeves that you gave me? Guess what I found in the pocket? Of course, you know. There it was – a pink envelope.

Before I reply to what you said, I need to tell you that you'd have been proud of me today. I asked the judge to let the boys work off their punishment by helping me build your stone wall. He should have seen his look – he must have thought I'd lost my sanity.

Hold on while I get the letter from my pocket. I'm back. Sorry, but I'm not sure I can reply tonight. Yeah, those nasty symptoms have reared up. No, not the flu. I'm pretty much over that. The tears are clouding my vision…so, until tomorrow, please know that I love you.

TUESDAY

I'm not sure how much I can write, Anne. You brought up how I found you in the garden, when you wrote that I saved your life. I, well, I haven't thought much about that day since then. To be honest, I thought you were gone. I ran to the phone and called, and in my head I was cursing the fact that we lived so far from a city, and how hard it is to get an ambulance into Pine Mountain Club. I felt like I had made a lousy decision to move there, and it would cost you your life.

We were in luck that day – there was an ambulance driving out of town after dropping someone off who had come home from the hospital. Wow, I can't believe how clear my memory is of those hours. Every minute felt like an hour. I couldn't tell if you were breathing. Hold on a minute.

WEDNESDAY

I had to take a walk, Annie. Remembering that day in the garden was not easy. I've tried very hard to not think about those minutes that became hours that became days. Unfortunately, I walked out by the very spot where you collapsed, and a flood of memories crashed back in. It's actually the middle of the night now. I guess it is Wednesday, so I wrote WEDNESDAY at the top of this paragraph.

I have to say that my walk around the garden allowed me to see that God granted me a real gift – to be able to be with you for a few more months. You mentioned that you learned how to let go of everything that is meaningless. Strangely, that seems to be a lesson I'm learning. Sadly, one of the most important things was you, and I had to let you go.

Paul and Sarah mean a lot to me, and I am trying to reach out, but, well, you know how hard that is for me. I won't quit on that, but I'm not sure I can tell them all I want to say. Too many problems in the past – too many misunderstandings, and, well, I suppose just too much stubbornness. That seems to run deep in the family.

You mentioned scrambling after the almighty dollar. When I look back now, after all of those years, I wonder if it was all worth it. I spent long hours at school, taking on all kinds of extra duties. Yes, we needed the money, but I feel like I lost all that time when our kids were growing up.

I talked to Paul on the phone the other day and after I hung up I start to cry. Anne, where was I when they were growing up? What happened to all of those years? No, wait. What happened to all of those decades?

We were just kind of shooting the breeze. I was trying, and you know I was. I wanted to find a way to connect, even if I don't know what I'm doing. He mentioned a concert in junior high school and, for the life of me, I couldn't remember. I sat down with a pen and paper and plotted out when he had been in junior high and I realized that was when I was coaching football.

I remember you telling me about some events at the school for our kids – and I remember how I had no time to get to those moments. How many years was I unable to go to the open houses or back to school nights at their schools because I was too busy at my own school? I used to think that being a teacher was good for the family. I was off from school when they were off, and stuff like that, but now I see that, for most of the time, I could not be a part of their school experiences.

I'm not sure if I ever thanked you for being there for them. I have to admit I feel bitter – no, not toward you, but toward, I don't know, maybe our system in general. All my life I heard, "work harder, work smarter, earn more," and every time we got a bit ahead there was always a bill due, or an unexpected expense.

I feel like someone in the financial world has rigged a system so you work harder and harder just to stay even. They don't want you to get ahead – I figure that if you get ahead they don't control you, and they want to control you. They make money off of you borrowing from them. Maybe I'm just a grouchy old man, I don't know.

I remember one time so well; it was when I taught summer school. This one hurt a lot. I had squirreled away a little money so we could make it through the summer without me getting a second job, and they asked me (at the last minute) to take over a class. You were all excited about how we could go to Zion National Park and camp, and we had to cut that down. We could get ahead, I said. Put some money in the bank, I said.

We camped for a week and, when we got home, we discovered something. Do you remember? There had been a water leak in the front yard and we needed a plumber to re-do a major pipe. Remember how much it cost? Yep, the same amount I had earned working in summer school. Remember how I never reconciled all of that? If we had just stayed home, would the expense have proven unnecessary? I have to find a way to let that go.

I really have to get to bed. Everything is getting blurry…

THURSDAY – ABOUT TWO WEEKS LATER. I THINK.

You know, I should have dated these things from the beginning. I hate to admit that Mary at the Post office was right, but I wonder if all of this will seem confusing and out of place to you. I was going to date this one, but then I said, what does it matter? We have all of time now. The days, well, they don't matter much now. I'll just keep doing this just, well, because I'm used to it. Yeah, I know. Stubborn.

THURSDAY – A WHILE LATER

Well, Annie, you mentioned that you hid these notes all over the place, and I realized that at this rate it WILL take me the REST of my life to respond to all you wrote! Maybe that's okay. Maybe you have found a way to help me in my time of aloneness.

You wrote that you worried about being crazy, Annie. No way, no how. If you are, then I am, too. Hah! Maybe THAT explains a lot! Don't get upset – I'm just teasing.

Someone recently asked me how were able to stay married for those 53 years. Since you've been gone I've seen that there were only a few "secrets" to our marriage. I thought I'd tell you here what I never really said, straight out, all those years.

JOEY AND ANNIE'S SECRETS

1. We truly, deep inside, cared about each other. I saw something very special in you, something that resonated inside of me. You had a sweetness that I was drawn to. You were always kind. You were patient. I believe you saw something that felt the same way for you – inside of me.

2. We saw that each of us had flaws, and we accepted that. I know we had many. I think we learned how to give up on the idea that someone is "perfect" (that princess and the prince idea) and to see who we are, just real people. I think early on you tried to change things about me, like how I always fidgeted with my second shirt button. I remember how your chewing your nails bugged me. Over time, however, these things seemed so small, so trite, so worthless…but we did have fights over them, early on. I'm sorry about those fights.

I want to say I'm sorry over that purple dress – one of your favorites. For some reason I got really upset about it, especially after we went camping and you wore it. I have no idea why I didn't like it, and now it seems so worthless. I saw a photo of you wearing it. I feel like whatever was going on inside of me had nothing to do with that dress, but I put it on the dress. And you got rid of it. I still feel bad about that.

My best guess now is that I never really liked purple, and when you wore it that made me feel like I didn't "control" you, or something like that. That's the best I can do. But now I see we had another secret…

3. We let the other person be who he or she really is. After a time I accepted you liked purple, and purple dresses. After a time I liked to see you in those dresses. Maybe I was learning, and I know it took too long, that you won't hurt me just because I can't control you, and when I let go of that idea, I could accept more about the "real" you. But, looking back, I see that it took a long time to get there. I'm sorry for all of the years when my fear kept us apart.

Gosh, I had a flashback about being bothered about how you ate pizza – from the crust end first. I see that it scared me, and there was no reason. I hope you were able to forgive me for such stupid things. Strangely, I believe you did. That's probably another secret…

4. We knew each other, and we felt genuine around each other. Harry (remember him from when I first started teaching? I can't remember his last name) once said knowing someone else really well is being able to scratch where it itches, in front of that person.

I suppose when you go through all we went through together we had few secrets…except for some pink notes you left around just recently! I sure chuckled about that! We never really kept secrets, but, boy, you hit me with a doozy!

5. Then there is fighting. Whenever we did, mostly in our early years together, we always made sure we didn't not insult the other person, or put them down. We never hit "below the belt". I know we respected those weak places that we knew we had, and never, no matter how frustrated we were, ever hit each other there. I remember we did once, early on, and saw how painful that could be if we kept at it. That's when we went back to Joey and Annie's Secret Number 1…we truly cared for each other.

6. I think we always had the long term in mind, Annie. There were times when just breaking up would be the easiest thing to do, not many, mind you, but I think we realized our marriage was bigger than just that moment. We have kids connected to us, and grandchildren. I now see that we were an example to them. We learn how a marriage works form people whose marriages work. I give you more of the credit, considering how messed up my family was.

I remember how I absolutely had to drive that old car back from Maine, because I didn't want you-know-who to buy it from my father's estate. You could not talk me out of it. I was stubborn, and then I drove across the United States being just as stubborn with Paul. Yeah, I know, I shouldn't use the same word twice in once sentence, but stubborn is a word that needs to be written twice in one sentence when I think about certain aspects of my life. Stubborn, stubborn, stubborn. There, three times in one sentence, if you don't look at the fact that there's no verb there.

When I was in court the day the teens were sentenced, I decided, for one of the few times in my life, to let go and take someone else's advice, Annie. It was from you, and I am so sorry you weren't around to see it. Or maybe you were. I knew you'd be compassionate to those kids.

You know I wanted the judge to throw the proverbial book at them. My heart and mind were made up. When I read your letter, and you said so many kids were dumped by their parents, I saw Tim, Shannon and Isaiah. Sadly, I remember how I wasn't there for our kids much, and now I am so thankful you were there for ours.

7. Well, one big "secret" we had was that neither of us was willing to give up. Quitting was just not allowed. I do see that it takes both people to feel that way, however. You remember a certain couple…darn, my memory is hazy again…when Paul was in high school. They lived next door to us. What were their names? I know if you were here you'd remember.

Oh, well (I use that phrase a lot about these kinds of things nowadays). The husband wanted to stay with his wife and she just up and left him, with his three daughters. Wait, I do remember he worked in a lab. Wore a lab coat or something like that. I think he drove a white truck.

I get so frustrated when something like a lab coat or a truck pops up but not a name. Sigh. Anyway, I remember how horrified we both were, and how we could not understand why she would do that. I'll never forget how three pretty little girls went from playing outside to being shut-ins who hardly every smiled – in the same week. The world became a harsh place for them on that day.

I wonder what became of them. Strangely, I still include them in prayers from time to time. I remember how pained the dad looked, and how overwhelmed he said he felt. They moved away after a while, and I saw him once after that, at the hardware store. He told me how much guilt he felt because his girls had to lose so much, in addition to their mom. I remember all I could do was just reach out and squeeze his arm. I wish I could have done more, but that has been a common theme of my life.

Well, I just saw a natural signal to stop writing. I really mean that – very natural. You won't believe this, but the sun is coming up over Pine Mountain. The old rock is telling me it's time to "hit the hay". Yep, the mountain still talks to me.

I'm a bit dizzy and blurry-eyed, but, for some reason, I am so glad I had this time with you, Anne. I really did have something special with you. Good night.

SATURDAY

Yes, I skipped Friday and I think you know why. I always hated going to bed at dawn. It really throws off my clock. I got up around noon, okay, maybe 2:00 PM, and I went out and stacked stones. I'm not going to say much today because I have to get back on schedule. I feel woozy tired. I'll write more tomorrow.

MONDAY, ABOUT A WEEK LATER, I GUESS

Hi, Anne. I've been busy dealing with the teens. Sorry if I'm not writing as much. I had to post some rules, like respect each other, no smoking or swearing, and to put the tools back. I'd forgotten what it was like dealing with teens – I guess I've been retired too long. I feel like two of the kids, Shannon and Tim, are figuring things out but I don't know about that Isaiah. He is quite a piece of work, if you ask me.

What bothers me is how they don't know much about proper meals – and I thought I was bad! I'm trying to teach them about regular meals and a balanced diet. Yeah, I know; don't laugh too hard. I can see you up there on Heaven's Chocolate Chip Creek, pointing at me and telling everyone, "Who is HE to teach kids how to eat?" Everyone's getting a big belly laugh right now, aren't they?

THURSDAY

It was cold out as I went to work on the wall, Annie. I slipped my medium work coat on and guess what I found in the pocket? Well, you know what I found – another note. I can't quite describe the feeling I get whenever I find one of these pink envelopes, but I want to try.

First I feel a lump in my throat; it's like I am able to touch you once again. Second, I take a deep breath and build up the courage to open it. I know you'd never put anything mean in these notes, and it's not really that. I'm not sure if I have the nerve to read what you write. I don't need a bourbon and lemonade any more, but I do have to sit down and take another breath.

This note was short, but it hit hard. Don't worry about not climbing Pine Mountain with me. In fact, I'll tell you what – I'll climb it with Tim and Shannon. Isaiah, well, I can't seem to find a way to reach him, but I have some hope for the other two. When we get the wall finished we'll do it. I promise.

Climbing Pine Mountain was easy to deal with but then you mentioned Paul, and how I called him that one day. Hard, hard, hard. That's a goal that I really want to work for – being able to reach him, being able to express myself in the way that I'd like to.

You know how I struggle to tell him that I love him, because of everything that has happened, and because of my own crappy background. I want to find a way to give him some hope that I do love him. Hope – there's the word. If he could find something to hold on to, something to cling to, maybe that could carry us until I figure this out. I've decided that I want to find a way for him to believe that I do care. I can't give up, even if it feels like I'm trying to stop the waves from hitting the beach.

My father, and you know this, was a hard man to get any expression of love from. It has always troubled me that I can't figure out how to show love to my children – at least not in a way that truly shows it. I just wish I knew how to do this. I hope I can get there.

A STORMY SUNDAY, AND I DON'T KNOW HOW MANY WEEKS LATER

I hope you don't mind, Annie, but I'm going to switch to writing to Paul for a little bit. I realized after I re-read that last entry that maybe I could write some things down, like a script, and maybe, just maybe, I could make sure he hears these words. Maybe is the best I can do. Perhaps this is just a set of desperate scribblings by a broken man who doesn't know how else to do this, but what do I have to lose? I'm just going to do it.

Dear Paul,

Before I write much about anything, I want to ask that you forgive me. I know I've been distant. I know I've not been able to fully understand you, and I see I have been the one who lost out because of that. I'm not going to make any excuses, but I will say that I want you to know that I am a man who has struggled with some nasty demons all of his life. Maybe, at your age now, you understand this.

You remember Grandpa, my father, and how cold he was. I remember trying to do anything that would get him to hug me, or smile at me, or praise me. I never learned how to be a dad, my son, except by trial and lots of errors.

It breaks my heart that you may have seen me in a way similar to how I saw my father. I hope I was a little better. I see that you are better with your children, so I think, just maybe, I was a bit better than my dad. Well, I hope. There's that word again.

Sometimes when we have little else, we can find some way to hope for something better. That's why I write this.

I can say that I love you, and I do, but I am praying for a way, some sort of a sign that will take you beyond hope, to a knowing deep in your heart, with certainty.

I hope there is something in any of these meanderings, somehow, that you can point at and say, "Now I believe." If I could know you felt that way, I would feel something deep inside myself, and we could share love, the true love between a father and his son. Maybe I don't make any sense at all.

I kind of figured that I'd write this down just in case I can't get it done. I've fallen short too many times. At least I wrote down that I love you with all of my heart, even if I had a hard time spitting the words out of my mouth.

One last request – just blurt out "I love you" when you see your own son next time. Break this stupid multi-generational chain…please.

To P.M. from Daddy. (Can you remember when I called you that decades ago?)

OCTOBER 11

Yes, there's a date, right there, which totally messes up my impeccable journaling system. I'll bet that Mary from the Post Office would cringe if she could read this lousy excuse of a journal. I'm, sure she'd never make it past the first page.

Oh, well, none of it really matters. What does matter is that it's our anniversary, and the first one since you left. Yes, I got your pink note about this day, and I saw the lipstick on the male duck. I almost went in and got your lipstick, put it on and kissed the female duck. Oh, what the heck, maybe I will.

You know what? I'm not going to tell you if I did it! Just take a peek down from heaven and see for yourself. I love you still…

MONDAY

Well, Annie, we found another note, in the first aid box. How did you know I'd need that sooner or later? I got hurt and Shannon helped me out. She's been such a great helper. That's why I said that "we" found the note.

Recently I've been kind of down, and feeling lost. Maybe I sound upbeat (I don't know), but I have some down times.

I wish they would leave me alone. When I read your words – the ones in which you remembered why you married me – I felt like I had a life raft to cling to. Your notes have done that for me.

You worried that I needed to forgive you. I cannot find anything you did that I should forgive you for. I mean that, but I know how this goes, though. We need to hear that we are forgiven, no matter what.

Anne, I completely forgive you for ANYTHING you want me to forgive you for, but I honestly feel no grievance against you. Your notes, these bits of love wrapped in pink, have more than covered anything you've said or done for our entire lives. I mean that.

WEDNESDAY

Well, Anne, I just had to let you know that I got a box of chocolate chip cookies from Maine! The note apologized to you for them being late, but I didn't care. Hey, look how screwed up my journaling system is! The cookies were great but what is really important is that someone has to teach Tim how to not eat and talk at the same time!

SATURDAY

Hey, Anne, can you see the stone wall? Check out these muscles! I'm really built now! Yep, I feel strong enough to climb Pine Mountain. That old man has been laughing at me - still. I think it won't be long before I take him down a notch or two…

TUESDAY

This is it, Annie. Tomorrow I'm attacking that old Pine Mountain. He has irritated me enough all of these years. Tim and Shannon will go with me, and I will make it to the top – I promise you. That crazy mountain will feel differently about me after this trip! I'll fill you in on how it goes after I get home.

I have to admit something to you. Like a man totally obsessed, I've looked all over this building for more of your pink notes. I feel like there's got to be one more there, somewhere. Where did you put it? I can't believe it is in this house. I've looked in just about every cranny. Maybe after I get back I'll find it.

I also have to admit that I never told you something. I would say that I forgot, but we've known each other too long. I didn't want to tell you, but maybe you already knew. Somebody stole your pearl necklace. I haven't forgotten, and I will get it back. I am pretty sure I know who has them.

Never forget that Joey loves Annie. And Paul, and Sarah. I love all of you, in my own, broken way. I hope you can hear this...

THE END OF THE
STONE MAN TRILOGY

www.ingramcontent.com/pod-product-compliance
Lightning Source LLC
LaVergne TN
LVHW051222080426
835513LV00016B/1366